"Heartland" English

"Heartland" English

Variation and Transition in the American Midwest

Edited by Timothy C. Frazer

A publication in the Centennial Series of
the American Dialect Society in celebration
of the beginning of its second century of
research into language variation in America

The University of Alabama Press
Tuscaloosa and London

Library of Congress Cataloging-in-Publication Data

"Heartland" English: variation and transition in the American
    Midwest / edited by Timothy C. Frazer.
        p.   cm.
    Includes bibliographical references and index.
    ISBN 0-8173-0675-7 (alk. paper)
    1. English language—Middle West—Variation. 2. Americanisms—
    Middle West. I. Frazer, Timothy C.
    PE2970.M53H43 1993
    427'.977—dc20   92-31253

        British Library Cataloguing-in-Publication Data available

For Charles R. Frazer and Barbara Nelms-Frazer, who gave me a desire to achieve and a lifelong pleasure in learning.

T.C.F.

Contents

vii

Preface

During the Chicago Cubs' surprising championship season of 1989, a television beer commercial played relentlessly between innings. On the soundtrack, a laryngealized male voice sang about a "dream" that "comes right from the heart of the heartland," while the visuals showed us a young man in farm clothes, against a rural winter landscape, throwing baseballs at a crude wooden sign. In thirty seconds, the legend of this interior Eden, unglamorous but home to simple virtues, was played out once again, courtesy of the G. Heileman Brewing Company, and once again the most misunderstood region of the United States was sacrificed in consumerist propaganda. No home to simple virtues or simple anything, the northern interior of the United States is a complex region of cultural clashes and little-known linguistic variation, seen by many only from thirty thousand feet as they jet from one coast to another.

A year later, as I began writing the introduction to this volume, a reporter for the *Philadelphia Inquirer* interviewed Dennis Preston and me about Midwestern place names. When the article ran, the teaser asked why the names of Midwestern places came from such diverse languages, when the language of the place itself was so absolutely uniform. During the interview I had denied any such uniformity, but as usual, formula triumphed over fact.

This myth of an undifferentiated heartland is probably the reason that linguists, except for those of us who have lived or studied there, have taken relatively little interest in the Midwestern United States. In fact, as this book will demonstrate, it is a region rich in variation, worthy of more study than has yet appeared. I will feel satisfied with this book if it results in a greater focus of attention and in an understanding that the phrase "Midwest English" is nothing more than a convenient label, not a description of an actual variety. The term *heartland* that I use in the title, then, is an ironic one. It describes a place that does not exist, save in the popular imagination.

Timothy C. Frazer

Acknowledgments

Assistance in preparing this volume was provided by Ronald Walker, chairperson of the English department at Western Illinois University, by the WIU College of Arts and Sciences, by the WIU Foundation, and by Kansas State University. I am also much indebted to Thomas E. Murray and Andrew Sledd. The initial stages of planning were supported by a 1987 Summer Stipend from the National Endowment for the Humanities.

An earlier version of Chapter 2 appeared in U. Ammon, ed., *Status and Function of Languages and Language Varieties* (Berlin: de Gruyter, 1989), 324–54, and was supported by a grant from the National Science Foundation.

An earlier version of Chapter 12 appeared in Gilbert Youmans and Donald M. Lance, eds., *In Memory of Roman Jacobson: Papers from the 1984 Mid-American Linguistics Conference* (Columbia, MO: Linguistics Area Program, University of Missouri–Columbia, 1985).

T.C.F.

"Heartland" English

1

Problems in Midwest English

Introduction and Overview

TIMOTHY C. FRAZER

ORE THAN FORTY years have passed since the first maps appeared representing data (Davis 1948) from the Linguistic Atlas of the North Central States (hereafter LANCS; McDavid et al. 1976). These data established a major dialect boundary extending well into the states of the Great Lakes. But one still reads and hears about "Midwestern English" as if no dialect boundaries crossed the Midwest region, as if no language variation took place there. The myth of a monolithic English variety throughout the vast heartland is not much different from the old "General American" myth. I hope this book will put that myth to rest.

General American, as readers of this book no doubt know, was posited as the dialect spoken by most of the people in the United States; its geographic delimitation was debatable, but it was generally thought to flourish everywhere that people did not speak "Eastern" or "Southern," including the Midwest (Van Riper 1973). If the term *General American* is heard less these days, the related belief that the Midwestern United States speaks with a single voice—a single, uniform "Midwestern" form of English—remains current. Linguists, unfortunately, often seem no better informed than the general public. Fromkin and Rodman (1983), as Dennis Preston observes in this volume, suggest by implication that standard (as opposed to regional) English is spoken in New England, the Middle Atlantic, and the Midwest. Misinformation about the Midwest appears even among some dialect specialists. Trudgill and Hannah (1982) include "Midwest English—U.S." as one of two American varieties (the other is "Eastern") on the tape that accompanies their

International English. Actually, their example is from Michigan, and the dialect they represent as Midwestern is really Inland Northern, a dialect with a very restricted geography in the Midwest, where it predominates only in Michigan, Wisconsin, and Minnesota, in northern Illinois, Indiana, Ohio, and Iowa, and in enclaves elsewhere. It was the Inland Northern dialect which for so many years was mistakenly identified as General American. If not everyone in the Midwest speaks Inland Northern, however, the belief that they do appears to be well established. Among laypeople, as Dennis Preston finds in several studies in perceptual dialectology, the "Midwest" is commonly imagined as a uniform, autonomous dialect area (see especially Preston 1986 and Preston 1989). A composite of hand-drawn maps of regional dialects as seen by Preston's New York City respondents identified a huge chunk of the north-central United States as a "Midwest" dialect area (1989: 114); a similar composite map was drawn by Hawaiian respondents, though for Hawaiians the "Midwest" overlaps with a "Northern" area similar in size and shape (32).

Not only is there an established popular belief in a uniform Midwestern dialect, but there seems to be some treatment of it as an accepted standard. Many of Preston's respondents in various parts of the country give "Midwestern" high scores for both correctness and pleasantness; in this volume, as Preston attempts to locate the perceived home of "Standard English" among laypeople, many of his Michigan and Indiana respondents give high ratings to a large area including New England, the Middle Atlantic, and the Great Lakes, suggesting a stubborn survival of a mythically uniform "General American" dialect perception.

Anecdotal evidence locates "Standard English" in an imagined homogeneous Midwest as well. An Ohioan interviewed for the film *American Tongues* says, "We're straight American. We're bland. We're just the normal stuff right here." Doing business in Tennessee, speech therapist Beverly Inman-Eble, another Ohioan, can charge Chattanooga clients $45 a session, as *Time* magazine reported (Conniff 1988), for "smoothing out the twang their daddies taught them and nipping off Mamma's drawl." *Time* identifies Inman-Eble's Ohio dialect as "anchor talk," suggesting a model for network newspeople and an unquestioned universality.

After two decades of study in language variation, I find something disturbing and pathetic about Inman-Eble's occupation. Her clients insert all sorts of useless contraptions into their mouths to "strengthen" their tongues, so desperate are they to get on in the business world. I get the same feeling watching a woman in *American Tongues* throw herself on the mercy of yet another speech therapist in order to rid herself of her Brooklyn accent. There is a sense of moral superiority in the work of these speech therapists, who teach Inland Northern (acronymed SWINE by Raven McDavid, for Standard White Inland Northern English) as something safely sanitized, a measure against which everything else is deviant.

The reasons for the enshrinement of SWINE lie in a complex history about which Thomas Donahue and I present differing but complementary hypotheses in this volume. Donahue finds a number of causes, including the former economic dominance of the Great Lakes region and its homegrown but highly mobile business class, as well as the authority of single scholar, J. S. Kenyon, and the many usage manuals and dictionaries he produced or contributed to. For me, all of these factors, including Kenyon's embrace of the "General American" hypotheses, spring from the neo-Puritan ideology of Inland Northern settlers who came west from New York state and New England in the early nineteenth century—an ideology, I believe, still very much alive in our politics and our educational system, as essays by Riney and Sledd in this volume show. In any case, the speech therapists have done their best to promote the ascendancy of Inland Northern. But it is not a "Midwestern English."

While the general nature of Midwestern language variation is well-known, it is complex and problematic[1] enough to warrant a review of earlier studies.[2] Most familiar to readers will be the Northern-Midland dialect boundary, shown in map 1.1. This boundary's position in the North Central states was established by Davis (1948) and in the Upper Midwest by Harold B. Allen (1964, 1973–76).[3] The boundary inscribes the southern limits of Inland Northern hegemony in northern Ohio and Indiana, in northeastern Illinois, in northern Iowa and northeastern South Dakota. Clearly, Inland Northern is restricted to only a portion of the Midwest.

On the other side of the boundary line was what the Linguistic Atlas scholars called the "Midland" dialect area. The hypothesis of a Northern-Midland dialect boundary influenced much of the research in Midwestern English for almost four decades (Davis and McDavid 1950, Potter 1955, Marckwardt 1957, Allen 1958, V. McDavid 1956, R. McDavid and V. McDavid 1960, Shuy 1962, V. McDavid 1963, Allen 1964, Hartman 1966, Carmony 1972a, Carmony 1972b, Carmony 1977, Frazer 1973, Frazer 1978a, Frazer 1978c, Frazer 1982, Frazer 1986, Frazer 1987a). But much of that research began to show that the Midwest was a highly complex dialect area inadequately described by a simple geographical division into "Northern" and "Midland."

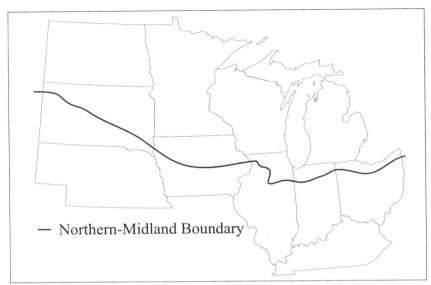

— Northern-Midland Boundary

Map 1.1. The Northern-Midland dialect boundary in the Midwest.

Marckwardt's (1957) maps of the North Central states, shown in map 1.2 as extended into the Upper Midwest by Harold Allen (1958), illustrate this point. Instead of bundling tightly, these lines spread widely apart, showing more divergent locations as they move farther west. An even greater complexity in the Upper Midwest is shown by Allen 1964. On Allen's 1964 map (not shown), the simple Northern-Midland boundary that appears in map 1.2 is shown with eight branches radiating in all directions. Each branch represents a significant case of Midland overlap on the Northern side or Northern overlap on the Midland side. Allen 1964 also identifies two speech islands (see below), a Northern island in the Midland territory of eastern Nebraska and a Midland island in the nominally Northern region of the Minnesota Mesabi range (but see Underwood 1981).

The phenomenon of overlapping isoglosses is one reason the Midwest cannot be defined in terms of a simple Northern-Midland division. A second reason is in the nature of the Midland itself. As originally conceived by Kurath, the Midland overlapped both Pennsylvania and the Southern uplands and at least three subdialect areas, North Midland, West Midland, and South Midland. Although these areas had some cultural and linguistic features in common, they have more differences than they do similarities, enough so that Carver (1987), as Kurath himself once suggested, has argued that the Southern

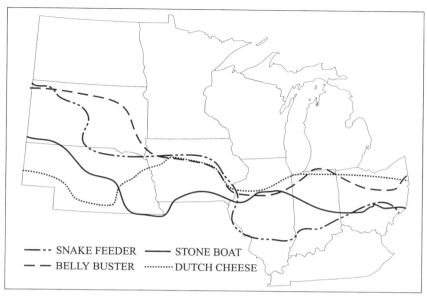

Map 1.2. Northern limit of *belly buster* and *snake feeder* and southern limit of *stone boat* and *Dutch cheese*.

uplands actually belong to the South proper, with which the uplands share a large regional vocabulary. Kurath, Carver argues, used only a small number of isoglosses to establish the Midland, not enough to justify treatment of the Midland as a dialect in itself. Carver relegates the Midland to the status of a very thin layer, a minor lexical distribution that straddles the Ohio River. For Carver, then, the principal dialect division in the United States is not Northern, Midland, and Southern, but Northern and Southern, each one composed of various subdialects or "layers." Instead of talking only about Northern-Midland divisions as if the Midland itself were a single dialect, then, we should examine the relative influences of those dialects (or subdialects) which underlie the Midland layer. (For convenience, I retain the term *Midland* throughout this discussion as a designation for the geographic area in which these overlaps take place.)

The most salient of these subdialects is the upland Southern or South Midland, since it shares with the South a large regional vocabulary along with a number of pronunciation and morphological features. The first large-scale effort to determine the northern limits of upland Southern speech was made in Robert F. Dakin's 1966 dissertation. Working with LANCS data, Dakin counted South Midland lexical isoglosses and determined that the "South Midland" dialect extended no further north than extreme southern Illinois and Indiana, with a tiny portion of Ohio around the mouth of the Scioto River.

Carver, working from the Dictionary of American Regional English (DARE) data, establishes the Ohio River and Missouri's southern state line as the boundary for his South II layer; his South I layer has the same boundaries except for the "Hoosier apex" in Indiana and Illinois and what we might call a "Show-me" apex, formed only by secondary boundaries, whose tip extends through Missouri into southern Iowa. Farther west, a secondary boundary separates Kansas from Oklahoma.

Largely because of my own observations after thirty years' residence in *central* Illinois, I have never been completely satisfied with Dakin's South Midland delimitation, which seemed to me to place the South Midland boundary too far to the south. A common experience for residents of central Illinois is to be told they have a "Southern accent." If Southern or South Midland speech did not go much farther north than the Ohio River, why are these speakers, located much farther north, so characterized? Carver's "Lower North," an extension of the "North" deep into the lower Midwest, raises similar questions.

In my own work I have demonstrated that at least some South Midland pronunciation features are found much farther north than the Ohio River (Frazer 1978a). This northerly distribution is apparent in the

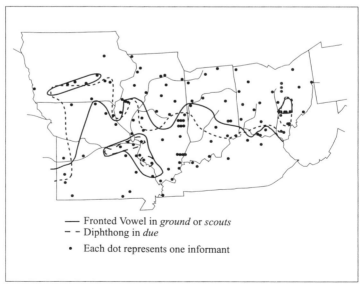

— Fronted Vowel in *ground* or *scouts*
- - Diphthong in *due*
• Each dot represents one informant

Map 1.3. Northern limits of fronted vowel in *ground* and *scouts* and the diphthong in *due*.

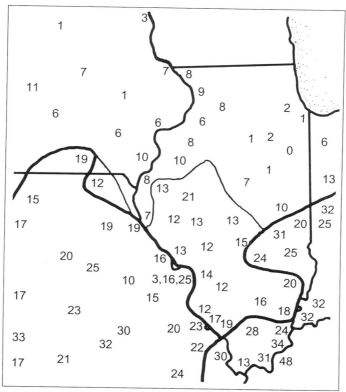

Map 1.4. Secondary and tertiary southern boundaries (after Carver 1986).

tape recorded readings of "Arthur the Rat" by 124 DARE informants in Ohio, Indiana, Kentucky, Illinois, Missouri and Iowa. These were the same DARE informants Carver studied, but while he reviewed their vocabulary responses as recorded on the DARE questionnaires, I examined their speech as recorded on tape. (Because DARE did not obtain as many interviews in west-central Illinois as planned, I added an additional reading of "Arthur" from McDonough County.) From these readings I mapped instances of raised diphthongs in /au/, inglides in *due*, flattened glides in /ai/, diphthongs in *cough/log*, inglides in *him*, *this*, *them*. The results are illustrated by map 1.3, which charts two of these variants. This map shows that the effects of Upland Southern accents range much farther north in the NCS than does the Upland Southern vocabulary, at least in Illinois. Map 1.3, moreover, shows a Hoosier apex like Carver's, but also includes more of Illinois.[4] The shape of my boundaries looks more like Carver's secondary and tertiary boundaries of the South in map 1.4 (Carver 1986), suggesting that some of his boundaries should be reweighted to include more than lexicon. Lance (1974a, 1974b, 1975, 1977), using traditional terminology, has called this area "ambiguously Midland." The chapter by Faries and Lance in this volume highlights the Midland ambiguity; rather than attempting to draw isogloss lines through Missouri—which would only add to the confusion experienced by earlier dialectologists in Missouri—Faries and Lance use numerical indices which indicate the *predominance* of one dialect over another. This rampant overlap and ambiguity, of course, indicates that the Midwest, at least this part of it, is a *transition* area.

Chambers and Trudgill (1980) call for more intensive studies of transition areas, because they believe "that transitions point the way to a deeper understanding of geographic variability than any other theoretical device posited so far" (142). The distribution of features in the Midwestern transitional zone may challenge classical notions of such regions. Trudgill (1983) describes such notions as follows: "If one moved across this transitional zone, one would have the impression of a continuum . . . an impression of gradualness" (48). Although Trudgill goes on to say that this model is "a distortion," the very example he cites to make his point (a vowel map of East Anglia and the eastern midlands of England) would seem to confirm the "continuum" model. His transition from Northern to "mixed," then "fudged" then "mixed" again and then Southern, would strongly suggest a continuum, especially as it depends on phonetic proximity. Change, spreading like a viral infection, moves from south to north in a predictable fashion through this zone. But the American Midwest is no such model of order.

Most linguistic models of change, diffusion, or transition have affinities with the continuum model. They usually suggest that change or transition should spread in some mathematically predictable way, like the laws of physics. While maps following these models capture an important part of the truth—as a *general* rule, for example, Southern dialect features do increase in frequency as we move South toward the Ohio River, as Carver suggests (1987: 102–03)—the often wide-meshed surveys on which they are based do not always allow them to take into account the cranky unpredictability of human movement.

In the Ohio Valley and points North, graded variation is interrupted by "speech islands," areas of dialect concentration which differ sharply from the surrounding area. Marietta, Ohio, a Yankee colony settled by the Ohio Company, emerges on LANCS maps as a Northern island in a Midland sea (Marckwardt 1957), although its Northern quality is eroding (Clark 1972). Louisville, Kentucky, sits right on the rim of Carver's Upper South, but its regional vocabulary is "chiefly

North Midland in character" (Howren 1958). Terre Haute, Indiana, is located in the center of Carver's Hoosier apex, but its regional vocabulary is also predominantly North and North Midland (Carmony 1977). In this volume, Thomas E. Murray reports on a massive study of the regional vocabulary, morphology and pronunciation of St. Louis, Missouri, a largely North and North Midland–speaking city in the midst of a more South Midland hinterland (see Faries and Lance, this volume, maps 16.6, 16.7, and 16.8).

Urban speech islands are not the only Midwestern exceptions to the continuum model of transition areas. The Lead Region of Illinois and Wisconsin is a famous largely rural Midland speech island (Marckwardt 1957, Shuy 1962). Moreover, in a study of Knox County, Illinois (Frazer 1986), I examined ten communities which were arranged in pretty much of a north to south direction. Seven were represented by LANCS checklist vocabulary questionnaires collected between 1950 and 1960; Wataga was represented by Roger Shuy's 1960 LANCS field interview; Galesburg by DARE's 1967 field interview. I added to the study Harold Allen's 1939 LANCS field interview record for Geneseo, a Henry County community several miles farther north. For the continuum model to be valid, we should find a decreasing number of Northern items as we move southward; conversely (since Shuy has identified "Midland" as the alternative to Northern for this area) we should find a decreasing number of Midland items as we move northward. To test this assumption, I counted the responses to questions which would elicit a Northern or Midland response (e.g., pail/bucket). Twelve such questions were common to all three kinds of questionnaires. Table 1.1, arranged from North (top) to South (bottom), indicates the results.

Column 1 represents the number and percentage of Northern words for each informant (note that three communities, Altona, Oneida, and Abingdon, have two informants); Column 2 shows the number and percentage of Midland words; and Column 3 shows the number and percentage of nonregional responses. Some similarity to Trudgill's continuum is apparent here. At the extreme North we have, respectively, the highest Northern number (7) and lowest Midland number (1); at the extreme South we have the lowest Northern number (2) and the highest Midland number (9). But towards the middle the continuum model runs into difficulty. Oneida 2 has as high a Northern number as Geneseo (7), although it is farther South, while Victoria has a higher Midland number than Wataga, Galesburg, Gilson, or Abingdon 1, all communities farther South. The reason for these anomalies is that settlement of Midwestern counties did not follow a

Table 1.1
Proportion of Northern and Midland Words in 11 Illinois
County Communities Arranged North to South
(13 respondents)

	Northern		Midland		Nonregional	
	#	(%)	#	(%)	#	(%)
Geneseo	7	(58)	1	(8)	4	(13)
Galva	6	(50)	4	(33)	2	(17)
Altona 1	6	(50)	4	(33)	2	(17)
Altona 2	5	(42)	4	(33)	3	(25)
Oneida 1	6	(50)	3	(25)	3	(25)
Oneida 2	7	(58)	3	(25)	2	(17)
Victoria	3	(25)	6	(50)	3	(25)
Wataga	4	(33)	4	(33)	4	(33)
Galesburg	3	(33)	5	(42)	3	(25)
Gilson	1	(8)	4	(33)	7	(58)
Abingdon 1	3	(25)	3	(25)	6	(50)
Abingdon 2	2	(17)	6	(50)	3	(33)
London Mills	2	(17)	9	(75)	1	(8)

graded pattern. Ontario Township, where Oneida is located, numbered New Yorkers and New Englanders most heavily among its early settlers—Oneida village was in fact named for Oneida, New York. Victoria, on the other hand, was settled largely from the Upland South, Pennsylvania, and Ohio, and lies several miles east of the railroad and the highway. Oneida looks like a tiny speech island of higher Northern usage than is found among its immediate, more "Midland" neighbors, which suggests that Shuy's designation of Knox County as "Midland" (1962)—based largely on the information in the Wataga LANCS interview—suffers from the weakness inherent in wide-meshed surveys, which may miss differences between communities only a few miles apart. Variation in this transition county, then, would seem to be somewhat unpredictable as far as any predetermined formula or model is concerned. Settlement history, which can be patchy, remains the only controlling variable.

Another Midwest example in which settlement history disrupts the expected continua appears in James Hartman's 1966 study of Hocking County, Ohio. Hocking, located about thirty miles east of the Scioto River in southern Ohio, combines forested, hilly, unglaciated country in its rough eastern half and fertile farming area in its western half. Because of this difference in topography, Hocking County was settled in the east by Upland Southerners, in the west mostly by Pennsylvanians and Germans. After interviewing twenty Hocking Countians with a

LANCS-type questionnaire, Hartman discovered a predominance of Southern and Midland features in the East. All of the eastern interviewees had a rounded low-back vowel in *fog*, while residents in the western half all said /fag/. The eastern half had raised or gliding vowels in *ash, fish*, and *rush*, an Upland Southern feature, while the western half had short monophthongs, as in the North and North Midland. The eastern half had these Upland Southern vocabulary items: *spigot, piece,* and *sook*. Common in the western half were *pail* and *stringbeans*, both Northernisms. The only deviance from this pattern was the occasional appearance of Midland *roasting ears* in the western half.

This unexpected east/west division in Hocking County contradicts the continuum model. The Southern nature of eastern Hocking County would not appear on LANCS maps or on the even more widely-meshed DARE survey. Isoglosses in this county will not run gradually east and west but from north to south, not necessarily connecting to other isoglosses outside this particular county. Again, the mostly unpredictable (except by landform) pattern of settlement history would seem to frustrate any posited model of the transition area.

Bruce Southard's contribution to this volume illustrates once more how settlement history contributes to the cultural and linguistic geography of the heartland, with which many Oklahomans identify (Zelinsky 1980). Southard's data—developed from the fieldwork done for the Linguistic Atlas of Oklahoma by Van Riper—show a definite clustering of Southern and South Midland terms outside the land rush areas of the 1890s. Elsewhere in the former "Indian Territory," mixed-blood Native Americans contributed to the perpetuation of Southern culture and language.

The patchwork nature of the settlement of Midwestern states is best illustrated by the 1850 census for three counties in southwestern Ohio. Just north of Cincinnati, Butler County, set off in 1803, was populated largely by Pennsylvanians, although New Jerseyans and Marylanders were concentrated in the southeastern townships of Monroe, Liberty, and Union. Germans were especially numerous in the town of Miami and in the northwestern township of Madison. The next county to the north of Butler was Preble, organized in 1808. Preble was very different from Butler in 1850. Here Virginians were the most numerous in all townships except the southern three, which were dominated by Pennsylvanians. A small colony of South Carolinians lived in southwestern Israel township, while Pennsylvanians and other middle staters predominated in the small towns of Lewisburg, Euphemia, Eaton, and North Westville. While Southerners dominated Preble County, Darke County, the next one to the north, was populated mostly by Pennsylvanians (Frazer 1978b: ch. 2, p. 14). If settlement largely determines language in the Midwest, as we have maintained up until now, then the linguistic geography of these three counties would be even more complex than what Hartmann found in Hocking. This suggests a major difficulty in Midwestern linguistic geography: while wide-meshed maps can represent *general* trends, a truly accurate linguistic atlas of this region would have to sample not just every county, but every township. Such an atlas for southwestern Ohio would actually show Southern features appearing farther *north* than some "North Midland" or "Lower Northern" areas, in contrast to Carver's gradually declining southern numbers from south to north (1987; see especially map B, 103). This discussion should also demonstrate the futility of efforts (including and especially, in recent years, my own) to apply a single dialect label to the lower Midwest. "Lower North," "North Midland," "South Midland," or just plain "Midland"—all of these fail to grasp the complexity of this region where every county may have its own internal linguistic geography, different from every other county.

An improvement over judgments based on wide-meshed maps is found in Thomas E. Murray's essay in this volume on positive *anymore*. His survey represents the evaluative responses of over ten thousand respondents, a more than tenfold increase in density over linguistic-atlas surveys and an even greater one for DARE. In some respects, his maps are reminiscent of the old Northern-Midland division, especially with the least-favored contexts such as clause-initial position. But more favored usages seem to have become established in urban centers, even in Northern territory.

Meanwhile, it is clear that the language of the transitional Midwest is so complex that we must buttress our geographical studies with other kinds of information. As Trudgill (1983) writes, "What we therefore require is a transfer of sociolinguistic methodology to the geographical plane" (50). That requires us to apply the techniques of urban dialectology to Atlas-type communities. One such attempt was made in a study of 50 adult speakers in rural Hancock and McDonough counties in Illinois (Frazer 1983b), both of which are right on the border for the raised/fronted /au/ and other Southern/South Midland pronunciation features. In this study, I calculated the frequency of raised and fronted /au/ in relation to age, sex, and urban/rural identification. Between the elderly (born before 1910) and the middle-aged, fronting/raising approximately doubled in frequency; it was also more frequent in the speech of females than among males. In this respect, /au/ fronting behaves like an advancing sound change. However, it was also more frequent (more than two and a half times) among rural than among urban residents, belying the notion that sound changes always originate in urban centers. Also, /au/-fronting received a negative rating on an attitudes test which rated for competence (Frazer 1987b). Subsequent examination of other features does not indicate the same patterns.

/au/-fronting, then, although it is accorded negative prestige at the "power" pole, is nevertheless expanding in frequency, at least between two generations. The behavior of this particular sound change is different from that of other Southern features, and circumstances suggest that it has been marked as a solidarity indicator for rural speakers. The middle-aged generation among whom this feature is advancing grew up during the agricultural depression of the 1920s and 30s. It is possible that when rural life was threatened, this linguistic marker took on new vitality. Labov (1963) reports a similar occurrence on Martha's Vineyard, where centralized onsets in /au/ and /ai/ began to increase in frequency when island life was threatened by "summer people."

Interestingly, although morphemes are supposed to be the smallest units of meaning in a language, features selected as solidarity markers like /au/ become signifiers in their own right, even at the phonetic level. We might expect that similar processes would take place elsewhere. Labov's evidence (1972b) about consonant cluster reduction among black adolescent peer groups and "lames" could be interpreted the same way. Herndobler (this volume) seems to have uncovered similar processes in a white ethnic neighborhood in Chicago. And something like this, too, may be going on in another rural community in this "ambiguously Midland" transition zone.

Habick, as he reports in this volume, visited yet another rural community in the Midwest transition area during the late 1970s. In Farmer City, Habick worked closely with a group of adolescents at the local high school and identified individual social networks. He concludes that the phonetic systems of the "burnout" group, the rebel adolescents, has a higher level of upland Southern features than the phonetic system of the group that accepts mainstream values. Apparently upland Southern speech has acquired a value as a rejection of certain bourgeois values and the Inland Northern speech associated with those values (again, Donahue's and my discussions of Inland Northern as "General American" in this volume shed some light here). To some extent this reflects a national trend in which upland Southern culture has become in itself a signifier for groups of alienated whites, a phenomenon which John Coggeshall (1985) calls the "rustification of America."

One problem with this idea, though, is that not all the phonetic variants which distinguish Habick's "burnout" group are Southern; fronted /o/ (which also appears frequently among young people in my sample) is part of the general contortion of the vowel quadrangle among Habick's adolescents. Fronted /o/ is not a traditional Southern feature (though perhaps a recent one—see Thomas 1989) but originates in western Pennsylvania, a source area which also influences the dialects of this region (Frazer 1978c, 1987a). Moreover, Habick shows that his young people do not exhibit all of the features used by his Kentucky subjects, true upland Southerners. That would suggest that Habick's adolescents select a set of features to distinguish their speech without consciously trying to sound "Southern," at least not in any accurate sense. This is classical behavior in the selection of solidarity variables: "any group of speakers of language X which regards itself as a close social unit will tend to express its group solidarity by favoring those linguistic innovations which set it apart from other speakers of X who are not part of the group" (Ferguson and Gumperz 1960: 7). That is certainly what Habick's subjects are doing and that is very likely what is happening among the rural speakers in McDonough and Hancock counties.

Foreign languages have played a large role in the linguistic diversity of the Middle West, although that role has attracted relatively little serious scholarship. The history of much of the area as a French colony led to the introduction of French dialects, some of which survived in isolated parts of Missouri until well into the twentieth century (Carriere 1939). The great European migrations in the nineteenth century led to the introduction of Norwegian into Wisconsin, Minnesota, and Iowa (Haugen 1953, Flom 1925) and German into Wisconsin, Illinois, Missouri, and Iowa (Johnson 1935, Harris 1948, Kehlenbeck 1948, Willibrand 1957, Eichoff 1971, Lewis 1973). The focus of most of these studies, especially Carriere, Flom, Willibrand, Eichoff, Lewis, and to some extent Haugen, has been to document the impact of English on these other languages, especially in terms of loans and loan translations. For example, the French studied by Carriere in Old Mines, Missouri, has introduced from English *traveler* 'to travel' in place of French *voyager*, and *watcher* in place of *surveiller*. English loanwords, Lewis finds, are also evident in the Swiss German dialect of New Glarus, Wisconsin, though the English impact on the dialect's phonology and morphology is minimal. Although these languages have all been alive in this region as recently as a few decades ago, they are now disappearing, and as Eichoff laments, it may be too late for studies of German or French on the scale of Haugen's work for Norwegian.

The Hispanic migration to the Middle West is more recent and has received even less attention from linguists, although Illinois and Michigan rank among the leading states in Hispanic population (Hart-Gonzalez 1988). The only published study of Middle Western Spanish to date is Gary Denning's examination of variants on the *ojala + (que)* construction in Kansas—variants which correlate with the origins of Kansas Hispanics in northern and central Mexico.

Of primary interest to this volume, of course, is the impact of foreign languages on spoken English in the Middle West. Of the studies mentioned so far, only Harris's study of St. Clair County, Illinois— where he finds a spoken English with features reminiscent of the Pennsylvania German area—assesses the impact of non-English speaking immigration on regional English. More recently, Larmouth (1990) finds traces of Belgian French in the English of Door County peninsula in Wisconsin. Larmouth reports expressions like *hairs*—possibly a loan translation for *cheveux*—and several borrowings for items of food and drink.

Given the rarity of such assessments, Donald Lance's chapter is particularly welcome in this volume. Lance reviews the influence of the German language in the German-settlement areas of what some call the "Missouri Rhineland." I have argued elsewhere that the non-Southern character of spoken English in the German settlement areas of Missouri and southern Illinois is due to the expansionist Yankee ideology and German sympathy to it (Frazer 1979), factors which, as I argue in this volume, contribute to the hegemony of the Inland Northern dialect. Lance, however, makes a persuasive argument that German-language influence can account for much of the North Midland character of these same communities. Just as important, he shows that in these rural communities, German influence on both English phonology and vocabulary is very common even among third-generation descendants of the German settlers.

The discussion so far suggests that the nominally "Midland" part of the Midwest is a region of considerable complexity, while the Inland Northern area was uniform, as Kenyon (1924) believed. This, however, is far from the truth. For one thing, what has come to be called the "Northern cities sound change" has been ongoing in the Northern dialect area for a century (Emerson 1891), and its frequency in Inland Northern dialect areas of the Midwest shows considerable variation (Callary 1975). Second, foreign—that is, non-English-speaking—settlement has been ongoing in this area too for the past century and a half, as documented by several of the studies mentioned above. Among the assessments of such impact, Linn (1980) has suggested that a definite influence survives in the heavily Scandinavian-settled areas around Lake Superior, to the extent that the interdental *th* fricative is realized as a stop (/t/ or /d/) among educated speakers. Linn also has found influences of European languages on the vocabulary, syntax and phonology of the spoken English of the Mesabi iron range in northern Minnesota (1984, 1988, 1990). Given these forces and changes, it would be hard to conceive of the Inland North as a uniform dialect area.

Two studies of Wisconsin, indeed, give notions of Northern uniformity the lie. Craig Carver examines the linguistic geography of Wisconsin by mapping items from Frederic G. Cassidy's 1950 survey; the resulting isoglosses divide the state into four distinct dialect areas. Moreover, continued ties to older English-speaking areas create some surprises. Donald Larmouth and Marjorie Remsing examine the remote community of a group of third-generation Kentucky migrants in the northern Wisconsin woods. Comparing his Wisconsin data with data drawn from the migrants' communities of origin in Kentucky, Larmouth finds that after ninety years, features of Kentucky speech survive in this isolated Northern woods community. In a study based on evaluation rather than production, Thomas E. Murray documents the apparent spread in specific contexts of a Midland phenomenon—positive *anymore*—into Northern areas far beyond the traditional Northern-Midland boundary. Erik Thomas documents a similar spread for constructions like *all the* + comparative structure. Both of these features—positive *anymore* and *all the* + comparative structure—are documented by Crozier (1984) as originating with the Ulster Scots, whose contributions to the Midland lexicon show a continuing dynamism outside the traditional Midland boundaries.

If Midwestern English is diverse and complex in rural areas, it is even more so in the cities. The best-known urban dialect project in the Midwest is of course the Detroit study by Shuy, Wolfram, and Riley (1967), and Wolfram's related study of Detroit Black English (1969). Before the Detroit project, however, and one year before Labov's landmark New York City study (Labov 1966), Lee Pederson's *Pronunciation of English in Metropolitan Chicago* examined the speech of 55 residents of that city and its suburbs (Pederson 1965). Pederson's findings cover the entire English phonemic inventory and are difficult to summarize, but several items bear particular attention. A short monophthong in words like *eight* or *April,* and /t/ for interdental fricatives "occur only in the speech of distinctive cultural groups, all of which are (with the exception of the Irish) bilingual" (1965: 65). In the pronunciation of *whore,* moreover, lower-class whites have /ʊ/ or /u/ (it is unclear whether this feature is lexically restricted or not). More discussion, however, has centered on Pederson's study of Black English, drawn from this same data base (Pederson 1964, 1966). Michael I. Miller (1989) subjected Pederson's data to statistical analysis and separated into groups those features that serve to distinguish white from black speech. "R-lessness," the vowel shape in words like *cut*, or *th* variables may distinguish white from black speech but do not show stratification within the black community, as do such features as consonant cluster reduction or nonstandard verb forms. In this volume, Miller employs Pederson's semantic fields to examine lexical differences between middle-class Chicago blacks and whites. While noting that differences in frequency may be found, Miller finds no evidence of either divergence or convergence between black and white middle-class speech.

Not since Pederson's investigation in the 1960s, moreover, has published research addressed the language of white Chicagoans, especially those in so-called ethnic neighborhoods. In this volume, Robin Herndobler performs a microanalysis of speech behavior on Chicago's "East Side," a largely working-class neighborhood so stable that four-generation families are common there. Herndobler's examination of stop variants for the interdental fricative *th* is one of the features mentioned by Pederson. That this and other nonstandard features are used by men more than by women is not surprising; however, Herndobler's closeness to the community and her understanding of the motives and desires of her informants enables her to provide some explanations for this gender difference, which sociolinguists have all too often taken for granted. Herndobler's data also include some surprises, especially in the linguistic behavior of fourth-generation, adolescent females who do not follow the traditional gender pattern. In addition, Herndobler's account of /æ/ raising's spread from what was then the Jewish neighborhood of South Shore into the speech of East Side women provides a human dimension and a deeper understanding of the dynamics underlying this well-known "Northern Cities" sound change. Analyses like Herndobler's and Habick's suggest that we need to get much closer to our subjects if we truly wish to understand all the processes underlying language change.

A third Chicago contribution comes from Andrew Sledd, who draws upon his own interactions with young black people in Chicago and upon his experience teaching predominantly black classes at Chicago's Harold Washington College. Sledd documents a number of Chicago Black English speech forms whose difference from Inland Northern can be explained by such operations as subject-raising transformations which counter a strong version of the creole hypothesis. But

Sledd is just as concerned with teachers' (and society's) attitude toward minority speech and the consequences of those attitudes. In particular, he questions the notion of whether or not economic or social advancement can be assured for minority young people who acquire Standard English.

Studies of urban dialectology and studies of Black English have concentrated on megalopolitan areas. But many residents of the Midwest live in smaller cities. Timothy J. Riney reports on one such city, Waterloo, Iowa. Riney tells us that Vernacular Black English is spoken in Waterloo, but that its presence there is denied by educational officialdom, specifically the Race Equity Commission of the Iowa Department of Education. Moreover, his study of language attitudes among students at the University of Northern Iowa—the source of most of the teachers in the Waterloo public school system—demonstrates that white Iowans assign low competence and intelligence scores to grammatically marked Black English and even to black-accented Standard English. Both Sledd and Riney remind us that after decades of civil rights activity and voluminous sociolinguistic discussion of race and language, negative attitudes—even deficit theories— toward the minority dialect and its speakers persists, not just in notorious megalopolitan enclaves like Howard Beach, but even here in the heartland, supposedly the home of the best of American values.

Thomas E. Murray's chapter on St. Louis rounds out the urban contributions to this collection. Unlike many urban dialectologists, Murray is conscious of the relationship between the city dialects he uncovers and the speech of the surrounding countryside; what is remarkable about his work is the differences he finds between St. Louis and the surrounding country, and between St. Louis and most of Missouri. Murray's work suggests too that regional dialects become class dialects in the city, with North/North Midland forms receiving preference from younger and more upscale speakers. Murray also offers a methodological innovation: his subjects are unaware that their speech is being recorded (the method has generated some controversy, which Murray addresses elsewhere; Murray 1985, Larmouth, Murray, and Murray 1992).

Until recently, studies in language variation have noted but otherwise paid little attention to gender as a controlling variable. Several years ago, Harold Allen began a large-scale quantitative study of gender variation among the LAUM informants (1985, 1986a, 1986b). In several additional studies of the Linguistic Atlas records, Virginia McDavid (1987) has discovered further insights on gender variation. In contrast to the large-scale work of Allen and McDavid, Robin

Herndobler's intensive study of a familiar neighborhood tells us much about the social forces and customs that account for gender differences in the first place.

The arrangement of this volume reflects the variety of interests, methods and subject matter included; the divisions are not always clearcut, but should make the contents more easily accessible. In Part I I have included chapters which address issues of "Power and Perception" as they relate to standard and nonstandard dialects. Contributors to Part I include Preston, Donahue, Sledd, Riney, and me. Part II includes chapters whose focus is both urban and/or small-group language. Included here are Habick, Murray (on St. Louis), Herndobler, and Miller. (Sledd and Riney could be included here as well, of course). In Part III, the chapters by Murray (on positive *anymore*), Lance, Faries and Lance, Carver, Larmouth and Remsing, Southard, and Thomas are geographic in focus, representing a considerable range of methodologies.

This volume does not, of course, cover in depth the entire area normally thought of as "Midwest," nor does it include all of the current research focused on the region. Ed Callary's longitudinal study of /æ/ raising, a followup to his 1975 paper, will have important implications for our understanding of sound change; that work is still in progress. Albert B. Cook's work on Kansas—a Midwestern state omitted, sadly, from treatment in this volume—is in preparation (Cook 1978). More work is needed on the English of bilingual ethnic groups throughout the region; my own data on the Mexican-American community of Sterling, Illinois—a small industrial city of fewer than twenty thousand—are still several years away from presentation. Chicago itself, where bilingual signs on elevated trains began to appear more than twenty years ago, needs much more attention. And as Herndobler and Habick have shown here, we also need studies of the dynamics of small peer groups and families. Finally, as I have argued at some length, we need a clearer understanding of the geographical dynamics of this region, particularly on the interface of historical forces like settlement history and contemporary forces like communication traffic patterns. The present volume, then, will do much to further understanding of this important region of the United States, but the amount of research being conducted could fill at least another volume of *"Heartland" English,* and the amount actually needed, many more. Maybe this is only a beginning.

I

Power &
Perception

2

Two Heartland Perceptions of Language Variety

DENNIS R. PRESTON

Language Standards in the United States

W HERE THE STANDARD variety originated is a historically apt question to ask of any language, but where it is spoken from a synchronic point of view is often the sort of information sought only by nonlinguists in the popular press. Although Oxford-Cambridge, Paris, and Beijing might once have been home only to local language varieties, they provided the norms which became prominent and widespread in countries which have a single standard (or aspire or even pretend to have one). In other areas (the United States and Canada, for example), the situation appears to be different. Whether or not regionally distinct patterns of syntax, morphology, and pronunciation are standard is troublesome in those settings.

In the United States, for example, metropolitan New York City's *stand on line* contrasts with the rest of the country's *in line* 'queue'; the North's *dove* with the South's *dived*; the North Midland's (though limited there) *my hair needs combed* with the rest of the country's *needs to be combed* or *needs combing*; some Northerners' *would you like to come with* is opposed to the rest of the country's need for a pronoun in such constructions—*with me* (or *us*, etc.). Differences in pronunciation from one area to another are even more numerous and better known.

Such regionalisms which are not glaringly nonstandard (at least not within their own areas) continue to remind linguists and nonlinguists alike that the promised leveling of variation which was to have resulted from universal opportunities in education and from the mass-media influence of film, television, and radio did not occur.

Although this is not the place to consider at length why that homogenization did not take place, some speculation is in order. First, perhaps foremost, universal education of equal quality is still only a goal, not a reality. Local schools, so prized as democratic institutions, are at liberty to hire spectacularly overqualified or underqualified teachers, depending on the wealth of the school district and on the importance its local taxpayers place on education. In addition, curricula, though mandated to some extent by state regulations, are not universally set. Although a school may be required to teach a certain number of courses in "English," the content of those courses may vary from stream-of-consciousness composition and diary writing through the reading of the classics or detective fiction to the parsing of sentences in old fashioned Reed-Kellogg diagrams. Finally, the growth of private schools in the United States (religious and secular, with qualities both superior and inferior to the public system) ensures even greater diversity.

Second, the single standard which the mass media were to evince turned out to be another fiction. Movies, radio, and television exposed an even greater diversity of regional types and allowed further solidifying of stereotypes and caricatures. The supposed single standard of newscasters is bogus, as three major networks in the United States demonstrate. The anchorman for CBS is Dan Rather (South Midland); for NBC, Tom Brokaw (North Midland); and for ABC, Peter Jennings (Canadian). Almost every evening, regional speakers from a variety of speech regions can be heard on all three networks; in recent years, even second-language-influenced varieties (e.g., Hispanic) have been present.

Lastly, regionalism is still strong in the United States in non-linguistic areas of concern. Northerners still know that Southerners are a slow, healthy, racist, conservative, anti-intellectual, Protestant lot, and Southerners know that Northerners are Jewish and Catholic, quick, dishonest, and lead morally questionable lives. Strong personal attachments to local values and norms and negative caricatures of out-groups help ensure that local language varieties persist.

Linguists and Language Standards in the United States

A commonplace in United States linguistics is that every region supports its own standard variety; that is, no one region is the locus (or source) of *the* standard. Historically, that is a fair assessment; no center of culture, economy, and government such as Paris or London ever dominated. Therefore, the truth in some texts is as Falk (1978) has it:

> In the United States there is no one regional dialect that serves as the model. What is considered standard English in New York City would not be considered standard in Forth Worth, Texas. *Each region of the country has its own standard.* (emphasis added; 289)

There is no doubt that speakers in each region could recognize their own local varieties which were more standard (the usage of the best-educated speakers). But it is not at all certain that they would adhere to a cultural-linguistic relativism that would admit to the existence of a standard in every region, and, more to the point here, that there is no region or area which is more (or less) standard than others. Falk's position is clearly a confusion of sophisticated linguistic relativism, deriving, perhaps, from well-intentioned attempts to debunk notions of so-called primitive and deficient linguistic systems with what she believes to be popular perception. The latter, of course, is the point which deserves investigation. At least in the United States (if not everywhere), it is not linguists who define language standards.

Other introductory texts use the national newscaster suggestion or have even proposed a mysterious, nonexistent variety:

> In America [*sic*], Standard English is the form of the language used on the national media, especially in news programs. (Akmajian et al. 1979: 181)

> SAE [Standard American English] is an idealization. Nobody speaks this dialect, and if somebody did, we wouldn't know it because SAE is not defined precisely. Several years ago there actually was an entire conference devoted to one subject: a precise definition of SAE. This convocation of scholars did not succeed in satisfying everyone as to what SAE should be. The best hint we can give you is to listen to national broadcasters (though nowadays some of these people may speak a regional dialect). (Fromkin and Rodman 1983: 251)

It is clear that Fromkin and Rodman contrast the standard with regional varieties, though they later show that they, too, are capable of confusing the two notions.

> It is true that many words which are monosyllabic in Standard American are disyllabic in the Southern dialect: the word *right,* pronounced as [rayt] in the Midwest, New England, and the Middle Atlantic states and in British English, is pronounced [raɔt] in many parts of the South. (249; NB: This pronunciation is, in fact, not disyllabic.)

Here, oddly enough, Fromkin and Rodman come much closer to the beginnings of an accurate folk linguistic description of a standard as their own prejudices peek through. *Standard American* is exemplified in the Midwest, New England, and the Middle Atlantic states (and even in

British English?) while the South has another variety (by implication, clearly not standard). Falk would have accused Fromkin and Rodman of regional prejudices (and she would be right), but a legitimate search for the source and locus of Standard United States English (SUSE) will have to consider just such prejudices. What linguists believe about standards matters very little; what nonlinguists believe constitutes precisely that cognitive reality which needs to be described in a responsible sociolinguistics—one which takes speech-community attitudes and perception (as well as performance) into account.

SUSE cannot be characterized as a simple socioeconomic reality. If it could, why do Fromkin and Rodman make the silly mistake of contrasting regional vowels in the South (used by the most privileged and impeccably educated) with those of SUSE, which they apparently locate in the Midwest, New England, and the Middle Atlantic states? They have committed the error of cloaking personal folk beliefs in the mantle of linguistic expertise. If they refer to varying attitudes about varieties, they should make clear whether they are drawing on research or citing folk linguistic information reflecting their own beliefs. To do otherwise confuses scientific reporting and hypothesizing with statements of linguistic prejudices. At least Langacker makes it clear that he is speculating about what many people may believe when he observes that "British English enjoys special favor in the eyes of many Americans. Boston English is considered by many people to be more prestigious than Southern speech or Brooklynese" (1973: 55). This is clearly true for Fromkin and Rodman, who believe that the Southern vowel system, despite its universal use by educated and uneducated speakers alike, is *regional,* and therefore not *standard.*

To correct even introductory linguistics textbooks, research must be done to establish the boundaries of SUSE from several points of view. An internal, linguistic view might describe the systems used by educated speakers and writers from various regions. Describing these as functional or productive standards for each region will capture part of the truth. A second sort of research concerns responses to varieties. What good will it do a speaker or a writer of a variety if his or her performance leads to conclusions about personality, intelligence, education, validity of content, and so on which do not correspond to the uses to which a standard variety is usually put? Surely one of the functions of a standard is to convey serious information in a variety which implies that the speaker or writer is well-informed and which disallows a caricature of the message itself on the grounds that it is delivered in "incorrect" language.

Language Attitude Studies

Language attitude studies have explored just such dimensions of diversity, beginning by sampling attitudes towards different languages (Lambert et al. 1960) and moving on to samples of attitudes towards different varieties of the same language (e.g., Tucker and Lambert 1969). Giles and his associates (summarized in Ryan and Giles 1982) have investigated a large number of such reactions (to taped voices) and have suggested a general pattern: speakers of regional varieties (where that suggests nonstandardness) find speakers of their own varieties warm, friendly, honest, sympathetic, and trustworthy, but often slow, unintelligent, and plodding; they often regard speakers of a superposed standard as cold, dishonest, and unsympathetic, but quick, intelligent, and ambitious. In short, to the extent that listeners find their own varieties less prestigious, they suffer from what Labov (1966) called *linguistic insecurity.* One suspects that some of this insecurity has its direct source in speakers' awareness that the local variety will not serve the function of a standard as outlined above. That is, it will not convince some listeners that the intelligence, education, and authority of the speaker or writer are high, and it will not, therefore, inspire confidence in the content of some messages. Of course, there are notable exceptions; information of the sort most likely to be delivered in a local or nonstandard variety (street-wise facts, farming information, sports calls and expressions, hunting and fishing facts) might, indeed, be seen as more trustworthy if delivered in a nonstandard variety, but the evaluation of other ("intellectual") characteristics of the speaker would not be improved.

Folk Beliefs about Language

Language attitude studies confirm, then, that regional varieties are not all equal, even when only phonological features are contrasted (that is, when lexicon and grammar are not variables). Such studies help establish the folk linguistic base for another perspective on standard varieties, an essential one for languages with a number of varieties and no clear-cut standard model. What is lacking in the study of standards in such settings is the account of what speakers of various regions (and classes, and sexes, and ethnic groups, and ages, and so on) believe. While language attitude surveys hope to avoid the *observer's paradox* (Labov 1972a), which here includes the effect awareness has on respondents' reactions to as well as their performances of language, other studies, perhaps of a more ethnographic nature, might seek to discover the overt categories and definitions speakers have about linguistic matters.

If speakers are confronted with the task of identifying the areas of the United States where the most "correct" English is spoken, how will they respond? If they are relativists like Falk, they will simply indicate that the task is impossible, claiming that each area supports a standard. If, however, as Fromkin and Rodman show (surely unintentionally) and Langacker claims, they have clear linguistic prejudices about the locus of SUSE, they will readily rank areas of the country for language correctness. Additionally, if Langacker is right, there should emerge some preference for "British" speech (however that may be represented in new world areas) and a preference for Boston over Brooklyn and the South; if Fromkin and Rodman's prejudices are widely represented, a preference for East Coast and Midwestern speech over Southern should show up.

Additionally, if the studies by Giles and his associates apply to United States varieties, one might also expect to find that speakers who consider their accents "regional" (that is, speakers who suffer from linguistic insecurity) will rank their home areas lower for correct speech than some other areas. On the other hand, since Giles and his associates found that there was a decided preference for the local area along affective dimensions (friendliness, honesty, and so on), one should find such a preference for the local area in a ranking task which asks where the most "pleasant" variety is spoken.

Such tasks are distinctly different from typical language attitude surveys. In the latter, respondents check off attributes which they assign to the speaker based on a short tape-recorded sample. A number of paired opposites (later factor-analyzed to produce groups of terms with similar ratings) are presented to the respondents while each voice is played; they usually include such pairs as the following, placed at the extremes of a seven-point scale:

Friendly __ __ __ __ __ __ __ Unfriendly

Such studies also often utilize a technique known as *matched-guise*, in which the same speaker (unknown to the respondents) provides samples of different varieties. This allows for assurance that idiosyncratic qualities of voice are not being rated.[1]

These studies generally conclude that attitudes to voices from here and there are thus and so, but they do not, as a rule, ask the respondents where they thought each voice came from. It is possible, then, that research which reports that respondents from Detroit believe that voices from Atlanta are "unfriendly," although it accurately represents the response to the voice sample, is misleading. It may be that (1) the respondents did not recognize where the voices were from (and might, in fact, have specifically believed the voices were from someplace else), and (2) the respondents might not have a cognitive speech area to which the voice sample might be readily assigned.

In summary, then, work on SUSE ought to involve, at least, the following:

1. descriptions of the structure of varieties used in various areas by well-educated speakers and writers (local "functional-performance" standards);
2. ethnographic accounts of nonlinguists' opinions about standard language—its shape, use, origin, and provenience (e.g., Niedzielski and Preston in progress, Preston in progress);
3. language attitude surveys of nonlinguists' reactions to a variety of regional standard and nonstandard voice samples (e.g., considerable work by Giles and his associates, much of it summarized in Ryan and Giles 1982);
4. determination of where respondents believe taped voice samples are from (e.g., Milroy and McClenaghan 1977, Preston in progress);
5. determination of nonlinguists' categories of areal language distribution, a "perceptual" rather than production "dialectology" (e.g., Daan and Blok 1970; Grootaers 1959; Kremer 1984; Preston 1982, 1985a, 1986, 1989, in progress; Preston and Howe 1987; Rensink 1955; Weijnen 1968); and,
6. ratings of the "correctness" and "pleasantness" of areas with no voice stimulus (Preston 1985b, 1988, 1989, in progress).

Such a many-faceted program of research puts the weight of describing SUSE precisely where it belongs—in the minds, out of the mouths, and from the word processors of nonlinguists. Of course, linguists (presumably sociolinguists, dialectologists, and ethnographers) will need to do the collection and interpretation, but there should be no confusing of their own feelings with their reports on and interpretations of the opinions of the respondents who count.

Indiana and Michigan Beliefs about United States English

The rest of this chapter reports, briefly, on an attempt to survey two regions of the United States in several of the ways described above. The two areas focused on are southern Indiana (an area suspected to have some linguistic insecurity stemming from its association with caricaturistic South Midland—"hillbilly"—speech) and southeastern Michigan (a typical Inland Northern speech community which should show little or no linguistic insecurity).[2] Although not all tasks and certainly not all subdivisions of the respondents studied are reported on here, the following research program was carried out:

1. Respondents drew (on a map containing only state lines) boundaries of where they believed the regional speech areas of the United States were; techniques developed by Preston and Howe (1987) allow computerized generalizations to be compiled from these individual responses.
2. Respondents ranked the 50 states, New York City, and Washington, D.C. on a scale of one to ten (1 = "least," 10 = "most") for "correct" and "pleasant" speech.
3. Respondents ranked the 50 states on a scale of one to four (1 = "same," 2 = "a little different," 3 = "different," 4 = "unintelligibly different") for perceived degree of language difference from the home area.
4. Respondents listened to nine voices which had been sampled from sites on a north to south line in the middle of the United States; the samples were all of male, well-educated, middle-aged speakers discussing a topic of general interest. They were presented in a scrambled order to the respondents, who were instructed to assign each voice to the site where they thought it belonged.
5. Respondents indicated which parts of the United States they had actually been in.
6. Respondents were interviewed after they had performed (1) through (5) to determine the etiology of their rankings, mappings, and identifications, and to allow them to express any other opinions about language distribution and status.

Processing of the data from (5) and (6) above is not yet complete and will not be included in what follows.

Correct English

Naturally, what pertains most to this study are the areas seen by the respondents as more and less correct. Map 2.1 is a map of grouped mean scores for the "correct" task from southern Indiana, and map 2.2 is a similar map for southeastern Michigan.

It should be noted that very few respondents complained about this task. That is, the relativist position taken by Falk above, though morally irreproachable, was not that taken by the great majority of respondents. Although they complained that they did not have information about this or that state, the ranking of most areas for correctness was for them a reasonable task and represented opinions overtly held about the sites where better and worse English was spoken.

Maps 2.1 and 2.2 show that for both southeastern Michigan and southern Indiana respondents, the areas most definitely associated with incorrect English are the South and New York City; they are the

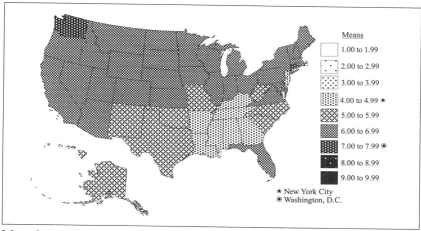

Map 2.1. Mean scores for 123 southern Indiana respondents' ratings of language "correctness" for the 50 states, New York City, and Washington, D.C. (1.00 = least correct; 10.00 = most correct).

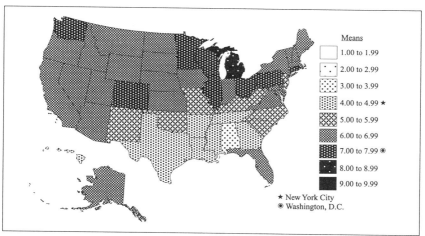

Map 2.2. Mean scores for 147 southeastern Michigan respondents' ratings of language "correctness" as in map 2.1.

only areas which have mean scores within the range 4.00–4.99 (and for raters from Michigan, Alabama even dips into the 3.00–3.99 range). Langacker's assessment of what nonlinguists believe about correctness and Fromkin's and Rodman's personal prejudices are upheld in this survey on at least two counts; the South and New York City (Langacker's "Brooklynese") are both rated low. In addition, areas which border on the South and New York City are given ratings in the 5.00 to 5.99 range, and their low ratings may be accounted for by noting their proximity to the lowest-rated areas. The other two sites falling in that range— Alaska (only for Indiana respondents) and Hawaii—must be interpreted differently. It is most likely that for many respondents the caricature of nonnative speakers for these two regions may be very high. Unfamiliarity is an unlikely reason for the low rating since these respondents are just as likely to be unfamiliar with some of the plains and mountain states (e.g., Montana and Idaho) which fall in the 6.00–6.99 range.

Turning to the other end of the scale, predictions about linguistic insecurity seem to be borne out. Michigan raters see themselves as the only state in the 8.00–8.99 range, exposing considerable linguistic self-confidence. Indiana respondents, however, rate themselves in the generally acceptable 6.00–6.99 range, but clearly regard some other areas (Washington, D.C., Connecticut, Delaware, and Washington[3]) as superior. This lower ranking of the home area must indicate some small linguistic insecurity. The Michigan ratings in map 2.2 suggest at least one of the sources of that insecurity. Those raters allow surrounding states to bask in the warmth of Michigan's correctness. Wisconsin, Minnesota, Illinois, Ohio, and Pennsylvania (all nearby states) earned ratings in the 7.00–7.99 range. Indiana, however, which actually shares a boundary with Michigan (unlike Illinois, Minnesota, and Pennsylvania) is rated one notch down, in the 6.00–6.99 range.

Two interpretations are available. Either Indiana is seen by Michigan raters as belonging to that set of states farther west which earn ratings in that range, or, much more likely, Indiana is seen as a peculiarly northern outpost of Southern speech. It is certain that internal and external perception of Indiana as a site influenced by Southern varieties (historically and descriptively an accurate perception, by the way) produces its linguistic insecurity. That Indiana respondents classify themselves along with Michigan, Illinois, Wisconsin, and other Great Lakes states in the 6.00–6.99 range in their own rating (map 2.1) may be interpreted as their attempt to align themselves with Northern rather than Southern varieties in order to escape the associations which form the basis of their insecurity. On the other hand, the narrower range of ratings provided by the Indiana respondents (4.00–7.99) compared to the Michigan raters (3.00–8.99) might indicate a more democratic view of the distribution of correctness in general. That alternative (and not necessarily contradictory) interpretation will have to await more detailed analysis of the post-task interviews. Other high ratings by both groups do indeed include some of the New England area Langacker indicated might be preferred (and might be associated with British speech). Quite unexpectedly, Washington, D.C., earns a high rating from both, an indication, perhaps, that the center of government is seen as an authority on matters linguistic, although its high rating might represent only a part of the Mid-Atlantic section of SUSE believed in by Fromkin and Rodman. Not mentioned either by Langacker or Fromkin and Rodman as a folk site for SUSE, however, is the West, but it is assigned generally high ratings by both Indiana and Michigan respondents. There is, doubtless, for both sets of respondents, a sense of a leveled, unremarkable speech in the West.

A factor analysis of the ratings provides a more subtle way of grouping together those areas rated similarly. Map 2.3 shows the factor analysis of the correct ratings from Indiana, and map 2.4 shows the same results for Michigan. The strongest factor group (#1) for both groups is the rather large western area to which both assigned high but not the highest ratings.[4] The second strongest factor group for both areas is the low-rated South, and, for Indiana residents, it reaches up to include the local area, strong proof that Indiana linguistic insecurity stems from associations with Southern speech. This same factor group

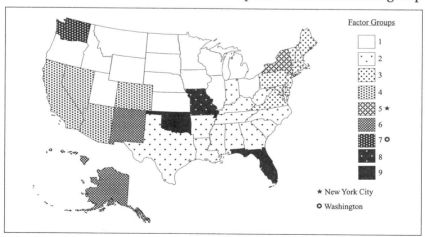

Map 2.3. A factor analysis of the southern Indiana correctness ratings from map 2.1 (1 = strongest factor group; 9 = weakest factor group).

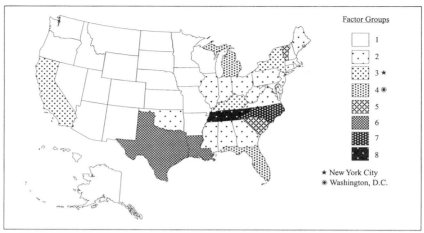

Map 2.4. A factor analysis of the southeastern Michigan correctness ratings from map 2.2 (1 = stongest factor group; 8 = weakest factor group).

is peculiarly divided for Michigan respondents; in addition to a small group of Southern states, there is a continuum of New England, Mid-Atlantic, and Great Lakes states in this category. Even these areas are broken up by a small number of idiosyncratic groups. These analyses suggest that the Indiana raters have a greater consistency in their perception of correctness as a geographical phenomenon. The third factor group for Indiana is a New England–Mid-Atlantic stretch; the fourth a generally southwestern group of states; the fifth New York and New York City, and the sixth an interesting confirmation of the suggestion that Alaska and Hawaii might be rated lower on the basis of their being perceived as sites with a high concentration of nonnative speakers. That they are joined by New Mexico in a factor analysis makes that interpretation much surer.[5]

Pleasant English

Maps 2.5 and 2.6 display the ratings of Indiana and Michigan respondents respectively for "pleasant" speech. The suggestion by Giles and associates that local speech is affectively preferred seems strongly confirmed, especially in the Indiana perceptions. Only Indiana is rated in the 7.00–7.99 range for pleasantness, and the Michigan raters put only Washington, Colorado, and neighboring Minnesota in the same

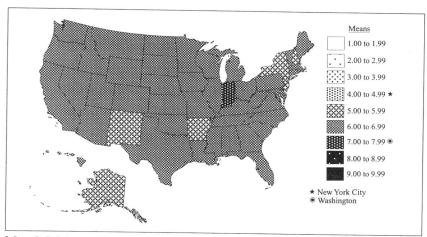

Map 2.5. Mean scores for southern Indiana ratings of language "pleasantness" as in map 2.1.

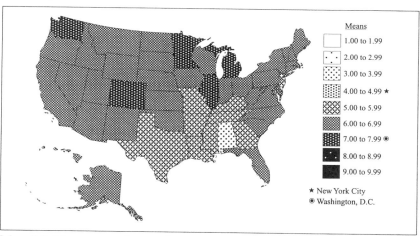

Map 2.6. Mean scores for southeastern Michigan ratings of language "pleasantness" as in map 2.1.

7.00–7.99 range along with their home site. These results suggest, further, that the preference for local norms along affective lines is stronger in areas where there is linguistic insecurity. At the other end, only a few areas are rated low. New York City is the only site put in the 4.00–4.99 range by both Indiana and Michigan raters. More interestingly, the ratings of the South, similar for the two groups in the correctness ratings, are very different for this task. The Michigan respondents continue to rate the South low, giving Alabama a score in the 4.00–4.99 range, but the Indiana raters, though they find the South incorrect, do not find it so unpleasant. In fact, New Hampshire, New Jersey, New York, and Delaware constitute a much larger pocket of unpleasant speech areas from the point of view of Indiana speakers. For

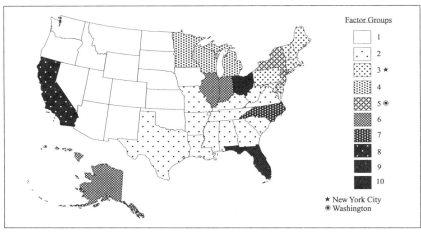

Map 2.7. A factor analysis of the southern Indiana "pleasantness" ratings from map 2.5 (1 = strongest factor group; 10 = weakest).

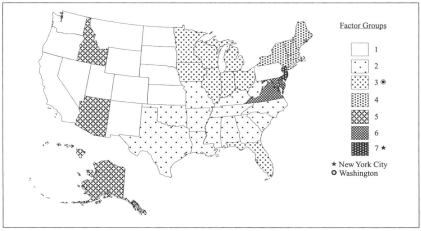

Map 2.8. A factor analysis of the southeastern Michigan "pleasantness" ratings from map 2.6 (1 = strongest factor group; 7 = weakest).

Michigan speakers this Eastern unpleasantness is associated only with New York City and immediate surroundings.

Factor analyses of these pleasant ratings (maps 2.7 and 2.8) show that Indiana speakers do create a little pocket (along with Illinois) for themselves (map 2.7, #6), but Michigan raters, more linguistically secure, extend the pleasant rating of their home site over the entire Great Lakes area (map 2.8, #3). The factor groupings for both sets of respondents show a greater consistency and internal agreement than for the correctness tasks and open other possibilities for interpretation not taken up here.

Mental Maps of Dialect Areas

How do these facts about the perception of correctness and pleasantness coincide with other studies of the perception and identification of regional variation? An important first task in determining such perceptions is one which establishes what the respondents' taxonomies of dialect areas are. It will not do simply to assume that those regions discovered by dialectologists form the cognitive set from which an ordinary speaker makes his or her assignment of regional identifications. I have studied the perception of dialect areas by respondents from the two areas under discussion here and have produced (through computer generation) mental maps of United States English varieties from those two points of view (maps 2.9 and 2.10).[6]

A comparison of the Indiana correctness map 2.1 with the Indiana mental map 2.9 showing regional speech differences demonstrates that correctness ratings do not necessarily change at the boundaries of perceived regional difference. While the low correctness ratings for the South and Outer South and for the Southwest are very good matches between the two representations, the Midwest, North, West, New England, Northeast, and East Coast, all seen as distinct speech areas, differ very little in their correctness ratings. Different dialect areas, then, may have equal status so far as a SUSE is concerned, but some areas are clearly inferior, and it seems to be the case that inferiority is more consistently marked than superiority. It is obviously more salient, since fully 86% (106 of 123) of the Indiana raters outlined a "South," while, for example, only 43% (53) outlined a "North."[7] Similarly, 94% of the Michigan raters marked a "South" (138 of 147) while only 61% (90) marked a "North." Although historical and popular culture facts as well as linguistic ones make the South geographically salient, it is not too

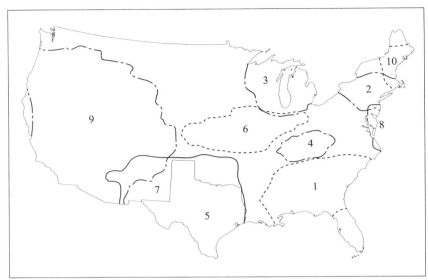

Map 2.9. The perceptual dialect areas of the United States from the point of view of southern Indiana respondents ($N = 123$).

Key: Area 1 = South ($N = 106$, 86% of total)
      Area 2 = Northeast ($N = 63$, 51% of total)
      Area 3 = North ($N = 53$, 43% of total)
      Area 4 = Outer South ($N = 44$, 36% of total)
      Area 5 = Texas ($N = 39$, 32% of total)
      Area 6 = Midwest ($N = 31$, 25% of total)
      Area 7 = Southwest ($N = 28$, 23% of total)
      Area 8 = Mid-Atlantic ($N = 22$, 18% of total)
      Area 9 = West ($N = 22$, 18% of total)
      Area 10 = New England ($N = 21$, 17% of total)

risky to suggest that there is a relationship between the perceptual salience of the South in the respondents' taxonomies of where dialect areas exist and their extremely low rating of that area. In support of this hypothesis, the second most salient area for Indiana respondents (51%) and the third most salient for Michigan respondents (54%) is the "Northeast," precisely the area where New York City, another poorly rated area, lies.

The Michigan map of perceived dialect areas (map 2.10) shows little correspondence with the detailed levels of correctness in the Great Lakes area which emerged in the correctness ranking study (map 2.2). Indiana is lumped together with Michigan, Minnesota, Illinois, Wis-

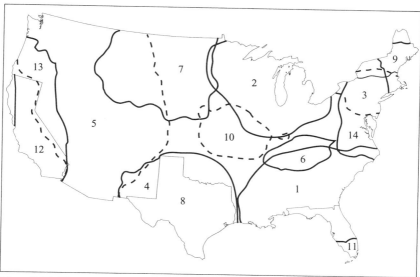

Map 2.10. The perceptual dialect areas of the United States from the point of view of southeastern Michigan respondents ($N = 147$).

Key: Area 1 = South ($N = 138$, 94% of total)
Area 2 = North ($N = 90$, 61% of total)
Area 3 = Northeast ($N = 80$, 54% of total)
Area 4 = Southwest ($N = 75$, 51% of total)
Area 5 = West ($N = 60$, 41% of total)
Area 6 = Outer South ($N = 44$, 30% of total)
Area 7 = Plains and Mountains ($N = 37$, 25% of total)
Area 8 = Texas ($N = 34$, 23% of total)
Area 9 = New England ($N = 33$, 22% of total)
Area 10 = Midwest ($N = 26$, 18% of total)
Area 11 = Florida ($N = 25$, 17% of total)
Area 12 = California ($N = 25$, 17% of total)
Area 13 = West Coast ($N = 23$, 16% of total)
Area 14 = East Coast ($N = 23$, 16% of total)

consin, and Ohio in a "North." On the other hand, the greater complexity of rankings in the Michigan correctness study is paralleled by a greater complexity of areal distribution in the hand-drawn map task. Considerably greater overlapping appears, corresponding to the more confused factor-analysis groupings derived in the Michigan ranking studies (map 2.4) and, again, suggesting that areas with less linguistic self-confidence may show greater uniformity and consistency in perception.

Degrees of Difference among Dialect Areas

Another task which elicits respondents' ideas of geographical language distribution asks them to rate the degree of difference between their own use and others'. Though rated by the respondents as 1 (no difference), 2 (slightly different), 3 (different), and 4 (unintelligibly different), the mean score ratings were divided into four groups as follows: 1.00–1.75, 1.76–2.50, 2.51–3.25, 3.26–4.00. Maps 2.11 and 2.12 illustrate the responses to that task. Again, Indiana linguistic insecurity emerges. Although in the correctness task the Indiana raters grouped themselves with areas to the north (map 2.1), presumably to avoid connection with the contaminating South, insecurity surfaces here (as it did in the factor analysis) since the Indiana respondents find a degree of difference between themselves and speakers to the north. In fact, the difference ratings from Indiana look more like the Indiana pleasantness ratings (maps 2.5 and 2.7); only the two latitudinally contiguous states (Ohio and Illinois) are regarded as exactly similar. Indiana respondents do not, however, associate difference from their own speech with nonstandardness. For example, the South (rated worst) is as different from Indiana speech as is the Northeast (generally rated well, with the obvious exception of New York City and nearby areas). In fact, Massachusetts, rated quite high, is the only area which might be regarded as having unintelligibly different speech. Michigan

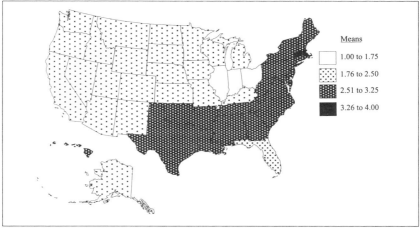

Map 2.11. Mean scores of the degree of difference seen by southern Indiana respondents between their local area and each of the 50 states (1 = same, 2 = slightly different, 3 = different, 4 = unintelligibly different).

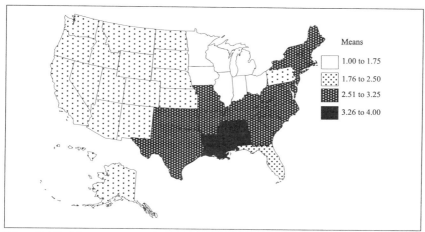

Map 2.12. Mean scores of the degree of difference seen by southeastern Michigan respondents between their local area and each of the 50 states (as in map 2.11).

respondents, on the other hand, are much harsher on the South and do seem to associate differences with standardness. The core of the South (Louisiana, Mississippi, and Alabama) is rated as most different.

Placement of Regional Voices

Finally, how precisely can speakers from the two areas place voice samples from different regions, and how might the boundaries which emerge from that task correspond to those already established for correctness and pleasantness? Map 2.13 shows the sites at which recordings were made for the recognition test; the voices (described above) were then played in random order and the respondents were asked to associate each voice with a site. Assigning the sites the numbers one through nine (from south to north) allowed us to calculate the mean score for the task. For example, if a respondent said the voice from Saginaw, Michigan, was from South Bend, Indiana, the number 7 was tallied for that response. If each voice were recognized perfectly by each respondent, the scores would read simply, 9.00, 8.00, and so on from north to south. The actual scores are presented in table 2.1.

What is most striking, though it is not particularly important to the focus here on correctness, is the fact that these nonlinguists were very good at arranging speech samples along a north/south dimension. If

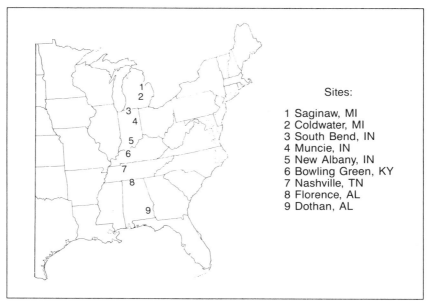

Sites:

1 Saginaw, MI
2 Coldwater, MI
3 South Bend, IN
4 Muncie, IN
5 New Albany, IN
6 Bowling Green, KY
7 Nashville, TN
8 Florence, AL
9 Dothan, AL

Map 2.13. Sites from which voices were sampled for the identification task.

Table 2.1
Scoring of Regional Voice Placement

ID	Site	Michigan Respondents	Indiana Respondents	Perfect Score
1	Saginaw, MI	7.0	6.6	9.00
2	Coldwater, MI	6.6	6.3	8.00
3	South Bend, IN	6.2	6.4	7.00
4	Muncie, IN	5.5	6.1	6.00
5	New Albany, IN	5.3	5.8	5.00
6	Bowling Green, KY	4.1	5.1	4.00
7	Nashville, TN	3.5	3.8	3.00
8	Florence, AL	3.1	2.6	2.00
9	Dothan, AL	3.7	2.5	1.00

one assumes that a greater distance between mean scores indicates a greater distinctiveness heard between two samples, then a convention of calling a 0.50 or greater difference a "minor" boundary and a difference of 1.00 or greater a "major" one is not unreasonable. Based on those calculations, a taxonomy of the respondents' areas of acoustic differentiation of United States dialects (along a north/south dimension only, of course) is as represented in maps 2.14 and 2.15.

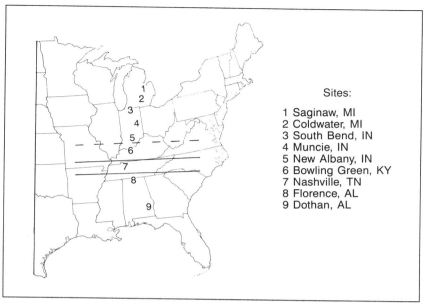

Map 2.14. Boundaries mathematically derived from the identification task for southern Indiana respondents.

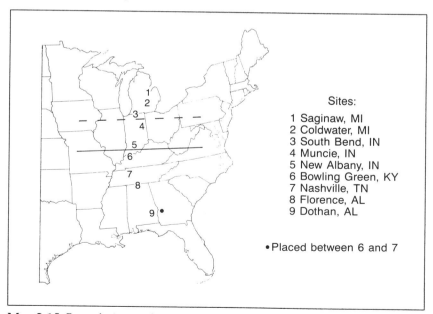

Map 2.15. Boundaries mathematically derived from the identification task for southeastern Michigan respondents.

Both sets correspond (and fail to correspond) in interesting ways to the data gleaned from the earlier tasks. Though Indiana residents, in their taxonomy of regional speech derived from hand-drawn maps (map 2.9), claim to distinguish a "North" from a "Midwest," there is no evidence that they hear any such difference strongly. The Michigan respondents, however, who taxonomize a similar distinction (map 2.10), do have a minor boundary between voice samples 3 and 4 (numbered as in map 2.13). Although both groups distinguish an "Outer South" from the "South," only the Indiana respondents have strong boundaries there. It would be premature, however, to suggest that the boundary between, say, site 7 and site 8 is the same as the distinction between those two regions as generalized from the hand-drawn map task. Similarly, the Indiana respondents hear two major and one minor Southern distinctions (map 2.14), but it is the Michigan hand-drawn map (map 2.10) which has an overlapping "Outer South" and "South," providing a three-way rather than two-way division. In summary, the Indiana generalized taxonomy of hand-drawn maps (map 2.9) results in a four-way division in the north/south continuum between areas 3 and 4, 4 and 5, and 7 and 8; the Indiana identification task (map 2.14), however, places major boundaries between sites 7 and 8 (suggesting that the "South" versus everything else is their strongest perceptual cut from at least these two points of view) and sites 6 and 7. Another boundary (albeit weaker) between 5 (the home site) and 6 serves, it might be suggested, to cut off local speech from anything that might be regarded as "Southern." That is, Indiana speakers, perhaps in another expression of linguistic insecurity, want to indicate that they belong to a large, undifferentiated "North," not to any of the several areas of "South" which they cut off below them. Michigan respondents have only one major boundary (map 2.15), between 5 and 6, again a differentiation between the "South" and everything else. This major division falls precisely in the area where both groups have a *trough* in their hand-drawn generalizations (maps 2.9 and 2.10)—a sort of no-man's land which arises where two perceptually different sites are seen as particularly distinct. The difference here is, of course, that the Michigan respondents hear that distinction strongly; Indiana respondents do not. The secondary distinction for Michigan respondents (map 2.15) in the identification task (between sites 3 and 4) is almost certainly a part of their awareness of the difference between "North" and "Midwest," even though their hand-drawn generalization does not have a "Midwest" which reaches far enough east (map 2.10) to be an actual part of the north/south continuum of voices.

When the identification task is compared with the degrees of difference task, the Indiana residents are again those who make the greater number of subdivisions in the north/south dimension.

One Michigan difference boundary (map 2.12, between Indiana and Kentucky) is precisely in the place where the major Michigan identification boundary (between sites 5 and 6) falls. Although the degree-of-difference task shows an even more radically different "Deep South" for Michigan respondents, their identification task does not reflect that. In the degree-of-difference task, the Indiana respondents make sharp subdivisions between Michigan and Indiana (map 2.13, sites 3 and 4), between Indiana and Kentucky (sites 5 and 6), and between Kentucky and Tennessee (sites 6 and 7). The latter two are parallels to differences heard in the identification task, but the first comes much closer to the distinction heard by the Michigan respondents but not taxonomized in the hand-drawn or degree-of-difference tasks.

Finally, correctness. The Indiana respondents' correctness map (map 2.1) is simple. There is a generally correct "North" (everything above the Ohio River assigned a score in the 6.00–6.99 range) and a generally incorrect "South" (all in the 4.00–4.99 range). The cut is precisely at the minor boundary in the identification task (between sites 5 and 6) which severs the home area from the "South." The Michigan correctness map (map 2.2) shows, however, a five-stage decrease along the line investigated in the identification task—Michigan 8.00–8.99, Indiana 6.00–6.99, Kentucky 5.00–5.99, Tennessee 4.00–4.99, and Alabama 3.00–3.99. The factor analyses of correctness (maps 2.3 and 2.4) reflect these same subdivisions, precisely in the case of Michigan and with Indiana grouped together with the "South" for the Indiana residents. Michigan respondents have a caricature of increasingly incorrect Southern speech—the farther south, the more incorrect. The Indiana respondents, though they too negatively evaluate Southern speech and are careful to cut themselves off from nearby varieties of it (which, of course, from a production point of view are not distinct), more simply dichotomize the middle part of the United States into a correct "North" and incorrect "South."

A similar stratification recurs in the pleasantness task. There are only two dimensions for the Indiana respondents; a most pleasant home area and not unpleasant surroundings, including a "South" which fares no better or worse than a "North" (map 2.5). The Michigan respondents, however, have a clearly stronger negative caricature of Southern voices along this affective dimension (map 2.6). Local speech is most pleasant (7.00–7.99), Indiana less so (6.00–6.99), Kentucky and Tennessee even less so (5.00–5.99), and Alabama as bad as New York City (4.00–4.99). The factor analysis for the Indiana pleasantness task (map 2.7) agrees with the means scores arrangement, but the Michigan factor analysis (map 2.8) reveals a simple dichotomy of "North" versus "South," again divided at the Ohio River.

In conclusion, it is tempting to note, simply, that the identification task shows that respondents hear more differences in areas which are closer to home. The Indiana respondents have internal Southern divisions; the Michigan respondents have internal Northern divisions. The other taxonomies, however, reveal that the areas where speech differences are heard as most distinctive do not necessarily correspond to the templates the same respondents have for the localization of such facts as dialect distribution and distinctiveness and for such judgmental considerations as the correctness and pleasantness of varieties.

Conclusions

Southern United States English (and New York City English) are clearly varieties prejudiced against. Northern speakers are prejudiced against Southern speech even along affective dimensions. There may be significant differences in the patterns of pleasantness and correctness when the perceivers groups are divided into groups with some degree of linguistic insecurity and others with generally good linguistic self-concepts. Insecurity may result in exaggerated isolation of the home area in affective evaluation and in exaggerated isolation from nearby "contaminating" areas in evaluations of correctness. Insecure areas would also seem to have a tendency to be less harsh in evaluating correctness in general, though Labov reports the opposite tendency for stigmatized speakers' evaluation of others with similar features in his study of attitudes and production differences in New York City (1966). Both secure and insecure areas agree, however, in assigning greater geographical salience to areas seen as incorrect.

Most importantly, these several approaches have shown that correctness and related affective dimensions, at least in United States English, are notions which, for nonlinguists, have geographical significance. Though it is not easy to arrive at the folk perception held of such concepts, it is important to seek it out, for, at least for United States English, it represents a set of beliefs both strongly held and influential in the linguistic life of large and small speech communities.

These data are being further analyzed for the consistency of general perceptions presented here with those of different age, sex, and status groups, and such subdivisions may have a great deal to say about the etiology of and change in the perception of language differences.

Such a multidimensional approach to what are ultimately folk linguistic questions provides a surer consideration of the limited data provided by language attitude surveys and from anecdotal and participant observer information. It serves, moreover, to help build a more complete and accurate picture of the regard for language use and variety within a speech community, providing questions about such issues as language standards with answers from communities themselves.

3

On Inland Northern and the Factors for Dialect Spread and Shift

THOMAS S. DONAHUE

THIS ESSAY WILL attempt to form the groundwork for future analyses of the spread of, and the native-area shift to, the Inland Northern dialect in the United States.[1] The analysis will formulate several hypotheses concerning the widespread shift to the Inland Northern dialect (the "General American" speech as described in the 1930s) between the Civil War and the mid-1950s. In addition, this analysis will suggest reasons why Inland Northern is sustained as a second, or alternative, dialect in most regions.

The method of analysis owes a great deal in its emphasis on practical facts and pragmatic theorizing to the work of Joshua Fishman on language maintenance and language shift. More specifically, this approach attempts to answer the question best phrased by Leo Lowenthal (1957: 56): "What are the functions of cultural communication within the total process of a society?" The most cogent political science argumentation in answer to this question has been provided in classical formulations by Karl Deutsch (1953): society is defined as "a group of people who have learned to work together" (61), and to assist in its work the society produces a culture composed of a "configuration of values" which impose "a common set of stable, habitual preferences and priorities in men's attention, and behavior, as well as in their thoughts and feelings" (62). When the culture then "facilitates communication" it may be called a community (62). The particular linguistic character of that communication may, of course, be characterized as a regional or social dialect; but the central fact about that dialect is that it unifies the speakers in subordination to, and in support of, the work of the society.

The basic reason for such an approach stems in my view from the fact that the Inland Northern dialect has for several decades been establishing itself as an instrument of the growth and stability of the United States economy. Because of the influence of a variety of social forces, and despite the fact that Inland Northern is itself merely a regional dialect, Americans in several regions are coming to accept the idea that the structural character of Inland Northern is "basic" and "correct." From the presumed nature of "standard" English in disciplines such as speech pathology to the social pressures involved in regularizing speech habits for the stage and screen, to enforced language rules taught to ethnic minorities, Americans have allowed a regional dialect to assume social-dialect importance, and have legislated public and private language policies accordingly. It is now time for a linguistic and political science perspective showing whether, figuratively speaking, the Inland Northern Emperor is wearing any clothes.

It is important to acknowledge that this particular approach emphasizes explanations other than those which attempt to trace the influence of formal, pedagogical prescriptivism on language behavior. The history of American prescriptivism is given by Drake (1977); this and similar treatments are admirable explorations of that peculiar American paradox in which governmental regulation is despised, but secular authority and various "self-help" sources are viewed as informal, yet binding, social legislation. The influence of schools on dialect spread during the first part of the century has in any case been overestimated. According to Boorstin (1973: 454), "In 1900, of Americans in the age group 14 to 17, only about one in ten was attending high school, and of those aged 18 to 21, only one in twenty-five was attending college. By 1920 the enrollments of high schools had quadrupled; by 1930 more than half the children aged 14 to 17 were in high school."

These figures indicate that by 1930 a large number of the high-school age students in this country could not have been getting the classroom message that there was a preferred American dialect. A sociology-of-language perspective would require that we start earlier and look elsewhere for our sources of dialect spread.

The Inland Northern region can be traced geographically starting at its easternmost point in upper New York State at the Vermont border in Lake Champlain, and then moving westward along the southern boundary of Lake Ontario and extending southward only to the outer reaches of the Iroquois nation at its height in the eighteenth century.

Next, Inland Northern passes along an area no more than 60 miles from north to south, a strip including all the major industrial cities of the Great Lakes, from Buffalo westward to Erie, Pennsylvania, continuing westward through Ohio's Western Reserve, then through Cleveland, Toledo, Detroit, and Chicago, and then north to Milwaukee with outlying areas reaching northwest toward the Twin Cities (cf. the treatment in McDavid 1958 and in the Linguistic Atlas of the Upper Midwest). The dialect itself shows most of the same characteristics as the dialect described for Western Pennsylvania in Kurath and McDavid (1982: 7, 17–18): there are full glides in /ai/ and /au/, a spelling pronunciation of the syllabic and the postvocalic /r/ phoneme, a merger of the /a/ and the "open o" /ɔ/ phonemes, and an absence of vowel lengthening before /r/. Inland Northern began as a geographical and regional dialect, but, as I will argue below, in the years since the period of post-Civil War industrialization, it has gradually become known as the "General American" dialect; it has shifted from its original status as a geographical dialect to its current form as a social dialect of such importance that nonlinguists might well understand the asperity with which a Southerner like the late Raven I. McDavid chose to characterize it when he gave Inland Northern the acronym SWINE (Standard White Inland Northern English).

For two of the three major phonological criteria which give SWINE its distinctive character, the historical facts are well understood and reliably described. The postvocalic /r/ phoneme, which is absent in dialects settling coastal New England and the coastal South in the eighteenth century because of the instability of the /r/ in Elizabethan English and the reinforcing effect of upper-class social contact with Britain in the nineteenth century, was reintroduced in the Inland Northern region because settlers moving there after the Revolutionary War spoke English dialects which themselves contained an articulated /r/—those coming from the northern and western areas of the British Isles.[2] At the time of the settlement of North America's colonial East Coast, the dialects around the city of London and in the southern counties preserved phonemic vowel length in diphthongs and in stressed syllables (see Lass 1976); vowel length did not remain phonemic in northwestern England or in the dialects that settled America from there one hundred years later.

The third of the major dialect characteristics of SWINE—the merger of /a/ and /ɔ/—has a more controversial history. The analyses of the problem by historical philologists schooled in the European tradition (compare Finnie 1972) show simply that "open o" coexists in America with an /ɑ/ (the low back version of the low central /a/). On the other hand, Terrill (1973: 353) proposes an historical process in which "open *o*" splits into a rounded and unrounded version, resulting in a central unrounded /a/ in the earliest Inland Northern dialects. The isophones in Shuy 1962 for *fog* and *on* as /fag/ and /an/ in northern Illinois illustrate this phenomenon. It is the task of the specialist in the sociology of language to find out what social forces secured the stability of the /a/.

In the hypotheses that follow, I propose that there are four factors underlying the geographical and social spread of Inland Northern toward the status of "General American": in the first instance, Inland Northern was carried to many other areas of the country with the basic social and economic influence of the growing wealth of the industrial Great Lakes region providing a motivating class, political, and cultural force behind it. In the second case, the educational influence of *Webster's Second International Dictionary* may have legitimized Inland Northern pronunciation through the prescriptive guidance of the scholar John S. Kenyon. Thirdly, the appearance of the *NBC Pronouncing Dictionary*, which was based on the advice given in *Webster's Second*, spread a characteristic Inland Northern usage throughout radio, television, and films, and further set a pronunciation standard in public discourse even when the journalistic and entertainment media were absent. Fourth, there was an independent and practically irresistible force at work in the 1930s—contemporary with the influence of the prescriptive pronunciation standards mentioned above—which spread the Inland Northern dialect with variously measurable kinds of penetration to all parts of the country. The impact of mass culture (the movies, radio, drama, and musicals) must be considered as a major but separate entity which nonetheless drew upon the first three sources of dialect spread for a powerful social authority that elevated the status of Inland Northern and established it as the basic dialect of first alternative choice in all regions.

I assume that the first cause of the spread of Inland Northern stems primarily from the economic and cultural importance (but with an underlying social dimension as well) of the growth of industrialization around the Great Lakes in post–Civil War America. We may suppose that that era began with the discovery of oil at Drake's well in August, 1859, at Titusville, Pennsylvania. This marked the end of what Lee A. Pederson has called the Water Transportation Era in the Midwest, and it began the Railroad Era, when coal could be brought more readily to the cities in the region for the rapidly developing steel industry (1965). Facts about subsequent industrial growth in this region as the economy developed between 1880 and 1920 are reported in the Fourteenth

Census of the United States (1923), which gives comparative figures, whenever possible, on the expansion in that 40-year period of manufacturing in steel, vehicles for land transportation, mining, coke production, and many other industries. By 1919, the Inland Northern dialect region contained a great portion of the nation's industrial wealth in blast furnaces, steel works, rolling mills, internal combustion engines, automobiles, and rubber goods.

Here we may invoke the general principle that the workplace is one of the institutional domains in the sociology of language, and that language behavior takes form and spreads outward from that domain. But more specifically, Inland Northern became the dialect model for generations of eastern and southern European immigrants who came to the Great Lakes cities for jobs in the plants and mills during this era. Mastering Inland Northern became a major route for assimilation and upward mobility for many generations of Slovaks, Poles, Czechs, Serbians, Italians, and Greeks who came to believe then (and still do) that this dialect was standard English itself.

In the spread of Inland Northern, research in the 1930s and 1940s on the geographical mobility of occupations is of crucial usefulness. In the first place, the professional, semi-professional, and business-elite classes prove to be more mobile geographically than any others (see Lipset and Bendix 1959: 206n). Next, migrant professionals ordinarily tend to be more successful than the average for their given occupation (see Blau and Duncan 1967: 257). Lastly, members of this group tend to be influential in the communities to which they move: they "typically achieve higher occupational status than non-migrants" in their new communities, especially when they have moved from large cities to smaller ones (Blau and Duncan: 272). In their study of the geographical mobility of the business elite in America between 1928 and 1952, Warner and Abegglen (1955) found that 45% of the managerial class had moved to a different region from the one in which they were born. About one-fourth of the business leaders in this period came from the "East North Central" (the Inland Northern) region; of this number, about 40% were mobile, with half moving to New York, Pennsylvania, and New Jersey, and the other half moving to the Upper Midwest, the South Atlantic states, and the Pacific States (1955: 182). The mobility of the managerial elite is a basic cause of the spread of Inland Northern.

In connecting dialect spread with an emphasis on immigration and geographical mobility on the one hand, and on the economy and aspirations for assimilation and social mobility on the other, we must adopt the perspective that Inland Northern is a mass dialect and that its spread is thus a mass culture phenomenon. We know for certain that

Inland Northern is not now, and never has been, the preferred dialect of upper-class segments of the population in such Eastern cities as Boston, New York, and Philadelphia;[3] hence the hypothesis that it has spread on bases other than social caste or social class interaction means that in principle this dialect is "carried" through relatively impersonal, economically-based broadcast methods. Overall, this signifies that people spread it for other than deeply personal social reasons, and at the same time that people learn it because of other than deeply personal and social motivations.

Inland Northern is a gesellschaft variety and not a gemeinschaft variety; by this distinction, I hereafter characterize it contextually as a mass culture dialect. For our immediate purposes, the salient feature of the gesellschaft/mass culture dialectal variety is that it is shared in interactive contexts away from the family and away from all kinds of gemeinschaft relationships; it spreads geographically from a given social class in any region to the same social class in another region, and generally it moves from one peer group to another analogously stratified peer group, and not from one generation to the next. For a variety of reasons, some deterministically based in class behavior and others loosely founded in political and economic ideology about industrial productivity and social unification (see Donahue 1985), our educational system in this country serves, promotes, and perpetuates the gesellschaft variety, as do the mass journalistic and entertainment media.

In this light it is amusing and instructive to view John S. Kenyon and his work in prescriptive pronunciation as a gesellschaft instrument. Kenyon, a respected philologist working in the 1930s at Hiram College in Ohio's Western Reserve, was the author of *American Pronunciation* (1924; 10 editions through 1954) and with Thomas Knott, coauthor of *A Pronouncing Dictionary of American English* (1944). But most importantly, Kenyon was the "pronunciation" editor of the second edition of *Webster's New International Dictionary of the English Language* (1934). A careful examination of Kenyon's work shows that he set up a group of patterned pronunciation contrasts: "American" was opposed to "British" and specific dialects were opposed to "the prevailing speech of the whole country" (p. xlviii). In the speech found in the "whole country" it was observed that the "open *o*" was disappearing in dialects outside of those on the East Coast and that the low central /a/ is preferred generally in much of the United States to the low back "open *o*" (see p. xlviii). Although in the "ES" (the Eastern and Southern regions in his *Pronouncing Dictionary*) postvocalic /r/ may be absent, Kenyon argued, it is to be pronounced elsewhere and generally. In his often-published and broadly-disseminated authority in these pronunciation guides, Kenyon was thus establishing as a de facto standard the cultivated speech found near him in Ohio's Western Reserve, and of course the speech of the managerial class in Cleveland as well: Inland Northern.

Kenyon is acknowledged to have had a major influence on the work of James F. Bender in his *NBC Handbook of Pronunciation* (1943; multiple editions following). The policy of this text, as described in the foreword by James F. Bender, is to key the pronunciation to the "General American" standard spoken by "at least ninety million" Americans (p. ix; Kenyon's estimates are quoted in the text).[4] The body of Bender's influential text preserves the /r/ phoneme in a direct spelling pronunciation pattern, and there is no attempt to indicate any kind of vowel length in 288 pages of prescribed pronunciations. Interestingly enough, the historical pronunciation differences between the "open *o*" /ɔ/ and the back /ɑ/ phonemes are retained in this guide: *not* is given as /nɑt/ and *nought* is recommended as /nɔt/. There is no mention of the already encroaching /a/, and I am at a loss to decide whether this is because Bender didn't hear it or didn't acknowledge it and was hoping that it would go away if he disregarded it; in any case, it would seem that broadcasters themselves chose to ignore this particular vowel distinction in their habits and practice (evidence is easy to collect: one might listen for example to broadcasters Dan Rather, Bob Schieffer—both former Texans—and Susan Spencer for CBS, and Don Harrison and Cathy Marshall for CNN). It can be claimed that Bender's volume became the prescriptive standard source throughout the broadcasting business, and from there it and its influence passed into use for the stage and films through such dialect guides as Herman and Herman (1943) and Blunt (1967 and 1980). Especially revealing is the emphasis in Herman (1967) on "Midwestern" speech.

Our last consideration of the possible agents for the spread of the Inland Northern dialect consists of an examination of the nature of mass culture itself. "Mass" or "popular" culture usually refers to the ways in which those people employed in an industrial and mass-production economy spend their time away from work. For our purposes, the most productive way of thinking about the effects of mass culture is to begin by characterizing American culture through the following hierarchical ordering (cf. Rosenberg and White 1957, 1971):

1. The classical artistic culture, elitist, individualized, and highly developed, produced by the most talented vanguard artists of their time.

2. A technocratic, research-oriented culture which ranges from academic research specialties on the one hand to technically accomplished leisure pursuits (computer programming, flying, sailing, crafting and building of all sorts) on the other.

3. A refined, interpretive culture which fixes its expository attention on groups 1 and 2 above, and which can slip into "cultural philistinism" by prescribing moral behavior on the basis of the artistic and cerebral products of group 1. Academic criticism is to be found in group 3.

4. A "middlebrow" mass culture (Broadway plays and musicals, large-circulation journals, newsmagazines, certain movies, etc.)

5. Traditional folk culture: handcrafts, self-schooled skills and talents of various kinds, older gemeinschaft wisdom and social practices.

6. A neo-"populist" youth culture—beatniks, hippies, punks, and so forth, together with older devotees of various self-indulgent countercultural persuasions.

7. A "lowbrow" culture attending to boxing, wrestling, football, and other such bread-and-circuses sports, together with a relish for films with explicit sex and violence, and so forth.

It must be remembered that Americans of all social classes have access to, and in many cases preferences for, the activities of any combination of the above culture groups; there exist no necessarily class-based correlations between social origin and cultural activities. Furthermore, a certain fluidity among these groups must be maintained, for the intellectually and emotionally healthiest Americans participate in a variety of the above groups and levels; a constant theme of writers on mass culture is that participation on only one cultural level results in narrowness, stultification, inanition, and vacuity.

The most sophisticated of analyses of mass culture insist on two points: participation in the lower behaviors in the hierarchy is "standardizing" or leveling, and a concentration on any of the lower behaviors is repressive: one loses the capacity to understand and appreciate the higher behaviors and to move toward them, and one then becomes an instrument of outside social and economic forces. The impact of any of these levels of culture upon the individual is variously measurable; for a specific illustration of group 5 (traditional folk culture) above, consider the following:

In the early 1930's . . . most Americans attended their local movie theatre an average of three times a week. In those days people went not just to be entertained or to escape the dreariness of their workaday lives but to gain an education, to see the world, to learn table manners and interior decoration, how to dress, how to kiss, how to laugh and cry, how to react to tragedy and happiness, how to be brave, evil and good. Hollywood was a silver-nitrate finishing school for a whole generation of Americans. (Heymann 1983: 169)

Here we see that Americans in the 1930s informally schooled themselves in dramatized life-situations and in appropriate speech through the lessons of mass entertainment, and further that mass entertainment served to fix a dialect promoted by language coaches who followed the pronunciation precepts of John Kenyon and his disciples. In addition, a number of the most successful and admired film actors and actresses of the 1930s spoke the Inland Northern dialect natively: a list of those who were either born in the region or pursued higher education there includes Mary Astor, Lew Ayres, Jack Benny, Richard Dix, Henry Fonda, Clark Gable, Bob Hope, Carole Lombard, Fred MacMurray, Fredric March, Adolphe Menjou, Pat O'Brien, William Powell, James Stewart, Franchot Tone, Spencer Tracy, and Robert Young.

Most important of all, we must consider that in the early twentieth-century American culture was "massifying" (to use Fishman's phrase) and modernizing at the same time. To claim that Inland Northern is the dialect of modernization is also to claim, according to Inkeles and Smith (1974), that the factory system governs learning behavior in at least as important a way as the school system, and that the workplace is a principal site of language and dialect shift and spread. Further, we must emphasize that massification, industrialization, and modernization were occurring at a particular time in immigrant history and in particular urban environments: the pressure to assimilate and to Americanize to some perceived supraethnic standard was exerted more heavily in Inland Northern cities like Chicago and Cleveland and less heavily in cities in such other dialect regions as those surrounding St. Louis, Memphis, and Atlanta—despite the paradoxical fact that the supraethnic, vaguely WASP-based model was more in evidence in those South Midland and Southern cities. The forces for assimilation were exerted most heavily in the region where Inland Northern was spoken.

In sum, these social movements and trends provide significant arguments for showing SWINE to be a gesellschaft dialect which has spread through the influence of the industrial economy, the mobility of the managerial class, and the impact of mass entertainment media on the American populace. Paradoxically, another major argument revealing the actual social character of this dialect would start from an exposition of the ways in which it is being supplanted in its original geographical region by the less urbanized North Midland dialect (please consult the careful argument on diffusion in Allen 1964). One may hypothesize that the Inland Northern dialect is in decline in reaction to the failure of the industrial economy in the rust belt: the ruralized speech of the North Midland area has encroached as the old social and economic promises implied in the mastery of SWINE have folded and all but disappeared. It would seem that a new kind of countrified American self-reliance ethic has sprung up (as Coggeshall 1985 suggests). The new order has appeared just as the old industrial dependency has been plowed under, and in reflecting that change the North Midland dialect has found a new social favor.

4

The Language of Yankee Cultural Imperialism: Pioneer Ideology and "General American"

TIMOTHY C. FRAZER

HE SELECTION OF a standard language or dialect is a political act, an exercise of power. In France and Spain, to cite two well-known examples, Parisians and Castilians have promoted their own dialects through the ruthless suppression of alternatives. Education policy, legal policy, and sometimes brute force have been used to promote a national "standard" (Ryan and Giles 1982). In the United States, on the other hand, individual states have dictated language policy (regarding, for example, the use of German in the Midwest [Jensen 1968] or Spanish in the Southwest). The federal government—so far, at least—has not been significantly involved in language planning or language policy, despite the efforts of groups like "U.S. English." Of the several spoken dialects of American English, moreover, none has received legislative sanction as the national standard (Kurath 1949, Kurath and McDavid 1982). Traditionally, local elites have continued to use local standards, evolved by unofficial consensus.

Nevertheless, it can be argued that the Inland Northern dialect, through a consensus of educators, scholars, and media people, seems to have emerged as a de facto standard without any government action. As "General American," Inland Northern has been promoted by numerous pronunciation manuals, dictionaries, and media guides. Among the most influential of these publications have been Kenyon's *American*

Pronunciation (1924, 1930), the second edition of *Webster's New International Dictionary* (1934), and Bender's *NBC Pronunciation Guide* (1943). In the previous chapter, Thomas Donahue argues that these reference works, along with the economic predominance of Great Lakes industry during the twentieth century, the rise of a mobile managerial caste based in the region, and European immigrants' identification of Inland Northern as the dialect of upward mobility, did much to promote Inland Northern as "General American." Donahue thus offers an answer to the question, "Why Inland Northern?" But his answer is a partial one. To complete it, we must learn what led to the establishment of Inland Northern as a prestige dialect in the Great Lakes region; we need to understand as well why scholars like Kenyon, George Phillip Krapp (1925), and Hans Kurath (1928), who later repudiated this position, embraced the concept of Inland Northern as a "General American" which was spoken everywhere outside the "East" and "South," implying a uniformity for American English which never existed. Why was the enthusiasm for "General American" so out of proportion to the facts? Scholars greatly exaggerated the geographical delimitations of Inland Northern, and Kenyon wildly overestimated the number of "General American" speakers.[1]

By the 1940s, linguistic atlases mapped the distribution of Inland Northern and demolished the myth of a uniform "General American" area outside the South and East. The Midwest, previously thought of as a homogeneous speech area, was crisscrossed by dialect boundaries. But in spite of these facts, "General American" persisted in textbooks and usage manuals (cf. Baugh 1957, Wise 1957). "Some scholars," writes William Van Riper, "responded to these facts by redefining the General American area," while "others ignored them" (1973: 235). How did Inland Northern as "General American" acquire this mystique, with this strong loyalty among people who should have known better?

For answers, this chapter will examine the original Inland Northern speakers themselves. These literal descendants of the Puritans came to the Great Lakes region from upstate New York and western New England during the early decades of the nineteenth century. The ethnocentrism of these people, commonly called "Yankees" in the histories, their elitism, and their church-based system of community organization are commonplaces for Midwestern social historians, but these factors have received little attention from linguists.

The original Puritan theocracy of New England is widely remembered for the religious sanction it gave to intolerance and expansionism. It viewed the wilderness as the domain of Satan, hence a territory to be conquered. Thus, interactions between the early Plymouth colonists and Native Americans foreshadow ideologies of conquest and destruction which surface later in American history: Manifest Destiny, gunboat diplomacy, paternalistic policies toward the Third World. In his *Historie of Plimmouth Plantation* (1624), William Bradford describes the slaughter of a surrounded Pequot village by Puritan militia. After the compound was set on fire, he writes, "those that scaped the fire were slain with the sword, some hewed to pieces, others run through with their rapiers." Although the resulting carnage filled Bradford with revulsion, he saw it as a beneficence of Divine Will: "It was a fearful sight to see them thus frying in the fire and the streams of blood quenching the same, and horrible was the stink and stench thereof; but the victory seemed a sweet sacrifice, and they gave the praise thereof to God, who had wrought so wonderfully for them" (McMichael 1974: 50).

If the original Puritans saw themselves as conquerors, the conquest two centuries later of the Great Lakes area and the West beyond by the "children of the Puritans" (Mathews 1909: 272) took place in the same spirit. As Thomas J. Morain writes:

> One of the most distinguishing features of the Yankees of the nineteenth century had been their confidence that theirs was a superior vision and that America's future depended on their ability to impose their order on the life of the nation. Faced with the declining fortune of New England, they set out to "save America" by converting the West to their standards. To a remarkable degree they succeeded. They established thousands of public schools and private colleges, filled churches and lodge halls with committed believers, and codified their version of morality in the statute books. Where there were still the unconverted in their midst, there was no mistaking who was in control. (1988: 256)

These beliefs echo in the nineteenth and early twentieth century histories of settlement. Neo-Puritan tracts in themselves, these histories uncritically elevate the traits of the Inland Northern settlers into myth: "New England is still a living force, and Puritan traditions and ideals still working models. Such an assertion is proved to be undeniable fact when the sons and daughters of the Puritans have been sought out in the West" (Mathews 1909: 272). The neo-Puritan histories also accept without question the religious zeal of their subjects and often speak an imperialist language. Thus the *Annals of Knox County, Illinois* (reprinted 1980) describe the first settlers there as "the advance guard of an army of occupation" (78); another Knox County history describes the founder of Galesburg, who "led a band of worthy pioneers to the wild prairies of Knox County" for the purpose "of founding a colony in the West" (Chapman 1878: 24–25). Apparently the language of the histories is an accurate representation of the thinking of the Yankee settlers themselves. The West, wrote a correspondent to the *Home Missionary* in 1841, would "yield to the plastic hand of a MASTER" [sic] (13: 266). Henry Ward Beecher predicted that "we are to have charge of this continent . . . and this continent is to be from this time forth governed by Northern men, with Northern ideals, and with a Northern gospel" (Power 1953: 11). A later, more objective historian labels this attitude "Yankee cultural imperialism" (Power 1953: 6).

As the Yankees moved west, they encountered others—Southerners, European immigrants, Mexican Americans—whom they regarded as inferior. Yankee-Southerner tensions were common in frontier Illinois and Indiana. Mutual hostility between the groups marked the frontier years in McDonough County, Illinois (Clarke 1878: 51). In McLean County, Illinois, "the Northerner thought of the Southerner as a lean, lank, lazy creature, burrowing in a hut, and rioting in whiskey, dirt, and ignorance" (*History of McLean County* 1879: 97). At first, such were to be excluded from the Northern colonies that began to dot the West: "By their laws no undesirable character could purchase land, while those who were worthy were in every way encouraged, which ensured good society from the start" (Power 1953: 13). Political power, not surprisingly, was not for non-Yankees. Wrote another Yankee from California about the Mexicans: "as yet the native 'greasers' rule, but a year or two more will put office out of their hands. We long for the day. They hate enterprise and public improvements . . . Well, the Lord cut short their day, and give His people dominion" (Johnson 1868; see Power 1953: 22n27).

Although the Yankee conquest was to be peaceful, military spirit was common: "Let missions, like freedom, follow the flag everywhere. The cannon . . . will open many a door" (quoted in Power 1953: 19). Clergymen and other Yankees on the frontier exhorted their friends back home to "come and help save the West for God" (Holbrook 1950: 74). The American Home Missionary Society sent "hundreds" of Congregational and Presbyterian missionaries to the West, and Catherine Beecher urged young New England women to enlist as teachers, to combat the "fearful scourge of ignorance" rampant on the frontier (Morain 1988: 9). And this peaceful conquest had its tangible victories. On convincing a Southern squatter to try mince pie and candles, a Yankee in Iowa exclaimed: "Thus has the power of example been felt widely; and the process of assimilation to New England tastes and the conquest to New England principles have been extended, until their complete triumph has been made certain throughout the whole Northwest" (Power 1953: 19).

If the Inland Northern Yankees viewed the settlement of the West as a military campaign, it was their economic and social organization which assured its success. Their most numerous competitors in the new territories, the Upland Southerners, left behind a loose social structure of rural "neighborhoods" based on kinship (Kenzer 1987); when Upland Southerners migrated—as individuals or in individual families—the neighborhood was left behind.

In contrast, Yankees often moved entire congregations or even communities. Sarah Fenn Burton's 1835 diary recounts the journey of 42 parishioners from Plymouth, Connecticut, to Mendon, Illinois. The group traveled by the Philadelphia Main Line railroads and canals to Pittsburgh, and then by steamboat to Quincy, Illinois. During the 25-day journey, "the Burtons' group tried to remain a New England community." Prayer meetings were frequent, and Mrs. Burton forbade her children to enter the "world of sin" represented by the theatres and museums of New York and Philadelphia. After a hard journey, "the Burtons' community arrived intact in Illinois and there discovered other communities which were nearly identical to the ones left in Connecticut" (Bracken 1981: 115–17).

Other communities were even more tightly organized into colonies on the frontier. Galesburg, Illinois, was one of the largest of 22 such colonies that Mathews counts in Illinois alone; in Ohio, Marietta, one of the first and most famous among dialectologists as a Northern speech island in Midland territory (Marckwardt 1957; Clark 1972), was joined by the Worthington colony in 1802, Granville a few years later, and Windham in 1811–1817. Other New England or New York colonies were found in Michigan (Vermontville), Indiana (Ovid), and Wisconsin (Beloit). In each case the colonies immediately founded schools and often a college (e.g., Beloit and Marietta Colleges; Knox in Galesburg; Denison in Granville). Thus, when the Inland Northern dialect arrived in the Midwest, it came complete with the social institutions which could strengthen its foothold.

Those Inland Northerners who did not settle the Midwest as colonists, moreover, still tended to gravitate to the towns and cities rather than to the countryside, living more often as merchants and professionals than as farmers. According to the 1850 manuscript census returns for Sangamon County, Illinois, Yankees made up only 9% of the rural population, but 17% of the adult population of Springfield, the state capital. In Madison County, Illinois, the wealthiest Yankee settlers in 1850 were almost entirely urban residents, while all but 2 of the 14 wealthiest Southerners lived in the countryside. Of the surviving Yankee "old settlers" still living in McDonough County in 1877, all were residents of the county's two largest towns (Clarke 1878: 594–601). Yankees, moreover, disproportionately gravitated to the professions and non-farm occupations; in Trempeleau County, Wisconsin, they made up over 80% of those in the professions in 1860 (Curti 1959: 249).

While many settlers in the Midwest sought only enough land to support their families through hunting and subsistence agriculture, Yankee ideology promoted the accumulation of capital; those who did not share the Yankee passion for "enterprise and improvements" were derided as shiftless and lazy. As a result, part of the Yankee conquest was economic: Yankees acquired a disproportionate share of the wealth. In Madison County, Illinois, Yankees represented a very small numerical minority in a county heavily settled by upland Southerners and Germans. Yet the "Yankees," boasted a history of the county, "set the examples of thrift and enterprise" (Brink, 1882: 11). According to the 1850 census, the wealthiest 1% of Madison County household heads were disproportionately Northern: fourteen of the wealthiest persons were from New England and another 3 came from New York. Only 14 of the wealthiest were from the South, even though Southerners outnumbered Northerners by more than 3 to 1. Three more of the wealthiest were from Pennsylvania, 2 were from Germany, 2 from Switzerland, and 4 were native Illinoisians. In Trempealeau County, Wisconsin, Yankees had the highest median property values (Curti 1959).

Yankee economic ideology, moreover, was readily adapted by many of the Europeans who settled the Midwest during the nineteenth century. Again, Madison County provides an example. Salomon Koepfli (1859: 18), an early Swiss-German resident of Highland, regarded his neighbors from North Carolina and Tennessee as "apathetic and unambitious," an attitude that mirrored Yankee prejudices. In Trempeleau County, where Yankee settlers lived among Poles and Norwegians, Curti writes that "the processes by which the foreign-born were increasingly assimilated into the community," along with a marked social conscience, "reflected the migration of New England social values to Trempeleau" (1959: 138–39).

Less evidence is available regarding the Yankees' linguistic attitudes, but what is available is instructive. Joseph Kirkland, a novelist with roots in New York who grew up in frontier Michigan, visited Tilton, Illinois, in the 1850s and later depicted a fictionalized version of Tilton in his novel *Zury*, which has been shown to be remarkably accurate in its treatment of dialect. A hint of Inland Northern language attitudes appears in this exchange between a Yankee schoolmistress and a child whose dialect is clearly South Midland:

"Please 'm, m'I g'aout?"
"What did you say?"
"I want ou'doors."
"You want out-doors."
"That's whut I said. I want aout."
At last she understood this Westernism, new to her.
To "want out" is to desire to go out.

This example shows us that from the novelist's perspective the Yankee teacher's speech is to be regarded as normative, while the child's Midland dialect is deviant. A real-life example of Yankee language attitudes came from southeastern Indiana in 1833. Reverend R. J. Wheelock wrote that his wife's school used "the most improved N.E. schoolbooks" for "correcting 'a heap' of Kentuckyisms" (Power 1953: 114).

It is clear from this discussion that the Inland Northern speakers who settled the Great Lakes region during the early nineteenth century set out to become the elite of frontier society. And as Brian Weinstein writes, "It is the cultural elites and political leaders working together who choose which linguistic . . . characteristics to emphasize or discount" (1983: 12). It is not hard to understand how a group who promoted their own culture and values so aggressively should have succeeded as well in promoting their own dialect of English as normative. Their social system—their tendency to settle in colonies—aided this effort. Since the Inland Northerners were more likely to seek the towns and cities, moreover, their dialect became a common urban dialect in the Midwest.

It remains to explain how scholars in this century could have been sufficiently mesmerized by the Yankee mystique that they so exaggerated the Yankee dialect's territory and the number of its speakers. Geneva Smitherman, however, has recently demonstrated the influence of ideology on linguistic scholarship (1988). The biological determinism of the early twentieth century, Smitherman points out, is reflected in Krapp's explanation of Black English as simplified baby-talk (1925). Neo-Puritan ideology surely affected Krapp just as powerfully as did the racism of his day, both ideologies having achieved the status of conventional wisdom. Although it was never articulated as doctrine, the myth of Yankee superiority was prevalent by the turn of the century and espoused by historians as eminent as Frederick Jackson Turner (Curti 1959: 138); no one examined it critically, as far as I can find, until Power's 1953 study. Under these conditions, the academic sanction accorded to Inland Northern as "General American" is not surprising.

Despite the accumulation of studies pointing to the diversity of American English, the belief in "General American" persisted. It appeared in succeeding editions of the *NBC Handbook*, the third edition of which proclaimed itself "the standard reference book on the pronunciation of General American Speech" (Bender and Crowell 1964: vii). And while the General American label is rarely used now, Inland Northern continues to be the pronunciation model used in most manuals and textbooks, even in those written by linguists, who ought to know better. Fromkin and Rodman imply that "Standard American English" is spoken in the Midwest, the Northeast, and the Middle Atlantic states; Akmajian et al. invoke "Standard English" as that "used on the national media, especially in news programs." Sounds an awful lot like "General American."

In the introduction to this volume, I mentioned the speech therapists who charge fees for teaching Inland Northern speech. These people are cashing in on Yankee ideology. How about those of us, however, who teach English in public schools and universities? The public's expectation of our duties, I imagine, would rank the impartation of "Standard English" much higher than teaching invention techniques, literature, or critical thinking. Is Standard English/Inland Northern absolutely essential? That seems a naive question, since the population at large does not share the cultural relativism of most linguists. Nevertheless, Andrew Sledd's chapter in this volume raises critical questions about educational policy. Timothy Riney suggests that "Yankee cultural imperialism" is alive and well in the Iowa Department of Education. What are we to do? I have no radical ideas for curriculum reform, but I do think that in training language teachers, we need to instill the historical knowledge that identifies the teaching of "Standard English" for what it is: a political act and an exercise of power.

During the 1820s, Lyman Beecher wrote that Yankees must make "the integrity of the Union a more homogeneous character, and bind us together by firmer bonds." A century later, scholars were working for a more "homogeneous character" by promoting Inland Northern as General American. Perhaps the language of "Yankee cultural imperialism" was appropriate for a century of corporate expansion, leveraged buyouts, and American military intervention in the Philippines, Central America, the Caribbean, Vietnam, and the Middle East.[2]

5

Black English and Standard English in Chicago

ANDREW SLEDD

HE BRUTAL HISTORY of segregation in Chicago, summarized in the first pages of this chapter, will serve to explain the persistence (or development?) over several decades of striking differences between the city's black and white varieties of English. Some of the most distinctive features of Chicago's African-American vernacular are the complex products of its unusually powerful system of verbal auxiliaries. These important and puzzling constructions are exemplified and described informally in the middle of the chapter, which I hope is accessible to teachers of literacy as well as to students of dialectology. A final section takes up some pedagogical issues related to this urban history and its intriguing linguistic landscape.

To end my guidance for the reader as she begins, let me anticipate two criticisms she may advance after she has finished. First, for expressing an unfashionable, left-wing politics I will make as much apology as conservative scholars should be required to offer for espousing their own persuasions. I do confess, however, to using an old-fashioned linguistic theory, but plead that my reader judge whether it accurately describes what it may not adequately explain. Even that partial success would put my effort half a step ahead of several others.

From the original inhabitants of *Chicagou* 'place of the bad smell' little survives but the name of the city (Drake and Cayton 1969, 1: 31).[1] The first new settler was a black man named de Saible; a trader from Santo Domingo, he built a cabin on the Chicago River around 1790. By 1860, fugitive slaves and free Easterners had established a settlement there almost one thousand strong. Chicago's first African Americans could not vote, marry the whites who had joined them as neighbors, go to school with them, eat with them in public places, or ride with them in public vehicles.

During the next two decades, neither the franchise, nor desegregated schools, nor legal access to public accommodations could break an evolving pattern of exclusion and exploitation which has continued until the present day.

By 1890, the bustling commercial city of Chicago had become a great manufacturing center, its militant working people, many foreign-born, embroiled in industrial strife from the railroaders' rebellion of 1877 through the Haymarket tragedy of 1886 to bloody Pullman in 1894. Amidst this turmoil and hysteria lived the city's underpaid, hardworking blacks, employed chiefly as domestics or in trades untouched by labor agitation. At home on the South Side, interspersed with whites, they were generally ignored. But as the city's black population swelled, indifference quickly gave way to hostility. When blacks sought more housing, whites grew anxious; and they feared for their jobs, especially since white employers used black strikebreakers. After World War I lured still more people from Southern farms to Northern cities, the working-class Irish and Poles, who lived west of Chicago's black belt, and the old middle class, to the south and east, all felt increasingly threatened. When milder efforts to intensify segregation failed, they resorted to violence.

By spring of 1919, a postwar recession had begun, and African Americans were being assaulted or their homes bombed almost daily. Local police and politicians protected the hoodlums, who were encouraged by such "respectable" organizations as the Kenwood and Hyde Park Property Owners' Association (Spear 1967: 212). On Sunday, July 27, race war erupted in Chicago. In six days, 38 people died; 500 were injured. Whites committed most of the violence, yet many responded by urging even stricter segregation. Twice as many blacks as whites were hurt in the fighting; and twice as many were brought to trial after it was over (Spear 1967: 216–17; Chicago Commission 1922: p. xv).

The report of the Chicago Commission On Race Relations was the only racial cooperation provoked by the riots (Spear 1967: 219); it blamed them on black migration, black entry into industry, housing conflicts, discrimination, and a climate of escalating violence. The report made 59 recommendations to limit segregation and assure African Americans of equal rights and opportunities. It did not say just how these recommendations might be implemented, or by whom. The report was much admired (Waskow 1965: 97–104).

The riot of 1919 had destroyed all hope for a peacefully integrated Chicago; black leaders concluded that their community should become self-reliant. It did become all black. But only briefly did the dream of a self-sufficient black city seem close to reality; for a few years, as prosperity eliminated racial conflict in Chicago's industry and still more migrants filled the ghetto market, its growing class of black businesspeople caught the optimism of the Roaring Twenties.

By August of 1930, however, every bank in the black belt had closed and white Chicago was firing its domestics. Factories, forced to cut production, let blacks go first. A boycott of white employers in the ghetto desegregated a few clerical jobs, but the campaign, justly scorned by Communists, did not touch the unemployed thousands, many of whom soon faced eviction. In August 1931, policemen killed three African Americans in a crowd trying to block removal of one such family. Before an integrated Red guard of honor, 18,000 people viewed the bodies. Thousands, black and white, marched in protest. Evictions stopped. Black leaders then advised city officials to undercut the "radicals" at once, and city and state began plans for relief, the first in Chicago (Drake and Cayton 1969: 87). As New Deal projects got under way and cotton tenancy declined, still more migrants came to Chicago. By 1940, one of every two black families in the city was reduced to dependence on public aid. The former sharecroppers seemed doomed to become a lumpen proletariat.

But first they went to war. As industry stepped up production, African Americans reentered mainstream economic life. By 1944, Chicago faced a labor shortage, and a new wave of migration began. But housing, recreational facilities, and schools in the overcrowded black belt decayed, and despite the Crusade for the Four Freedoms, African Americans still faced discrimination in Chicago, as in the armed forces. They also worried that peace would again mean depression and unemployment. So did big businesspeople and federal officials, who used victory to achieve full employment through overseas expansion, an enlarged welfare state, and burgeoning military budgets.

Cold war prosperity completed the urbanization of black America. To black Chicago's South Side, which continued to fester and spread, a poorer West Side ghetto was attached (see Hirsch 1983). Then, as automobiles and freeways multiplied and the city's manufacturing declined, white flight to the suburbs began and the inner city was "reconstructed," increasing segregation. Soon, black unemployment often tripled that of whites.

After Watts in 1965, African-American leaders scrambled to find a nonviolent strategy for Chicago. They invited Dr. King to lead an open occupancy drive into white neighborhoods; he was met with bitter violence, and Chicago's racial problems made headlines nationwide.

There was arson and looting on the West Side. Mayor Daley the First extracted a promise from protest leaders to halt the marches. Business promised to abolish the dual market in real estate and to hire more blacks. Prominent citizens vowed to curb police brutality (Drake and Cayton 1969).

Hearings into the ongoing tragedy of police brutality in Chicago held by the City Council during the summer of 1989 revealed an African-American citizenry now full of frivolous complaints or a black police chief and an Office of Professional Standards skillfully used to insulate the department against public scrutiny, legal action and professional reform. However, it did not take two dozen years for the West Side to be convinced it had been swindled. When Dr. King was assassinated in April 1968, the neighborhood went up in angry flames. Nine persons were killed, 500 injured, 3,000 arrested. Property damage exceeded $11,000,000. The community became home for the Black Panthers, whose youthful state chairman, Fred Hampton, was murdered there in his sleep in December, 1969, by the FBI and local police (Churchill and Vander Wall 1988: 64–77).

Fraternal conflict and suicidal impulses joined repression in scattering the mass mobilizations of the 1960s. As the U.S. destruction of Indochina wound down, the right orchestrated populist backlash. Postwar fiscal crisis and stagflation ate away at gains the civil rights and black power movements had won from prospering cold war liberalism, and Chicago remained one of the nation's most segregated cities. When open-housing marches resumed in 1976 and demonstrators were stoned, with the connivance of the Nazi party and Chicago policemen, it was hardly news anywhere.

Public scandal followed the assassination of Hampton and his comrade, Mark Clark, speeding an African-American revolt against the Daley machine. Throughout the long years of economic crisis and conservative restoration—under Nixon, Carter, and Reagan—blacks in Chicago struggled for political influence. Finally, in 1983, after an ugly, racist campaign, a reformed machine politician, the late Harold Washington, was elected the city's first black mayor. Much of his term was wasted by an obstructive bloc of white aldermen. His death after reelection in 1987 dealt one more blow to black Chicagoans.

Yet Washington came to power in a city on skids greased by bigger villains than bad white mayors. Federal policies and the routines of corporate profit-search went on stripping Chicago's industry and immiserating many citizens. These forceful patterns of ruling-class decision crosscut the city's perennial racism (and the recent mobility of its black elite) to further isolate and demoralize the black poor, sinking them deeper into hopelessness, self-defeating street crime, and drug abuse (see Markusen 1989; Wilson 1987).

The history of Chicago is, with local variations, the history of New York, Detroit, Los Angeles, and so on. It makes clear how the structure and rhythms of American life prevent significant, durable African-American progress. In good times and under liberal regimes, blacks share in the general well-being and even improve their relative status; but under conservative rule and during lean years, they suffer first, most, and longest, while their previous advances are rolled back. Only a basic change in the dominant society, one which benefited working people of all colors, could alter this dreary cycle.

It is not surprising, given this history, that the originally rural and Southern-derived speech of poor black people may depart strikingly from the local standards in Northern cities. And white Chicago's Inland Northern dialect profile, now shifting toward national urban uniformity, is often far removed from the language of its West Side slums and the housing projects on South State Street.[2] What is surprising is the conviction (or pretense) of many linguists and teachers, reiterated through decades, that they could provide good jobs for all, and thus change the course of history and the shape of American society, by drilling ghetto kids on standard verb forms during their English classes. The generous grants such programs once received were sure signs that the roots of unemployment and degradation, among blacks and whites, lie much deeper in our way of life than in its stigmatized patterns of speech. The frequencies of such patterns are hardly as important as the distribution of wealth and power, which would be a first object of genuine reform. Establishment reforms have merely strengthened, modestly, the African-American middle class, now expected to mediate the impact of white power on ghetto life. And programs of forced oral bidialectalism have been failures, unable, in segregated schools, to provide most pupils with healthy motives for mastering standard English, or with the necessary natural exposure to it.

Thus, many black students in Chicago continue to display the stigmata of lower-class speech. Among the young, kaleidoscopic slang is common, so a white teacher hardly knows whether charges who leave will *raise, space, hat up, book, break, push (out),* or what when class is over. She will also be puzzled or annoyed by many features of their pronunciation, from the front-shifting of primary stress in *police* and *insurance* to substitution of /d/ for *th* in *dis, dese, dat, dem,* and *dose.*

In their morphology, noun plurals and possessives will come and go, depending, probably, on phonological cues; the pronouns *mine, himself,* and *themselves* may analogize to *mines, hisself,* and *theirselves,* while demonstrative *dose* becomes *dem* and *theirselves* further disguises itself, by various devices, as *theyselves* or *theyself*; adjectives may compare themselves twice and *more better*, but adverbs lose *-ly*; the third-person singular verb ending may vanish or appear in other persons; the forms of *be* will not agree, as in *you is* or *we was*; past tense and past participial inflections may be absent, perhaps to simplify final consonant clusters; the principal parts of irregular verbs may be irregular; contracted forms of *be* and *have* may disappear or be negated as *ain't*; and so on.

Trivial syntactic differences will also be common, as in *I wonder did she leave, That's the man stole the car,* and *It's a dog in here.* More significant ones include: multiple negation as in *Don't nobody know nothin'*; durative or habitual *be* as in *She be readin' to us all the time*; perfective *done* as in *He done lef' already*; and remote perfective *been* as in *Oh I been knowed that.*

However, great as the distance between poor black students and middle-class white teachers may be, it is not so large that they really speak two languages with separate histories and distinct rules of phrase structure. As far as can be seen, historic and structural overlap are predominant between African- and Anglo-American speech, even in their systems of auxiliary verbs, where the greatest differences in grammar have repeatedly been alleged.[3]

Contrary, sensational claims may have pleased black nationalist sentiment and been profitable in the golden era of liberal funding, but anyone who has studied the testimony of Irish philologists on durative *be* will not be immediately convinced by the theory of its creole origin, no matter how scarce the form may have become today in white American folk English—where it does survive, in some locales, at least among the elderly (see James Sledd 1983; Bailey and Bassett 1986).[4]

Perfective *done,* more prominent in the data presented here, has also been claimed, most implausibly, to be a surviving creolism, notably by J. L. Dillard (1972: 220). It actually descends from the causative *do* of Middle English. As the work of Elizabeth Traugott (1972: 138–41) Joseph M. Williams (1975: 272–73), and others has shown, it is introduced into sentences of various Southern dialects, black and white, by a rule of phrase structure reading

Perf → *have* + *en* (*do* + *en*).[5]

Perfective *been,* the most famous deeply divergent "Africanism," seems well known, curiously, in Newfoundland (Noseworthy 1972, 21–22);[6] and, in this country, it is merely one of a fascinating complex of related auxiliary constructions, some shared, at least superficially, by

Southerners of both races, all having many parallels, even in Northern, standardized dialects, indeed, some theorists would say, in all the languages of the world.[7]

These numerous and peculiar auxiliaries, unknown in the language of white Chicagoans, include multiple modals as well as perfective *been* and several other apparent anomalies. They can be heard in sentences like *He may could get me some type of job; I been finished that book*; and *They shoulda been did that before, I would have been done took it, John'll be done consumed everything.*[8] Such sentences can be paraphrased, closely, as 'Maybe he could get me some type of job', 'It has been true that I finished that book', 'It should have been the case that they did that before', respectively; these glosses providing rough clues, presumably, to underlying structures.

Like perfective *done*, the double modals are also inherited from Middle English; they can still be found in Scotland as well as the white South (Visser 1963–73: 1751, 1789; Sir James Wilson 1926: 91). Analogues of these ancient constructions also occur in the English creole spoken in Jamaica (Bailey 1966: 45, 66–67). In the black English vernacular (BEV) they apparently result from raising transformations which apply to "deep structures" like *NP^e may be [he could get me some type job]* and lift the lower subject noun phrase to replace the higher, semantically empty one. (*Be* is then deleted.) In some white dialects, on the other hand, double modals may actually be single lexical items, though not by all accounts (see Di Paolo 1989; Boertien 1986).

Perfective *been* simply extends the transformational pattern of BEV to structures like *NP^e has been [I finished that book]*. In such cases, underlying *been* is not deleted, but forms of *have* are removed phonologically, by the process in BEV Labov done made so familiar (see n5). Since this auxiliary *been* is actually derived from the main verb *be*, it obviously does not reflect a great and persisting difference in deep structure between black and white dialects. Rather, the case for creole influence in African-American English has once again been somewhat exaggerated.[9]

Nevertheless, a sharp-eared racist native to Chicago could probably hear enough of this raising construction alone to persuade himself that black people can't even speak English. The double modals, for example, enter into a number of combinations, many with one member negated: *You don't know what I might would do, We might could get together, You may can help me too, I might not can read fast but I CAN read slow, Larry might not would ever walk again, I might not could do that, He may not can speak the language, Monday it [the weather] may still won't be good, Write me a pass in case I might can't get out of class.*[10]

Sometimes, though apparently not in white dialects, the second, negative element is a form of *do*, not another modal, as in *You must don't get out til nine o'clock* or *The other plan must didn't work.*[11] This *do* can be emphatic, however: *She may DO be saying that.* Closely related are sentences like *He mighta couldna stopped* and *She mighta didn't come*, in which the leading modal is followed by a reduced form of *have*. The syntax of such forms is by now transparent: *NPᵉ might have been [he could not have stopped]; NPᵉ might have been [she didn't come].*

Perfective *been*, which often appears without any preceding auxiliary, is also occasionally found following *have*—or its negation, *ain't*: *He been had that paper for three months, I been knowed that all these years, I been quit [my job], He been took his bath,* but *She have been told me "Don't say that"* and *I ain't been had to get up that early for a long time.* It is common, though, for *been* to be heard after a modal and *have*: *Some fool woulda been grabbed that apple by now, I am thirteen—I should have been met someone, They woulda been throwed me out, Jack.* Of course, these last examples are produced by transformations similar to those suggested earlier. Thus, *NPᵉ should have been [I met someone]* becomes *I should have been met someone.*

When the higher and lower clauses in such underlying structures both contain perfect aspect, the result is sentences like *You've been done found somebody?* or, when the first *have* deletes rather than reducing, *I been done already found a parking space.* If the higher clause also involves a modal, even lengthier constructions will occur: *We coulda been done run down [to the corner] by now, He don't want to do that or else he would have been done went an' did it.* These elaborate auxiliaries make clear the syntax of many similar ones from which the higher underlying *have* is missing, so that *been* appears without its participial ending as simple *be*: *I'll be done got confused, If I get ranned over, it'll be you—you'll be done did it, Call me soon's you get in, cuz somethin' may be done jumped up, We'd be done went 'n had steak, I could be done vacuumed the whole house by then, You not eatin'? Love must be done got your heart, We can be done walked down to Wendy's by then, I won't be done missed nothin'* and *Please don't be done lost it!* Again, the raising rule transforms *NPᵉ will be [I have done got confused]* and *NPᵉ may be [something has done jumped up]* into *I'll be done got confused* and *Something may be done jumped up,* and so forth.

As the number and variety of these examples make clear, *be + done* is a common construction in black Chicago, though it has been termed "infrequent," by Wolfram (129), for example, as recently as 1990. Rare or not, Wolfram understands the form pretty well, paraphrasing it as "an analogue of the standard English future perfect" but "with some [mysterious] specialized emotive connotations." Wolfram also notes that "it hardly seems to be . . . evidence for the significant reorganization of the tense-aspect system," but he does not describe the construction beyond implying that it could be called a "quasi-auxiliary" similar to southern vernacular *liketa* (129).[12]

In fact, as we have seen, this entire extensive and superficially bewildering array of auxiliaries can be explained quite simply by subject-raising transformations operating on the copula, transformations similar to many used with other verbs in standard dialects of English. It must be admitted, however, that this explanation, proposed and argued in considerable syntactic detail as early as 1976 (Herndobler and Sledd), has apparently not caught the attention of sociolinguists wedded to strong versions of the creole hypothesis concerning the history and structure of contemporary BEV. Perhaps, if evidence (such as that reviewed by Wolfram) continues to weaken these hypotheses, then this transformational account of BEV's multiple modals, perfective *been, be + done,* and so on, will be heard more clearly, even though it may anchor these auxiliaries deeper in the history and syntax of other dialects of English than in some earlier African-American creole. But you do not need to know the creolists' theory or its factual limitations to know that black students, even the impoverished ones, speak English. Anyone at all acquainted with black speech, in Chicago or elsewhere, understands most of it, if she wants to, almost at once, and the rest after a very short time.

The problem, of course, is to get acquainted. Many, including some teachers, do not. They may fear or dislike their students (who will return the compliment), just as they often despise their language. In that context, teaching becomes an act of flight or aggression and failure a form of disguise or resistance. For if sociolinguistics should teach teachers anything, it is that they cannot teach anyone whose language and humanity they will not respect. That is an unvarnished gloss of Labov's finding that "the principal problem in reading failure is not dialect . . . differences but rather a cultural conflict between the vernacular culture and the schoolroom" (1970: 43). Nor is it just a matter of class or ethnicity, for the sissified speech of schoolmarms, male or female, can hardly sit well with the tough talk of tough kids. And matriarchal classrooms do threaten young masculine egos.

However, the educational crises for the 1970s and 1980s have not been in nonstandard speech, but in freshman composition and just about everybody's literacy.[13] A cynic might suggest that even after the ghetto youngster had been forgotten, the college classroom still seemed too crowded. Of course, crises, real or imaginary, are a necessary political and scholarly fashion, though it must be doubted, on the record, that American academics or pedagogues will do much about them but lament, reapply for research monies, and return to their old ways. The limited power of linguists and teachers, of dictionaries and rhetorics, to channel the waves of language use or change is often overestimated. It is not, as purists charge, that linguists or trendy teachers no longer uphold a common standard of excellence. Most linguists are firm in their approving belief that American English is commonly spoken, at least on formal occasions, according to the local standard, one shared by almost everyone in the speech community, including the misfortunates who approximate the norm most inadequately and even reject it in rebellious moments. Teachers generally enforce an ideal, sometimes imagined, standard, more bookish and conservative than actual prestigious lingo. Unfortunately, furthermore, the study and teaching of proper usage are both characteristically devoted to trivialities, mere etiquette, not more substantial matters affecting communication.

Standard English is more than a grab bag of socially superior synonyms. However, since it emerged in London, long ago, it

> has been the language used with approval from our rulers. It is many other things as well; but first it is an instrument of power. The mere existence of a dialect judged superior, sole vehicle for public celebration of established values, gives the system of class distinctions a moral sanction and builds that system into the most inward reaches of each child's humanity. (James Sledd 1976)

This indoctrination is one thing a prestigious dialect is for—and public schools support the elitist enterprise. There is little effort to tally any costs of the idiotic self-conceit so taught or of its converse, tragic self-denial. We do hear a great deal, however, of the itch to get ahead, as if human life must forever remain a nervous rat race, and of the need for efficient communication, hardly impaired among willing speakers and listeners to any American dialect.

But however brutal or foolish, power does not idle. Standard English has been used for five hundred years in public affairs, legal proceedings, private enterprise, literary production, philosophy, science, medicine and works of engineering. It has become everything from a private tongue for friends and lovers to history's premier world language, and has in some respects been made superior, for some purposes, to other languages and dialects. For contrary to careless linguistic relativism, languages are equal only in potential, not in actual development. And what history has invited at one time or place, it may then forbid in others: equality of endowment simply does not guarantee equal opportunity. The effort to legitimize, codify, and cultivate a nonstandard dialect so that it could serve as a written medium might well cost more than attempts to teach children to write in something like the standard one even if they do not speak it. Still, judgments of relative merit must be cautious. When an upwardly-mobile scholar elaborates on the restricted code of working stiffs, it is not unreasonable to suppose that the pickpocket, like Moll Flanders, may be blaming his own victim. Labov has stressed the defensive character of monosyllabic lower-class speech; voluble and ostentatious equivocation is often a middle-class phenomenon. It is dangerous to ignore these cruel paradoxes. Our language, a means to domination at home and abroad, is contaminated with the worst but enriched by the best of our values. No one should be forced to speak standard English, least of all children, who are too young to reflect on what else they will acquire and what they may lose of family or friends. If we want our students to speak as we do, we ought not to try to dupe or coerce them, but to set a good example and help them when we can and they want us to.

Good English is not good because of the pigment of its speakers or the size of the wad in their pocketbooks. Good English does what decent people want it to; it speaks truth; it is not self-deceptive or misleading to others; it does not seek to harm. It is rarely heard on Capitol Hill or along Madison Avenue, though it may be spoken in unheard-of places.

By no means should students be left indefinitely to write however they will. Writing is not an innate ability. It is an acquired skill, even among the gifted. A student's natural idiom must serve as the foundation, flawed or not, for the building of her craft, which the language of business, government, and the academy would often undermine. Still, the literary language, not easily mastered, makes the best servant for those with the will and a way to control it. For that language to prosper in its proper service, it must make room for renewal of its native habits and garb by the words and wisdom of fluent strangers, the young of rising classes and foreign faiths or nations. Otherwise, the decline of English, so long lamented, may yet commence. Good teachers, accordingly, will learn to avoid linguistic prejudice as well as naive relativism, and their instruction will respect the traditional use of our written language and whatever is valuable in the many other varieties of English.

Of course, that is more a declaration of principles than the statement of a program. In some small way, teaching fundamental linguistic concepts like those implicit in this chapter may help to put the ideals into practice. However, lessons on language, which are secondary, ought to grow from reading and written work. Reading and writing come first. For we must strive to prevent our overburdened schools from graduating students untouched by literate culture and its liberatory threat but immersed in the state and corporate propaganda which saturates the new electric media with disabling venom.[14]

Thus, students should know something about the biological nature of language, which suggests the innate equality of the species. They should be shown the complexity and elegance of linguistic structure, particularly in nonstandard speech; that may counteract misguided notions about superior and inferior dialects. It is hard to see, for example, why habitual *be,* multiple modals, or perfective *been* should not be permissible in writing; they give direct expression to nuances of meaning which the present literary language can only circuitously convey. Snobbish readers could learn to accept them just as underprivileged writers must now assiduously avoid *s/he don't.*[15]

Students should also examine variation, style-shifting, and change in language, along with the role prestigious groups may or may not play in directing them. From that they may learn something important about history and sociology as well as language. They should discuss the uses and misuses of writing and speech, their advantages and shortcomings. Here a reasonable rather than a bigoted conception of good English can develop.

Meanwhile, there is much for us to learn about writing and teaching it. Here at Harold Washington College in Chicago, dialect interference is an insignificant cause of the empty or garbled prose so often produced by disadvantaged remedial students. Missing inflections and double negatives may offend a reader; they do not really confuse one. Much more important are inexperience, self-deprecation, and fear—fear of a strange endeavor and the strangers who teach it.

People accustomed only to the give-and-take of speech have unusual problems with the solitary act of writing. It is so much harder, for example, to spell a sentence than to say one, that its beginning may simply be erased from memory before the end is reached. Anacoluthon then represents success, but grammatical crazy quilts are likely, since the explicit precision and complexity that writing requires will consistently strain a beginner's competence far more than conversation has. And when a new student has heard the academic tongue but is not yet speaking on its terms, then inflated diction and dynamited syntax will conspire to subvert meaning.

Caught in the resulting chaos and grotesque parodies of professional or bureaucratic jargon, a teacher takes shelter wherever she can, often in old-fashioned or newfangled prescriptive grammatical doctrines. Thus, instruction in writing is trivialized and enervated. Instead of promoting new and useful skills which a willing student might acquire, it attacks old, insignificant habits that are hard to break. Failure is thus built into the system, whether pupils are evaluated by real or irrelevant criteria. Their distrust of teachers understandably becomes dislike. If they have ever thought of themselves as having anything to write, and they often never have, they soon learn not to write it. Surely, at that price, valuable lessons in the composing process, in reading and proofreading, in rhetoric, logic, and argument, in matters of style and our Latinate vocabulary, even in pattern practice, sentence combining and paragraphing should not be sacrificed to the whimpering task of aping pedants or their masters.

We ought to teach our students to read: it is the surest way we can show them to understanding the world and their places in it. We should teach them to write: some of what they learn may help them improve their lot as well as the life we all must share. But we should not waste our energy or dissipate our influence in vain or trivial pursuits.

6

Linguistic Controversies, VBE Structures, and Midwest Attitudes

TIMOTHY J. RINEY[1]

STUDIES OF VERNACULAR Black English (VBE) continue to evolve through controversies that do not seem to get neatly resolved or accurately communicated to the public through the press. Still little understood is the longstanding controversy about the possible pidgin origins of VBE. And likely to be little understood by the public is the more recent controversy surrounding "the divergence hypothesis," which centers on whether VBE is becoming more different (Labov 1987) or less different (Butters 1989) from surrounding American dialects. While the linguistic debates continue, linguistic topics such as "pidgins" and "divergences" continue to provide the press with material for creating "good stories" (Wolfram 1990), and these stories in the press continue, as I shall show below, to play a major role in forming public attitudes about language (Algeo 1985).

No linguist has maintained that pidgin-creole continua or dialectal divergences are unnatural or bad developments. Yet throughout the VBE controversies, and perhaps partly as a consequence of them, stories in the press have continued to scatter doubts about the legitimacy of VBE as a language, and its position as a peer dialect among American dialects. To the extent that linguists are willing to take responsibility for conveying the nature of "language" and "dialect," and "standard" and "nonstandard" to the public, linguists may have to hold themselves accountable for the progress, or lack of progress, that has been made on this front. According to Labov (1987: 12), "we linguists have yet to make a significant contribution to the school curriculum that will put our linguistic knowledge to use."

More than a decade ago, in 1979, in a case known as the *King* decision (Labov 1982, Scott and Smitherman 1985), Labov and J. L. Dillard testified in Ann Arbor on behalf of black plaintiffs (parents) who were concerned that their children's language of the home, VBE, was a barrier to educational opportunity. The parents were not asking that VBE be standardized, or that their children be taught in VBE. The argument of the black parents was that teachers perceived and rejected their pupils' native language, VBE, as intellectually inferior, and that this rejection left the VBE-speaking children discouraged and unmotivated as students. The *King* decision ruled in favor of the black parents, and required that the teachers in the school district concerned take a series of workshops that would enable these teachers (1) to understand the concepts of "language" and "dialect," (2) to be sensitive to common public attitudes toward dialects, and (3) to be able to describe some of the basic structures of the home language of their students (in this case, VBE). This chapter investigates, a decade later, whether or not schools in the Midwest may still be in need of such workshops.

The investigation was conducted in northern Iowa in the adjoining cities of Cedar Falls and Waterloo, whose combined population in 1980 (112,307) was similar to that of Ann Arbor (107,000). The investigation, which determines that VBE is spoken in Waterloo, explores (1) to what degree the VBE presence is acknowledged by the educational establishment in the community and in the state, and (2) attitudes toward VBE and the social and educational significance of those attitudes. I hope that the results of this investigation will provide one measure that could be used in conjunction with others to assess to what extent, if any, a decade of efforts by some linguists and language educators have affected Midwesterners' perception of VBE since the *King* decision in Ann Arbor in 1979.

The first part of the chapter provides background information about Cedar Falls/Waterloo, Iowa. Next, I document what has previously gone unacknowledged—that Waterloo has a VBE-speaking population. The third part of the chapter describes an attitude study that involves Iowans' subjective evaluations of four matched guises, including one VBE guise. Finally, I consider the educational implications of this investigation and suggest some possibilities for future research.

Background

When I moved to northern Iowa in the fall of 1988, I noted a conspicuous presence of VBE in the city of Waterloo, where I lived, and a conspicuous absence of black Americans in the adjoining city of Cedar Falls at the University of Northern Iowa, where I worked. When I looked through descriptive language studies that had included Iowa, however, I could find no mention of VBE. When I called the Iowa Department of Education in Des Moines to get an estimate of the number of VBE-speaking students in Waterloo schools, the "race equity consultant" (C. Reed-Stuart, personal communication, September 1989) informed me that "that population is not in Iowa" and therefore posed "no problem." When I called back for clarification, and asked if I could quote her, she told a different story: VBE is, in fact, spoken in Waterloo, but because "Black English" is so widely "misunderstood" by the public, it is probably better not to call attention to the presence of the dialect. Of eight public officials and teachers, black and white, whom I have consulted, seven seemed to share this viewpoint: if "Black English" is present, it is better for all that it not be perceived as an issue. Many appear concerned about what the press might represent as "poor grammar" and "more lack of progress," a concern they may share with some linguists (e.g., Labov 1982, 1987; Vaughn-Cooke 1987; Wolfram 1987, 1990). Considering the manner in which some linguistic studies and claims about VBE continue to be interpreted by the press (Wolfram 1990), one can sympathize with the desire by a public official to avoid more "good stories" and pretend that VBE is not present.

But VBE *is* present, and dialectism, a language prejudice that cuts across social categories of race and gender, is present, too. It does not simply go away if you ignore it. I have reported these possible symptoms of dialectism in Cedar Falls/Waterloo (Riney 1989): (1) During the 1988–89 school year, the black enrollment in the Waterloo Community School District was 1,190 of 5,678, or 21%. Yet the black student population at the neighboring University of Northern Iowa, the only university in the area, was 2% in the fall of 1988, and only one of 206 undergraduate English majors was a black American. (2) On a diagnostic questionnaire administered in the first week of class (involving a total of some 200 university students in eight classes) one open question asked students to name (not circle—names were not given) one of their most and one of their least preferred "varieties" of English. "Most preferred" varieties were "American English," "Iowa English" and "British English." "Least preferred" varieties included "Southern English," "Black English," and "Ghetto English." Not one student named "Black English" or "Ghetto English" as a preferred variety, although VBE was the only dialect other than the majority dialect available to the students in the vicinity of their university. (3) Black educators in the Cedar Falls/Waterloo area offer estimates of the percentage of "monodialectal Black English" speakers (of the total number of blacks in Waterloo) that range from 10% to 90%. The 10% figure comes from the race equity consultant who had initially asserted that "that population is not in Iowa." The 90% figure comes from a black educator and outsider who appeared to have little in common with Waterloo blacks. Because VBE in Iowa has never been publicly acknowledged or studied, these widely varying estimates are difficult to assess.

But privately, if not publicly, no one denies that a variety of Black English is spoken in Waterloo. Previous studies (Scholl 1977, Riney 1989) indicate that the first large settlement of blacks in Waterloo occurred in 1911 and 1912, when hundreds of blacks from a rural community in Holmes County, Mississippi, were brought in (on railroad boxcars) to replace white workers who were on strike. In the decades that followed, the black population in Waterloo gradually increased, largely because of continuing migration of family and friends from Holmes County. By 1984, Waterloo, the fifth-largest city in Iowa, had the largest urban concentration of blacks in Iowa.

For decades, a speech island of VBE, unique in Iowa, has been maintained in Waterloo. As late as 1962, 50 years after the first large migration of blacks into Iowa, one of the two large public high schools in Waterloo was still 100% white. As late as 1967, one elementary school was still 100% black. Between 1970 and 1980, as the schools became more integrated, the black and white housing patterns remained segregated. By 1980, a few more blacks were found scattered in outlying areas, but the urban concentration of blacks in Waterloo remained relatively constant. In 1984, only one of 34 census tracts in the Cedar Falls/Waterloo area was more than 50% black. That tract was 89% black (Riney 1989).

The pattern of VBE migration and segregation described above accounts for the linguistic features of VBE observed in Waterloo and described in the section that follows.

Linguistic Evidence of VBE

Most studies of VBE have concentrated on the metropolitan North or the rural South. Few studies have examined middle-sized urban communities in the Midwest. No VBE studies, to my knowledge, have included Iowa. The purpose of this part of the chapter is to document that Waterloo, Iowa, does in fact contain a community of VBE speakers, and to document how Waterloo VBE contrasts with the surrounding vernacular Midland. *Vernacular Midland* is used here as a convenient label and to emphasize that Waterloo Vernacular Black English is distinct from both formal and informal varieties of the surrounding majority vernacular dialect. I do not address "Upper Midwest" or "Midland" distinctions, layers or subvarieties; for a discussion of these see Allen (1964), Carver (1987), and Frazer (1987c). In order to distinguish Waterloo VBE from vernacular Midland, Wolfram and Fasold (1974), who compare and contrast VBE with other social and vernacular dialects, are used as a point of reference below.

VBE and Vernacular Midland

Waterloo VBE and vernacular Midland share a number of common grammatical structures, such as *ain't,* two-part negatives, *at* in *Where's it at,* and demonstratives such as *them* in *leave them girls alone.* Shared phonological structures include items such as [d] for [z] in *isn't* and *wasn't,* and [ɪn] in *ing* suffixes.

Other structures of Waterloo VBE, however, seldom or never occur in vernacular Midland. The examples of Waterloo VBE that I report below all came from a single one-hour observation, Sunday afternoon, May 27, 1990, at a softball game in a park in Waterloo. I arrived in midgame, sat by myself in the bleachers, and took notes in a book. I listened to about 30 men and women, fairly evenly distributed in age from 12 to 35. The mood was informal, and a number of spectators and players were drinking beer. I transcribed examples of what I heard both in the bleachers and on the field.

I do not claim to be describing a representative sample, and I do not attempt to address variation, bidialectalism, code-switching, gender, age-grading, degrees of phonetic differences, northern-southern VBE differences, or the divergence hypothesis.

Phonological Evidence of VBE

Cluster Reduction

In vernacular Midland, word final consonant clusters that end in a stop are frequently reduced when both consonants are either voiced or voiceless and followed by a word initial consonant (Wolfram and Fasold 1974, 129). In VBE (hereinafter Waterloo VBE), this type of reduction also occurred before word initial vowels in *find out* ([fajnaut]) and *just in* ([dʒʌsɪn]), and before pauses, as in *you lost* ([yulas]).

The [f/θ] Correspondence

Waterloo VBE [f] corresponded to vernacular Midland [θ] in a medial position (in *nothing* and *bathroom*) and in a final position (in *both* and *bath*). Two Waterloo VBE exceptions to this pattern (see Wolfram and Fasold 1974: 135), were *with* as [wɪt], and *throw* with [t] instead of [θ] in word-initial position before [r].

The [d/ð] Correspondence

Waterloo VBE [d] corresponded to vernacular Midland [ð] in initial position in *the, that, them*. Waterloo VBE [v] corresponded to a vernacular Midland [ð] in intervocalic position in *mother* (Wolfram and Fasold 1974: 135).

Deletion of [r]

Little to no vestige of [r], consistently intact in vernacular Midland, appeared in Waterloo VBE pronunciations of *more* [moə], *four* [foə], *sure* [šoə], and in unstressed *for* [fə]. After the [ɛ] in *there*, an [r] vestige did appear (Wolfram and Fasold 1974: 140).

Other Phonological Structures

Waterloo VBE [æks] (Wolfram and Fasold 1974: 133) corresponded to Midland [æsk] for *ask*. Waterloo VBE glottal stops (Wolfram and Fasold 1974: 139) corresponded to vernacular Midland final stops, as in *look* as [lʊʔ].

Grammatical Evidence of VBE

Auxiliary Deletion

VBE deletion (Wolfram and Fasold 1974: 158) corresponded to Midland reduction of *are* to [r] in *they gone, I know you bringing me something, see if they still partying at home,* and in *hit the ball, that's what you up there for.* VBE deletion corresponded to Midland reduction of *is* to [z] in *she just in tenth grade.* VBE deletion corresponded to a Midland reduction of *is* to [ə] and [z] in *this a demonstration of what he gonna do.* VBE deletion corresponded to Midland reduction of *have* to [v] in *I should had one of them.* VBE deletion corresponded to Midland reduction of *will* to [l] in *I be back here* (for *I will be over here*).

Distributive be

Two examples of distributive *be,* a structure which, according to Wolfram and Fasold (1974: 161), occurs only in VBE, occurred in *he be there at night* and *I ask him why he be going over there.*

Subject Verb Agreement

VBE regularization of the third person singular form of the verb (Wolfram and Fasold 1974: 154) included the following: *the way he sound, he talk just like his dad,* and *he act like he bout twenty-one.* (These may be related to phonological cluster reductions, above.)

Other Grammatical Structures

Also noted were high frequencies of *you all* (Wolfram and Fasold 1974: 176) as a plural form of *you,* and one instance of generalized *is* (Wolfram and Fasold 1974: 157) in *here they is.* Structures commonly cited as VBE structures but not noted in this limited observation were *ain't* in the preterite, absence of possessive [s], the "remote time" use of *been,* as in *I been told you,* and the completive use of *done* in *I done tried* (Wolfram and Fasold 1974: 152; Labov 1987: 7; Wolfram 1990: 129). A more thorough investigation may turn up some of these structures.

Certain structures above suggest, along with the pattern of migration from Mississippi reviewed above, that Waterloo VBE is related to a southern VBE variety. These structures are (1) southern VBE [f] (and not northern VBE [t]) for [θ] in *nothing* (Wolfram and Fasold 1974: 135) and (2) the absence of any word final [r] vestige after [o] and [u] (Wolfram and Fasold 1974: 140). Those interested in the divergence hypothesis might note that these data include structures (e.g., the [f/θ] correspondence and *be* + verb + *ing*) that have been discussed (Labov 1987, Butters 1989, Wolfram 1990) as possible candidates for divergence.

Attitudes Toward VBE

The sections above have briefly described to what extent VBE has been acknowledged in Iowa, how VBE came to Waterloo, and how it continues to be spoken there. This next section describes an experiment intended to investigate the social significance of VBE and to measure attitudes toward VBE by some non-VBE speakers.

Subjects

This experiment (Riney 1989) involved 61 students who attended the first two class meetings of three sections of a course I taught at the University of Northern Iowa during the fall semester of 1989. The course served as the introduction to the study of language and was a prerequisite for further studies in linguistics and English structure. Personal data sheets served to identify 61 students who were undergraduates, U.S. citizens, Iowa residents, and who had had no previous course in linguistics. Of the 61, 70.5% (43 of 61) indicated that they were majoring in English, a foreign language, or education. (The personal data sheets also identified approximately 20 international students who were distributed evenly throughout the three classes, and whose performance is not included in the discussion below.)

I personally administered the experiment in all sections at the second class meeting of the semester, before students had had any exposure in the course to sociolinguistics or language attitudes. All students were non-black, and they were similar in age (mostly 19 to 21 years old), and two-thirds were female; in the weeks after the experiment, I observed that all were native speakers of a Midwest variety of English.

Materials and Procedures

The experiment involved a commercially available cassette recording produced by the Ohio State University Department of Linguistics (McManis et al. 1987). The cassette contains four female voices or "guises." Each guise is approximately ten seconds in length, and each involves a semantically similar utterance.[2] Two of the guises involve the same bidialectal female speaking in two different dialects, one of which is VBE.

This cassette was designed to demonstrate "that speech characteristics clearly influence the way one is perceived by others" (McManis et al. 1987: 363). I used the cassette not only for this purpose but also to illustrate the sociolinguistic "matched guise" technique (Lambert et al. 1960, Lambert 1967, Tucker and Lambert 1975) and to conduct the experiment I describe here. Students-raters did the activity described below first (without any sociolinguistic explanation) and discussed the results and implications two weeks later.

With the exception of the order of the guises (see below) I conducted the experiment in the same manner in all three sections. First, I explained how raters were to use the questionnaires. I then told the raters to prepare to rate "the four speakers" on four copies of the same questionnaire. After hearing each guise one time, raters had three minutes to complete the questionnaire and to rate aspects (e.g., intelligence and education) of that guise before listening to and rating the next guise. All raters appeared to have sufficient time to complete the questionnaire, and in a class discussion after the rating all students who spoke up indicated that they assumed that they were rating four different people.

The guises, referred to below by number in the order that they appear on the cassette, are as follows: Guise 2 is VBE, and grammatically marked as nonstandard with deletions of third person singular *s*, deletions of auxiliaries and *got*, and the deletion of one indefinite article. Guise 1 and Guise 3, labeled "network English" in this chapter, are grammatically and phonologically standard American English guises. These Iowa student raters later reported that they considered Guise 1 and Guise 3 either regionally unmarked or "slightly Eastern."

Guise 4 is a mixture of standard English and some elements of VBE. Although it contains none of the heavily marked VBE grammatical structures of Guise 2, it does exhibit suprasegmental and phonetic traces commonly associated with the speech of black Americans. Guise 4 also contains one structure that Wolfram (1990: 129) might interpret to be the "historical present" and common in all vernaculars. Labov (1987: 8) might interpret this structure as a variation of what he calls a VBE "narrative *s.*" I interpret this structure in Guise 4 to be the historical present, and common among speakers of both VBE and vernacular Midland in an informal story-telling mode. I have labeled Guise 4 "black accented English with historical present," to distinguish its grammar from the other guises. Each section of raters heard and rated the four guises in a different order: 1-2-3-4, 2-3-4-1, and 3-4-1-2. These orders always separated Guises 2 and 4 (the same person).

Results

Most items on the questionnaire were distractors. Of primary interest are parallel ratings of three items: (1) highest level of education completed, (2) smartness, and (3) intelligence, all three of which formed a similar three-tier pattern across the three types of guises and dialects. The ratings for intelligence are used to illustrate this pattern below.

Of the 61 student raters, 72.1% (44/61) rated both "network English" guises as more intelligent than average; 49.2% (30/61) rated the "black accented English with historical present" guise as more intelligent than average; only 18.0% (12/61) rated the VBE guise as more intelligent than average. Again, the raters were not aware that the VBE guise and the "black accented English with historical present" guise were the same person speaking different dialects.

These raters may appear to be making an assumption about relationship between intelligence and race. The three levels of intelligence ratings, however, correspond more closely to three types of grammar than they do to two types of race. The most formal and standard English guises ("network") receive the highest rating (72.1%), the second most standard ("black accented English with the historical present") receives the middle rating (49.2%), and the least standard guise (VBE) receives the lowest rating (18.0%).

As I noted above, 70.5% of these students had indicated on earlier personal data sheets that they were majoring in English, a foreign language, or education. In addition, during the 1989–90 school year, the year after this attitude study was conducted, 31 of 45 (68.8%) newly hired teachers in Waterloo public schools were graduates of the University of Northern Iowa (personal communication, Gladys Brummer, Office of Human Resources, Waterloo Schools, June 21, 1990), where I conducted the attitude study.

Discussion

A university with a student body that is only 2% black supplies a neighboring school district that is 21% black with the majority of the district's teachers. That district sends very few black high school graduates back to the neighboring university. Some of the blacks in the school district speak VBE. Some of the current and future teachers in that school district associate VBE with less intelligence. Correlations between language attitudes, teacher expectations, and student performance have been established (e.g., Williams 1976), and the apparent relationship among these factors provided the rationale for the *King* decision more than a decade ago. Nevertheless, some Midwestern educators appear deliberately to ignore the presence of VBE.

Educators in Waterloo and elsewhere in the Midwest may want to follow up on this study and investigate whether their students and teachers assume that some inherent relationship exists between intelligence and native dialect. If that attitude is widespread, then issues of equity identified by a federal judge in Ann Arbor in 1979 must be addressed in Midwestern communities today.

How do such attitudes emerge, and why do they persist?

Wolfram (1990) identifies racism as their source. My focus is dialectism, and how dialectism is both disseminated and reflected by the press. I mentioned above that the press sometimes exploits linguistic controversies about VBE. Press stories may play a major role in forming public opinions about language (Algeo 1985). One such story circulated in Iowa the year before the study reported above. It involves Orr's widely reviewed study (1987) of the language of black children as they studied mathematics in Washington, D.C. Orr, an educator but not a linguist, associates the difficulty that students have learning mathematics with the structure of their native dialect, and attributes misunderstandings between students and teachers (which contribute to poor performance) to the differences between their dialects.

Orr's conclusion, however, was altered in reviews in the press. The heading in *The New York Times* was "Why Black English Doesn't Add Up" (Countryman 1987). In Iowa, the heading of the review in *The Des Moines Register* (Heys 1988) was "Black English Hurts Academics." According to Heys, Orr contends (though in fact Orr does not) that VBE "lacks the prepositions, conjunctions, and relative pronouns necessary to communicate quantitative concepts in math and science." (It is frightening to imagine what a racial analogue to these alleged linguistic deficits would be, but it is certain that it would not appear in *The Des Moines Register*, and that it would not be accepted by the public if it did.)

Heys manages to make a "good story" even better by capitalizing on the ongoing controversy about the origins of VBE. While appearing to base his story on Orr's discussion of the possible pidgin origins of VBE, Heys describes VBE in such a way that suggests that VBE is a pidgin! Heys provides no assessment by linguists of Orr's work (which he misrepresents); Wolfram and Christian (1989: 59), however, assess Orr's conclusions as "premature."

Implications and Future Research

Descriptive Studies

The presence of a VBE speech island isolated for decades in a smaller urban community in northern Iowa raises a number of questions that future studies might want to investigate. What is the structure of Waterloo VBE today, and what is the structure of VBE in the linguistic source, Holmes County, Mississippi, today? In a smaller urban community, with a continuing history of tightly segregated housing and only recent experience with integrated schooling (and more opportunity for interethnic contact), is a dialect shift occurring across age groups? If so, are code-switching and bidialectalism also occurring, and how are they distributed across age groups?

Language Attitudes

It is important to remember that this attitude study never isolated the variable of race from the variable of the degree of the standardness of the grammar. Future studies of language attitudes might do so. How would raters evaluate a phonetically black guise that is unquestionably morphologically and syntactically standard English (i.e., without the marked and informal "historical present" or "narrative s")? Or a phonetically non-black "vernacular Midland" guise that contains a number of nonstandard grammatical structures? Would they rate the standard black guise higher than the nonstandard white vernacular Midland guise? I think they might. During the two years I spent in northern Iowa I encountered no one who expressed a belief in any inherent racial superiority, but I encountered many people, black and white, who expressed a belief that some dialects are somehow inherently superior to others.

Language Education

Does the rationale of the *King* decision of 1979 need to be considered in Iowa and elsewhere in the Midwest today? One of the first steps in language education should be the careful study of the languages and attitudes in the community being considered. As I have pointed out, in Iowa today VBE is not even publicly acknowledged. It is uncertain what a department of education can do for its students if it does not first acknowledge their native language and consider their teachers' attitudes toward that language. The workshops mandated by the *King* decision were intended to address precisely this kind of educational oversight, and should be offered to Waterloo and other communities that may need them.

Until they are, or some other solution is found, the educational prospects for monodialectal VBE children entering schools in the Midwest are likely to be bleak. Racial relations in the United States may still be in trouble, but most discussions of racial relations have at least risen to a level of sophistication beyond questions of legitimacy and equality. The legitimacy and equality of all dialects, however, has never been accepted—not even in principle—by the public at large. The *difference is deficit* assumption about nonstandard dialects continues to go largely unopposed in the media and must be exposed, challenged, and overcome. Linguistic controversies about VBE must not be used to divert the public from the important issue, which is not linguistic inadequacy (and perhaps not even racism), but the continuing ignorance about the nature of language on the part of the press and the public—and what linguists and language educators should do about it.

II

Urban Studies & Microanalyses

7

Farmer City, Illinois: Sound Systems Shifting South

TIMOTHY HABICK

RECENT ADVANCES IN both instrumental phonetics and socio-linguistic theory have allowed researchers interested in the nature of sound change to examine sets of data that are much more reliable and revealing than was previously thought possible. By use of the sound spectrograph (or one of its computerized successors), it is now possible to obtain an objective visual (or digital) record of speech sounds, which can then be measured or interpreted, often with a high degree of confidence.

These procedures are perhaps a far cry from any ever imagined by Louis Gauchat (1905) or Eduard Hermann (1929) when they investigated the dialect of the Swiss village of Charmey, but they allow us to take giant steps towards goals those early dialectologists held dear: capturing in a systematic way the essential dialectological facts of a small speech community, and perhaps gaining some insight into the processes by which dialects and their sound systems change. Having discarded the Neogrammarian notion that sound change is by its very nature imperceptible, contemporary linguists are now in a position to observe sound change as it progresses within communities of speakers. The work begun by Gauchat and Hermann—and later abandoned by other dialectologists in favor of large atlas studies—is now continuing, if not with chocolate-factory workers in Swiss mountains, at least with farmers in Illinois cornfields.

Armed with Labov, Yeager, and Steiner's (1972) methodologies of spectrographic dialectology and the microsociolinguistic model in Labov (1973), I set out to document the vocalic system of one small community in as much detail and historical depth as possible. I chose Farmer City[1] (population 2,200) in central Illinois, simply because the friendly people there were willing to participate and the town was close to my home base of Urbana-Champaign. As a Zen master once said, "If you can't find it where you are, where will you wander in search of it?" As it happened, I wandered no farther than 20 miles northwest of Champaign.

I was also attracted to Farmer City, as Gauchat and Hermann were to Charmey, because its ethnic homogeneity and physical distance from the myriad social influences of large cities reduced the number of variables to be considered.[2] Farmer City's settlement history also was not terribly complex. The initial, late nineteenth-century population of Farmer City and surrounding communities was composed primarily of white settlers from North Midland dialect areas such as Ohio and Pennsylvania and from the South Midland area of Kentucky. At the present time, many members of the younger generations of Farmer City can trace their origins to ancestors from both regions. In the early decades of the twentieth century, Kentucky was an important source of laborers for established farms in central Illinois, and many such transient workers eventually made their homes there. Immigration from Kentucky still continues today, though at a greatly diminished rate. Thus, Farmer City dialect, although essentially North Midland, is strongly influenced by the speech of Kentucky. This latter settlement pattern offers the major complication in an otherwise uniform state of affairs.

The Sample

The 40 speakers in the study were drawn from Farmer City and some small surrounding communities.[3] In addition, a sample of seven speakers from Somerset, Kentucky,[4] was collected for the purposes of comparison, because many Farmer City families originally derive from that town. The Farmer City sample includes 20 speakers from two opposing teenage peer groups, which constitute the focus of the study. This original group was expanded later to include seven parents and six grandparents of the peer group members, to enlarge the age range and thus gain insight into earlier stages.

Though social stratification occurs in all communities, the degree to which the particular senior class of 1978 at Farmer City-Mansfield High School was polarized was unique and the subject of much discussion. In this report, the two major peer groups are often identified as groups X and Y. The group members themselves, however, had more descriptive epithets for each other. Group X was called the "burnouts" for their openly admitted involvement with drugs (mostly marijuana), and group Y was called the "rednecks" because of their more conservative values. From casual observation and the students' own descriptions, group X could be characterized as individuals with a marked nonacademic persuasion and a fondness for mild drugs, alcohol, and "partying." As two group X girls put it, emphasizing the misunderstanding they have endured, "They think of us all as burnouts. Anyone who smokes marijuana is automatically addicted to all kinds of drugs, you know, hard drugs. . . . They just stereotype all of us into. . . . We're all burnouts." Group Y, on the other hand, was composed of students who took part in school activities and sports and also tended to do well academically. They rarely indulged in alcohol or drugs. The use of the term *redneck* to describe such model college-bound students is somewhat puzzling until we realize that from the burnouts' point of view, their rivals' attitudes seemed repressive and provincial, as opposed to their own expansive and innovative behavior. One group X member provided the following clarification: "A redneck is a person, like in this age group, who goes to all the school things, goes out for all the sports, gets good grades, or else brownnoses good enough that they get good grades, and they talk to the teachers all the time, and just general brownnose, and they don't, they won't associate with people like me." The burnout/redneck distinction among Farmer City teenagers is thus analogous to the polarization between "burnouts" and "jocks" noted for Detroit by Eckert (1989). It is *not* socially comparable to the "lame"/ in-crowd distinction in New York City street gangs made by Labov (1973a), but to the opposition of structurally equivalent social categories occurring in public secondary schools across the United States (Eckert 1989).

As expected, there was a considerable amount of rivalry and antagonism between the two groups, stemming from the burnouts' jealousy of the rednecks' achievements and consequent privileges at the school ("The rednecks get so much more and we're so discriminated against"), as well as from the rednecks' superior attitude. In the words of one repentant redneck, "I think [we've] just, basically been a bunch of snobs. We just thought that we were so much better, so college-oriented, that of course they resent it, because we've been almost mean and nasty up until now." When I heard this self-critical assessment, I protested that it was the burnouts who appeared more exclusive. The same individual continued: "I think they are more, I mean, they make it a more elite type, but I think that we've basically driven them there, because we have, we act like they're, you know, it's us and them, you know, there's such a definite break." This break, it should be noted, had existed for no more than 5 years, considering that several burnouts and rednecks, including leaders from both groups, were best friends in elementary school.

The basis for the development of the two rival groups was attitudinal rather than socioeconomic. Members of both groups were sons and daughters of farmers or businessmen in the community and thus came from comfortable middle-class homes. There were differences in the personal lives of the two groups: two group X members came from less-than-ideal family backgrounds, one living with foster parents, the other with parents anticipating divorce, and had frequent run-ins with the police and caused minor disturbances at school. But in terms of material wealth and the parents' own social position, it would be hard to differentiate the two groups. A few lower-class students, sometimes referred to collectively as the "scruffies," did attend the school, but in Labov's terminology, they were "lames" and did not constitute a coherent social group.

The sociometric diagram (figure 7.1) illustrates the degree of separation between the two groups. The diagram was constructed on the basis of the students' response to the question, "Who do you consider your best friends?" The numbers within the circles refer to individual speakers. Numbers 1 through 7 refer to burnout males; numbers 11 through 17 identify redneck males. Numerals over 40 refer to group members not interviewed or analyzed. To simplify the figure, only the most frequently mentioned boys are represented,[5] and some peripheral individuals who were mentioned only once were not included. Table 7.1 contains a key to other speaker codes used throughout this paper.

Table 7.1
Key to Speaker Codes

Code	Group
1–7	"X" boys
8–10	"X" girls
11–17	"Y" boys
18–20	"Y" girls
21–24	FC fathers
25–27	FC mothers
28–30	FC grandfathers
31–33	FC grandmothers
34–40	Kentucky family
34	male, 17 years
35	female, 16 years
36	grandfather
37	male, 24 years
38	female, 22 years
39	female, 39 years
40	grandmother

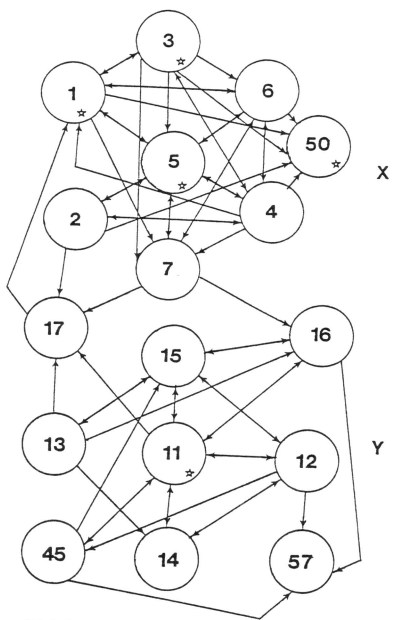

Figure 7.1. Sociometric diagram. The numbers refer to individual speakers, as explained in table 7.1. Group X indicates the "burnouts"; group Y represents the "rednecks."

The arrows in figure 7.1 indicate friendship or association. When one member mentioned another as his friend, the relationship is indicated with an arrow directed from the first to the second. When the second individual also identified the first, the reciprocal relationship is indicated by an arrowhead placed at the other end of the shaft. A star within a circle indicates a group leader (identified by direct statements from group members), and those individuals were naturally mentioned more often. Figure 7.1 thus reveals the degree of coherence within the two groups, as well as the social distance that separates them. In all the interviews, only four instances of intergroup association were noted; these involved speakers 16 and 17, who still had ties with the burnouts.[6]

Speech Styles

As has been demonstrated amply by Labov (1971, 1973), the most innovative speech style, the vernacular, is more likely to occur in "unobserved" casual conversation than in reading passages or word lists. In an effort to simplify the analysis of raw data, however, and because I was interested in charting a set of phonemes in the same coarticulatory environments for each of 40 speakers, the word-list style seemed most appropriate. Only in this way was it possible to construct 40 phonemic systems and have them clearly comparable to each other. Thus, in attempting to improve on the comparability of the charts in Labov et al. (1972), which were based on different allophones for each speaker, I willingly sacrificed the chance to consider the most advanced sound changes in the dialect. Nevertheless, the relative performance of each individual is still telling, as the same speech style was collected for each speaker.

Recording, Analysis, and Charting

I taped the interviews in Farmer City on a Nagra IV-D recorder with a Shure SM54 unidirectional microphone. Recording was made at 7.5 ips on Scotch 250 tape. A well-maintained Kay Elemetrics 6061B Sonagraph produced both wide band and 37.5% magnified narrow band spectrograms for each signal. I measured from 60 to 100 spectrograms (90 words) to establish the vocalic system of each speaker.

In accordance with standard practice in the field, spectrographic data collected in this study have been interpreted phonologically by charting the first formant as a function of the second. The two-formant graph represents two fundamental phonological feature sets commonly referred to in articulatory terms: high/low (acoustically, F_1—the higher in frequency, the more "low") and front/back (F_2—the higher in frequency, the more "front").

Although the ellipses and phonemic symbols that I have used here to delimit phonemic boundaries are similar to those found in Labov et al. (1972), the ellipses often have different underlying meanings. One important difference is that in the present study the entire trajectories of diphthongs are represented, the direction of movement being marked with an arrow. The meaning of the ellipses' sizes also deserves comment. Unlike the ellipses in Labov et al. (1972), those in the Farmer City charts can be understood to vary in size as a function of (1) fundamental frequency (the higher the speaker's F_0, the larger the ellipses) and (2) the care that certain speakers take to avoid the effects of coarticulation. In other words, if fundamental frequency is constant, speakers with smaller ellipses (such as the group Y male of figure 7.2) hit their acoustic/articulatory targets with more precision than those with larger ellipses, for whom the effect of an adjacent /r/ or /l/, for example, is more exaggerated. This added specification can be made because the ellipses are based on the *same* allophones for each speaker.

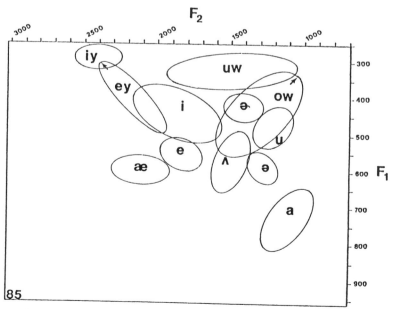

Figure 7.2. The vocalic system of Group Y Speaker 13. This speaker's relatively small ellipses for some phonemes imply precise articulatory gestures.

The Acoustic Variability of Phonemic Systems

One of the most serious limitations on the use of spectrographic evidence for dialectological research is caused by the acoustic relativity of many phonemic features. A researcher who plots the phonemic systems of speakers of different ages, sexes, and social backgrounds may well be startled at first by their dissimilarity. The /ʌ/ in *Monday*, for example, may have an F_1 value of about 550 Hz for one individual, but about 900 Hz for another speaker of the same dialect, and such differences can be found even when the sample is restricted to males (cf. figures 7.3 and 7.4). The frequency range used to establish phonemic systems varies considerably from speaker to speaker, and so phonemes cannot be reliably identified acoustically by reference to absolute values in two-formant space. Each speaker organizes this space in his or her own way, on the basis of a variety of constraints, some beyond the speaker's control.

An understanding of the nature and causes of acoustic variability is naturally crucial to the use of spectrographic analysis for any type of linguistic evidence, especially when comparisons are to be made be-

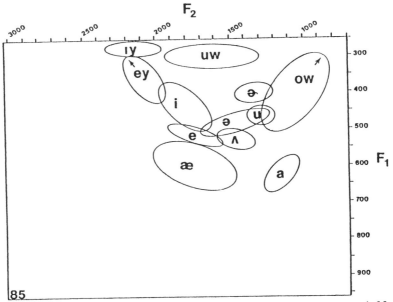

Figure 7.3. The vocalic system of Speaker 22 (male, second generation). Note the difference in the F_1 level of this speaker's phonemes from that of Speaker 28 in figure 7.4.

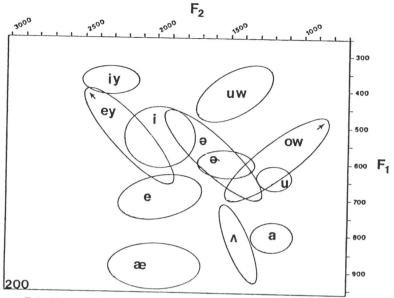

Figure 7.4. The vocalic system of Speaker 28 (male, first generation). The numbers in the lower left corner of the chart indicate the speaker's average fundamental frequency.

tween the systems of different speakers. To study one phoneme effectively, the analyst must first orient her- or himself by plotting the entire vocalic system, or at least several cardinal vowels for each speaker. Many points in two-formant space—apparently not all—are dependent on their relationship to other points in the system for a judgment of vocalic quality (Ladefoged and Broadbent 1957), and so formant values alone do not necessarily have dialectological significance.

The Farmer City project is ideally suited to a study of acoustic variability, since it involves such a large number of speakers from the same town pronouncing the same words. With so many variables accounted for or controlled, it was possible to move beyond some of the monolithic explanations found in earlier studies. Vocal tract size, for example, is undoubtedly important in determining the levels of a speaker's formant frequencies, but the evidence from Farmer City suggests that such invariant anatomical characteristics combine with a quite variable articulatory setting to determine the true resonating properties of that vocal tract. A speaker's characteristic articulatory setting, that general arrangement of the organs of articulation that the speaker maintains while speaking, itself is complexly determined, for

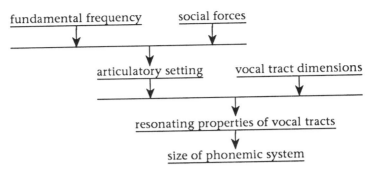

Figure 7.5. Determinants of the "two-formant size" of the phonemic system.

example, by fundamental frequency and social forces. These relationships are summarized in figure 7.5.

The issue of acoustic variability is discussed in Habick (1980: 129–55), and detailed arguments are offered in support of the claims made earlier.[7] For present purposes, it is important to note that the systems of speakers with different fundamental frequencies cannot be compared in absolute terms; such comparisons can have little meaning. A speaker with an 85-Hz fundamental frequency is playing a different instrument than one with a 170-Hz fundamental, such that a second formant value of, say, 2,800 Hz must be interpreted differently for each speaker (remarkable for the first, normal for the second). For this reason, the average F_0 in hertz of each speaker's normal voice is noted in the lower left corner of the vowel chart. In fact, as so many variables are involved, the prudent analyst will avoid absolute comparisons even between same-sex speakers with similar fundamentals, though such comparisons would be the least subject to distortion.

Acoustic variability means, in effect, that we must be cautious not to overrate the objectivity of formant measurements when comparing different speakers' systems. Statements such as "This speaker's /u/ is relatively closer to his /i/ than is the case for that speaker" are more realistic and potentially less misleading than are comparisons in terms of absolute frequencies: "There is a distance of 200 Hz between this speaker's two phonemes, whereas that speaker's are separated by only 100 Hz." If we generate and analyze a sufficient number of spectrograms for each speaker, we can now achieve a higher level of objectivity than was the case with the aural judgments of prespectrographic phonetics. But until we understand and control for all of the variables that determine the levels of a speaker's formant frequencies, our final interpretations must still be somewhat subjective.

Characteristics of the Farmer City Dialect

From the field records of the Linguistic Atlas of the North Central States (as presented in Marckwardt 1957), central Illinois is a transitional area between North and South Midland speech. It is especially difficult to classify central Illinois into a discrete dialect area, since so many lexical isoglosses pass right through the region.

In terms of the dialect groupings used by Labov (1992), Farmer City in particular has a predominantly Northern dialect, but with strong Southern influence. There the farmers *shuck* corn (Southern) rather than *husk* it (Northern), though strong Southern usages such as *y'all* were never observed.

Phonologically, Farmer City is once again basically Northern, with many Southern features variably appearing in certain age and peer groups. Some speakers displayed the drawling features of monophthongization, lengthening, and medial amplitude drop, but only variably and not strongly. The state of Kentucky, on the other hand, is in the Southern dialect area, and the seven speakers from Somerset were found to use many more typical Southern forms, especially drawling.

The Southern Drawl

In its most basic sense, drawling can be defined simply as a type of tempo, indicating lengthened as opposed to shortened ("clipped") syllables. In its practical realization in Southern dialects, however, drawling has become a complex phonetic and phonological development characterized by a large number of features and systemic implications, many of which are discussed in Sledd (1966). Drawling is by no means expressed in the same way in each Southern dialect, nor, of course, by each speaker of the same dialect. The drawled syllables of the Farmer City and Kentucky samples, however, can be described spectrographically in terms of three major features which may occur singly or in combination: lengthening, breaking, and amplitude drop.

For some speakers, drawling often involves only lengthened monophthongs. More often, however, at least in Somerset, the secondary features of breaking and amplitude drop also occur. Breaking refers to the development of lengthened monophthongs into diphthongs or triphthongs. Actually, the breaking that has traditionally been termed "ingliding" (as by Kruse 1972) is a triphthongal, not a diphthongal, contour. Sometimes a drop in composite amplitude (or "loudness") occurs at the middle of a lengthened monophthong. Other times, amplitude drop is observed at the high front apex of what are usually fronting-raising/backing-lowering triphthongs. It appears that breaking and amplitude drop both function to demarcate the center of lengthened syllables. Habick (1980: 181–87) provides graphic illustrations and a more detailed description of these drawling features.

In Farmer City, a slight amount of drawling occurs, and this is expressed by amplitude drop patterns on lengthened monophthongs, rarely by breaking. In the sample analyzed, amplitude drops are found especially in the younger generation (in burnout speakers generally and in redneck Speakers 14, 15, and 16). In the second generation, the patterns are found especially in the speech of Speakers 22, 23, 24, and 25. It is interesting that the first generation members analyzed (the grandparents) do not exhibit this feature. For those speakers who do have this type of drawling, it occurs variably, but almost exclusively on lax vowels.

Schwa Raising and Upglide Insertion

There is a clear tendency for the younger speakers of Farmer City to avoid certain stereotypical Southern features of pronunciation[8] such as schwa raising and upglide insertion before shibilants (table 7.2). Raising of final schwa to [i] or [ɪ] level in such words as *soda, idea,* and *opera* occurred in the speech of three Kentucky subjects, but only one (first-generation) Farmer City resident. Six of the 7 Kentucky speakers had upglides in the words *tarnish* and *fish,* as did 5 of the 6 grandparents from Farmer City. But only 2 of the 7 parents (second generation) had upglides for *tarnish* and only 4 of the 20 teenage peer group members. Similarly, for *pleasure,* none of the teenagers produced an upglide, but 6 parents, 4 grandparents, and 3 Kentucky speakers retained the dialectally marked pronunciation.

Education may well be responsible for the younger generation's shift away from these socially disparaged Southern features in favor of dialectally unmarked pronunciations. Two first-generation subjects, in fact, observed that the young people in Farmer City are "more precise" in their speech and use more "correct grammar" than older people, who tend to "let you guess what they're talking about." It is not surprising that the grandparents focused on such surface features in assessing their grandchildren's speech, as most people attend to their close relatives' lexical choices (and perhaps voice qualities) more than to their realizations of individual phonemes. What is surprising is their conviction

Table 7.2
Raising/Upglides before /š/, /ž/

No.	Speaker Group	Sex	pleasure	tarnish (t)/fish (f)	mash
1	X	M		t	
2	X	M			
3	X	M		t	
4	X	M			
5	X	M			
6	X	M		t	
7	X	M			
8	X	F			
9	X	F			
10	X	F			
11	Y	M			
12	Y	M			
13	Y	M			
14	Y	M			x
15	Y	M			x
16	Y	M			
17	Y	M		t	
18	Y	F			
19	Y	F			
20	Y	F			
21	2	M		t/f	
22	2	M	x		x
23	2	M	x		
24	2	M	x		x
25	2	F	x	t	
26	2	F	x		
27	2	F	x		
28	1	M	x	t/f	x
29	1	M		t/f	
30	1	M	x	t	x
31	1	F		t/f	x
32	1	F	x	t/f	x
33	1	F	x	t/f	x
34	KY	M			x
35	KY	F		t/f	x
36	KY	M		t/f	x
37	KY	M	x	t/f	
38	KY	F	x	t/f	x
39	KY	F		t/f	x
40	KY	F	x	t/f	x

that their grandchildren's linguistic performance was generally more correct and acceptable than their own. As we will see presently, it is the teenagers, not the octogenarians, who have vowel systems that depart more from the norms of network English.

The Southern Shift

The overall vocalic systems of the first generation of Farmer City are characterized by the fronting of /uw/, initiating the Southern Shift discussed by Labov (1992), and sometimes by raised schwa. Only the fronted /uw/ feature, however, was inherited by the second generation (figures 7.6 and 7.7). /uw/ fronting was probably introduced to Farmer City by the early Kentucky immigrants. For comparison, figure 7.8 shows the vocalic system of a 17-year-old Somerset male, and figure 7.9 shows that of his grandmother.

Only in the third generation does the Southern Shift continue, and among the burnouts the change is dramatic. The differences in the phonemic systems of the two peer groups can be seen most clearly by considering the vowel charts of their group leaders: the males rated

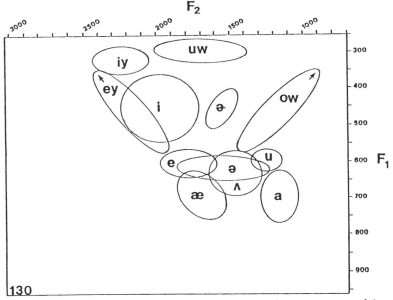

Figure 7.6. The vocalic system of Speaker 21 (second generation, male).

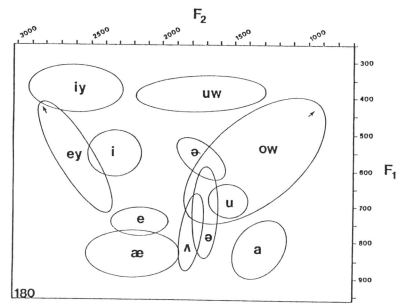

Figure 7.7. The vocalic system of Speaker 26 (second generation, female).

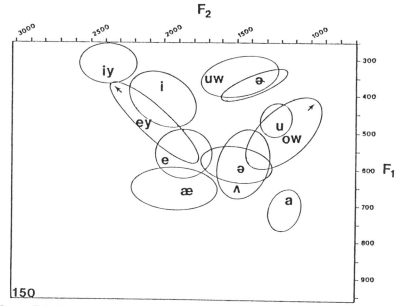

Figure 7.8. The vocalic system of Speaker 34 (Somerset, KY, male, 17 years).

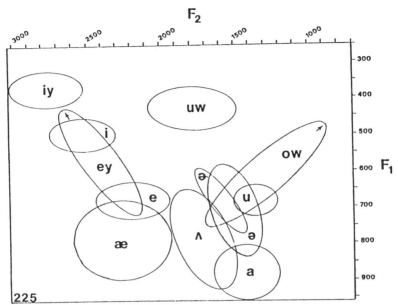

Figure 7.9. The vocalic system of Speaker 40 (Somerset, KY, female, 80 years).

most popular and influential by other members of their groups. Figure 7.10 shows the vocalic system of a burnout leader and figure 7.11 shows that of a redneck leader. In general, both systems exhibit /uw/ fronting, but now this fronting has become a process that progressed to include /u/, /ow/, and /ʌ/, especially among the burnouts.

The typical redneck's vocalic system is thus more conservative; the burnouts', more innovative. In fact, the rednecks' systems tend to resemble those of their parents or grandparents. (See figures 7.12, 7.13, and 7.14.) The burnouts' systems, on the other hand, show a continuation of the Southern Shift; the vowels have collapsed in on themselves, taking the shape of a parallelogram, rather than that of the traditional vowel triangle or trapezoid, as figures 7.15, 7.16, and 7.17 also illustrate.

The particular sound changes that have contributed to the burnouts' unique collapsed systems are considered in detail next.

/uw/ Fronting

As /uw/ fronting is the initial change in the generalized fronting process occurring in Farmer City, it is found in almost every speaker in a rather advanced form and does not constitute the most diagnostic sociolinguistic variable in the community. Nevertheless, using relative

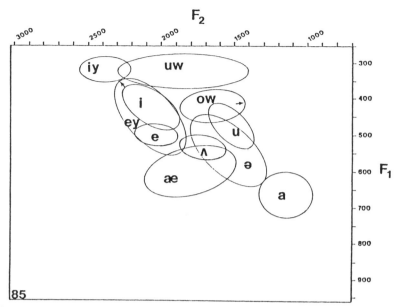

Figure 7.10. Speaker 1 (Group X leader, male). This vocalic system illustrates the effect of the generalized fronting processes favored by Group X, producing a peculiar "collapsed" system.

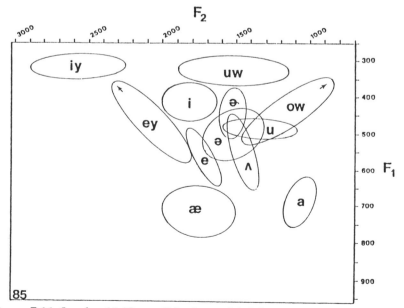

Figure 7.11. Speaker 11 (Group Y leader, male). Like most Group Y members, this individual has less extreme fronting of back vowels.

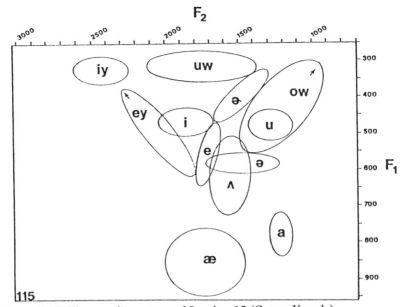

Figure 7.12. The vocalic system of Speaker 12 (Group Y male).

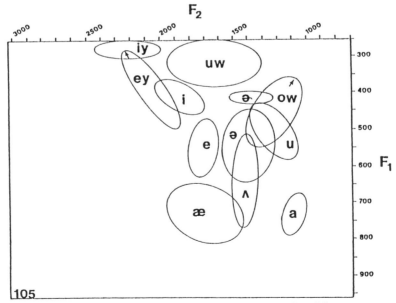

Figure 7.13. The vocalic system of Speaker 14 (Group Y male).

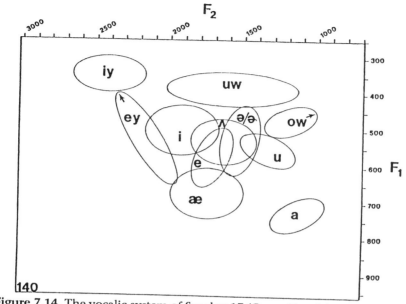

Figure 7.14. The vocalic system of Speaker 17 (Group Y male).

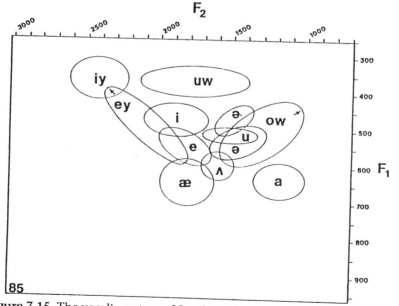

Figure 7.15. The vocalic system of Speaker 2 (Group X male).

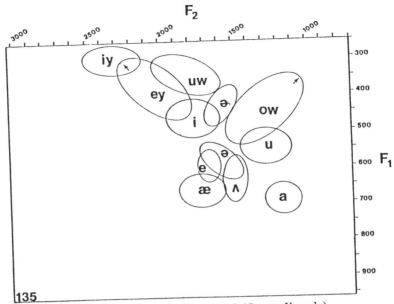

Figure 7.16. The vocalic system of Speaker 3 (Group X male).

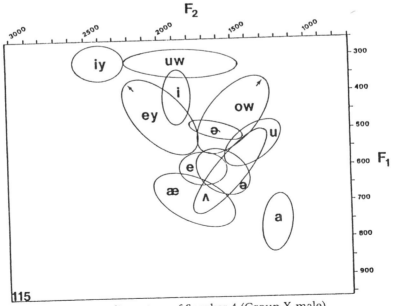

Figure 7.17. The vocalic system of Speaker 4 (Group X male).

comparisons, it is possible to identify certain speakers as having less fronted realizations of /uw/ than others. These are presented in table 7.3 along with a list of those who have very fronted pronunciations (clearly the majority) and those few who have the unusual fronting diphthongal contour of [u^y], which is opposite to the common backing direction of [iu^w]. For some dental-initial words for three burnout speakers and one father, there is a clear fronting contour from the dental position to a high front target of [ɨ] or [ü]. This contour is also found in one word spoken by one Kentucky subject. Such a development is an indication that the nucleus of /uw/ is shifting to the front of the system, and that this target is becoming more important than the high back [u] target to which some of these speakers' /uw/ lexemes still glide. And although it is natural for dental-initial words to occasion a fronting contour to a target such as [ü] or [ɨ], one would expect relatively steady vowels with palatal-initial words. This expected situation is found in a few such words for some speakers, though most retain the common backing direction from these high front targets. Two speakers, however, have fronting contours, even for palatal-initial /uw/ lexemes. Significantly, these are both burnout leaders. For one, the transitions for *shoot* and *chew* start at the palatal targets and move front to the periphery of his /iy/ ellipse. For the other, the tendency is so progressed that, at least on the basis of two-formant spectrographic evidence, *shoot* might be classified in his /iy/ phonemic category. The transition starts well within his /iy/ phonemic domain, moves to an even more front position, to a point slightly more front than even his /iy/ vowels reach, and then moves back to an [ɨ] or [ü]. It is this subsequent backing movement that helps maintain *shoot* within his /uw/ phoneme.

For the other speakers, the binary distinction of "fronted" and "less front" suggested in table 7.3 should be interpreted as suggestive approximations. More accurate data can be found in Habick (1980) in the detailed appendix of /uw/ gliding charts for each speaker. Nevertheless, from table 7.3, it can be seen that some redneck speakers have relatively less fronted realizations than burnout speakers, and that a few parents and grandparents also have relatively less fronted vowels.

/u/ Fronting

Although Sledd (1966) mentions the general fronting of both /uw/ and /u/ ([ʊ]) as a feature of the dialect of Atlanta, Georgia, /u/ fronting was not observed in the Kentucky sample. Kruse (1972: 28), on the basis

Table 7.3
Fronting in /uw/, /ow/

Speaker			/uw/			/ow/		
						e/ow		i/ow
No.	Group	Sex	[üʸ]	Fronted	Less Front	Overlap	Close	Overlap
1	X	M	x	x		x		
2	X	M		x		x		
3	X	M		x				
4	X	M	x	x		x		
5	X	M	x	x		x		
6	X	M		x			x	
7	X	M		x				x
8	X	F		x		x		x
9	X	F		x		x		
10	X	F		x		x		
11	Y	M			x		x	
12	Y	M			x	x		
13	Y	M			x		x	
14	Y	M		x				
15	Y	M		x		x		
16	Y	M		x		x		
17	Y	M		x				x
18	Y	F		x				x
19	Y	F		x				
20	Y	F			x			
21	2	M	x	x			x	
22	2	M		x				
23	2	M			x			
24	2	M			x	x		
25	2	F		x				
26	2	F		x			x	
27	2	F			x			
28	1	M			x		x	
29	1	M			x		x	
30	1	M			x			
31	1	F		x				
32	1	F		x				x
33	1	F		x				
34	KY	M			x			
35	KY	F	x	x				
36	KY	M			x			
37	KY	M		x				
38	KY	F		x				
39	KY	F		x				
40	KY	F		x				

of linguistic atlas records, however, observed that some centralized variants of /u/ are found in that state. Nevertheless, it appears that this feature is unevenly distributed among Southern dialects and has arisen independently in several of them. One such dialect is that of Farmer City.

In Farmer City, /u/ fronting is strictly limited to the younger generation and thus can be considered a recent innovation. Three words in the word list are members of the /u/ phonemic class: *shook, book*, and *look*. Of these, the vocalic target of *shook* is naturally more susceptible to fronting, as a result of the influence of the palatal [š]. The targets of *book* and *look*, under the influence of a labial or liquid, are noticeably more back spectrographically, though perceptually they still have a fronted quality, especially among burnouts.

It could be argued that because *shook* is under the influence of a palatal consonant, there is nothing unusual in the lexeme having a fronted /u/ target. But clear evidence that /u/ is beginning to pattern with the general fronting process is found when transitions for the first two phonemes of *shook* for the younger speakers are compared with those of the other groups in the sample. Speakers from the older generations in Farmer City and all of the Kentucky speakers have transitions that start in the high front, palatal area but move to an [o] target that is fully back. But with the exception of four redneck speakers, most younger speakers' transitions do not move farther back than the central portion of their systems. These distinctions are summarized in table 7.4. Those speakers not marked either "fronted" or "back" can be assumed to have intermediate realizations. Once again, the actual transitions are detailed for each speaker in appendix 2 of Habick (1980). As will be true with the other secondary fronting processes, more burnouts than rednecks have participated in this change.

/ʌ/ Fronting

Aside from the fronted targets of /uw/, one of the most striking characteristics of the Farmer City dialect is its realizations of /ʌ/. For many speakers, there is a marked transfer of /ʌ/ nuclei to within the phonemic space of /e/ ([ɛ]); for others /ʌ/, though distinct in two-formant space, has a noticeable [ɛ] quality. In fact, there appears to be no difference in the pronunciation of *money* and *many* for several speakers. This fronting is the opposite of the backing of [ʌ] in the Northern Cities Shift (Eckert 1992: ch. 7).

Spectrographically, actual overlaps of phonemic boundaries were

Table 7.4
Fronting in /ʌ/, /u/

Speaker			Proximity of /e/ and /ʌ/			/u/-Fronting (in shook)	
No.	Group	Sex	Overlap	Close	Far	Fronted	Back
1	X	M	x			x	
2	X	M	x				
3	X	M		x			
4	X	M	x			x	
5	X	M		x		x	
6	X	M	x				
7	X	M		x			
8	X	F	x			x	
9	X	F	x			x	
10	X	F		x		x	
11	Y	M		x		x	
12	Y	M		x			x
13	Y	M		x			x
14	Y	M			x		x
15	Y	M		x		x	
16	Y	M	x				x
17	Y	M	x			x	
18	Y	F	x				
19	Y	F		x			
20	Y	F		x			
21	2	M		x			
22	2	M	x				x
23	2	M			x		x
24	2	M		x			x
25	2	F			x		x
26	2	F			x		x
27	2	F			x		
28	1	M			x		x
29	1	M			x		x
30	1	M		x			x
31	1	F			x		x
32	1	F			x		
33	1	F			x		
34	KY	M			x		x
35	KY	F			x		x
36	KY	M			x		x
37	KY	M			x		x
38	KY	F			x		x
39	KY	F			x		x
40	KY	F			x		x

observed primarily among burnouts and almost exclusively in the younger generation. Six burnouts have overlaps between /ʌ/ and /e/, along with three rednecks and one father, as shown on table 7.4. Most younger speakers who do not exhibit actual overlaps in the test words have quite front realizations of /ʌ/ that are very close to the boundary of /e/. In this category could be classified the other four burnouts as well as five rednecks, two fathers, and one grandfather. No Kentucky speakers, however, show the /ʌ/ fronting tendency; this process is an innovation of Farmer City (and possibly other related dialects).

/ow/ Fronting

The conservative phonetic realization of /ow/ is [ʌoʷ], and this phoneme has also undergone the fronting shift and is realized as [ɛoʷ] in the speech of many individuals. As with /ʌ/-fronting, /ow/-fronting is most common in the younger generation, especially burnouts, and is found in the systems of a few speakers from the older generations of Farmer City. Once again, there is no sign of this later fronting process in the Kentucky family.

Some speakers have more raised starting positions for their fronted /ow/, resulting in overlaps with /i/, rather than /e/, usually involving the word *lip*. Of the /ow/ lexemes, *show, choke, go,* and *joke,* all under the influence of palatal or velar consonants, share in this development. Speakers whose /ow/ transitions overlap with either /e/ or /i/ (or have starting positions for /ow/ that are close to those phonemes) are noted in table 7.3.

Articulatory Settings

Although the generalization of /uw/ fronting to other back vowels accounts for the collapsed appearance of some of the burnouts' phonemic systems, it does not explain why the frequency range of F_1 in these systems is so restricted. The burnout speaker of figure 7.15 and the redneck speaker of figure 7.2, for example, are both males with average fundamental frequencies of 85 Hz, yet in figure 7.2 the F_1 of /a/ moves as low as 850 Hz, but in figure 7.15 no lower than 670 Hz. These differences appear to result from the preferred articulatory settings of most burnout males and two redneck members, one of whom still maintains some contact with burnouts. Referred to in other dialects as a "lockjaw" setting, this articulatory strategy appears to have been adopted by some burnouts as part of their "tough guy" postures. Note that the two redneck males of figures 7.18 and 7.19 (speakers 15 and 16) also have restricted systems. These atypical redneck speakers also have advanced fronting; however, their systems do not appear quite as collapsed as those of some burnouts. Whatever its origin, the acoustic consequences of this habit are easily demonstrated (Habick 1980: 164). In terms of articulatory/acoustic correlations, the more the jaw is lowered when pronouncing a vowel such as /a/, the higher will be the frequency of F_1; the more closed the jaw, the lower the value of F_1.

It would be interesting at this point to consider whether the closed-mouth articulatory setting is related causally to the Southern Shift occurring in Farmer City. In other words, one could hypothesize that a closed-mouth setting, which produces a restricted system, could also lead to a collapsed system. A case for such a development could be presented. In a closed-mouth setting, articulatory gestures in general are abbreviated; they involve less movement than the corresponding

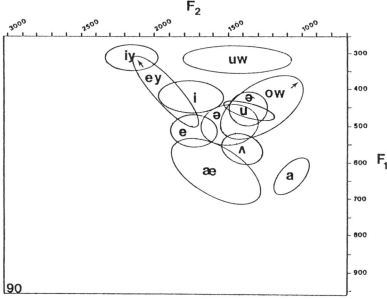

Figure 7.18. Speaker 15. This is a core Group Y member who apparently has little association with Group X. Nevertheless, his system is both "restricted" and somewhat "collapsed."

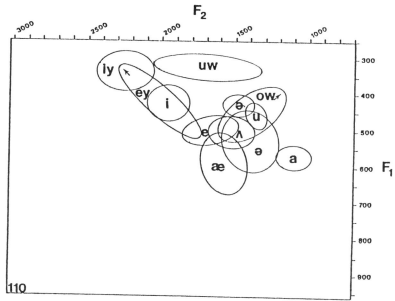

Figure 7.19. Speaker 16. This Group Y member still claims at least one Group X male as his friend. This individual speaks with a "lockjaw" articulatory setting, which is responsible for the "restricted" nature of his vocalic system.

gestures that produce the more expanded systems. It is also likely that the same motor tendencies that favor shortened articulatory gestures also incline toward less precise phonemic boundaries (greater coarticulatory effects). The burnouts, with the more restricted systems, also tend toward the more collapsed systems, for that group most favors the generalized fronting process. Those rednecks with the more expanded systems also put forth the additional articulatory effort necessary to keep phonemic boundaries more discrete.

The effect of articulatory setting on the overall structure of the phonemic system can thus be seen as having implications for systemic phonological change. The suggestion by Labov (1972a: 40) and Macaulay (1976: 269), that many otherwise unconnected segmental changes occurring in a dialect may be based on alterations of the dialect's typical articulatory setting, has obvious value for a theory of sound change. Such a holistic point of view of articulation complements and strengthens Martinet's observation that phonemic systems strive for economy and balance.

Conclusion

The most important sound change observed in progress in Farmer City involves a community-internal generalization of the /uw/-fronting feature common to most Southern dialects. As such, it provides a vivid example of how communities in the path of a transdialectal sound change spread will adopt the new feature and integrate it into their own phonological systems in different ways. Analysis of the speech of a sample of speakers from Kentucky, as well as the published dialect atlas materials from that state, showed that the immigrants from Kentucky brought no more than /uw/ fronting to Farmer City. Other elaborations of that feature must have developed independently in Farmer City (and possibly other central Illinois communities).

An understanding of the tendency of individual communities to handle changes adopted from other communities in different systemic ways represents an advance over the Neogrammarians' view of sound-change spread. For those early scholars, sound changes lose momentum as they travel geographically. But whereas some changes actually do die out as they progress farther from their original location, others find new vitality, new applications. It is possible that insights into other currently spreading sound changes, such as the well-known /æ/-raising process in the dialects of New York, Philadelphia, Detroit, and Chicago, could be gained from a consideration of the systemic implications of this process in each community. At the same time, a reconsideration of the work already done by classical dialectologists in many of these communities will add historical perspective to these developments.

8

The Language of St. Louis, Missouri: Dialect Mixture in the Urban Midwest

THOMAS E. MURRAY[1]

FOR ALL OF the numerous dialectological and sociolinguistic studies that have been done in the United States over the last several decades, a review of the literature in 1982 revealed one pocket of virtually untouched wealth in the city of St. Louis, Missouri. This lack of investigation was surprising for a number of reasons. First, St. Louis has an especially colorful settlement history, which suggests that the language spoken there today may be an equally colorful mixture of regional dialects. Second, the city has grown into one of the largest metropolitan centers in the country and one of the most important focal points of commerce and transportation in the Midwest, which suggests that any regional dialects present there may also have stratified along socioeconomic lines. And finally, there has been widespread disagreement among scholars about the dialectal character of the area's speech, which suggests the need for a larger, more thorough, and more definitive study.[2]

Preliminary work for a Missouri Linguistic Atlas—in which the language of St. Louis would certainly have received at least some attention—was begun more than a generation ago (Malmstrom and Ashley 1963: 17), but those data have apparently never been edited or published. It is true that independent scholars have studied various aspects of Missouri's language, including its lexicon (Faries 1967), the eastern affiliations of its speech in general (Pace 1965), geographic dialect boundaries within the state (Lance 1974a, 1974b, 1975, 1977), the language of the Ozarks (see Randolph and Wilson 1953 and the many references therein), its creole dialect (Carriere 1939), and even its speechways as they were interpreted and used by Mark Twain in *Huckleberry Finn* (Pederson 1967, Carkeet 1979). But each of these studies is somehow inappropriate—either because of the restricted demographic breadth of the informants, the methods of analysis, or the extremely limited scope and purpose of the research—so that very little information concerning the language of the Gateway City can be deduced. In fact, prior to 1986, the most extensive conclusions published were those of a master's thesis (Johnson 1976), and they were based on data from only eleven informants. Clearly, a thorough investigation of the language of St. Louis was warranted; thus I began such a study—encompassing 46 aspects of phonology, 110 aspects of morphology and syntax, and 96 aspects of lexicon—in June of 1982 and published the complete results in late 1986. This chapter is a synopsis of part of that study.

Methods

The methods of this study can be divided into two distinct categories: those that parallel the traditional methods of dialectology as practiced, for example, by the fieldworkers of the various Linguistic Atlas projects, and those that fall squarely into the realm of sociolinguistics as practiced by a growing number of ethnographic participant-observers. Initially, the project summarized here was intended to be strictly parallel and complementary to the several Linguistic Atlas projects: suitable and willing informants would be located, data would be collected through the use of questionnaires and personal interviews, and valid conclusions would be drawn concerning the language of St. Louis. Unfortunately, so many of my informants displayed such an obvious unrest at having me observe their pronunciation—an unrest that could not be allayed even through the use of the well-known "danger-of death" question (Labov 1972a: 92–94)—that I had to experiment with other techniques, foremost among which was the frequent adoption of the role of participant-observer.

For the phonological portion of the study, I therefore resorted to the surreptitious recording of St. Louisans speaking in a number of different contexts.[3] The recordings were all made in nonethnic portions of the city,[4] and they concentrated on sounds that my own experience as a native St. Louisan as well as my earlier unsuccessful attempts at interviewing suggested would reveal salient variation; they involved a wide demographic range of informants, including three social classes (estimated on the location of the recording), ages ranging from under 20 to approximately 80 (estimated, but verified in a 10% cross-section of informants to be more than 90% accurate), both genders (also, in some cases, estimated), but only the white race; and they were divided into three levels of contextual formality (based on whether the utterance was initial or repeated, what purpose it served, whether the interlocutors seemed to be strangers, and so on).

No such linguistic self-consciousness was displayed with regard to morphology, syntax, or lexicon; thus my methods for the collection of data in those areas closely paralleled the methods of the various Atlas projects.[5] Ethnically-mixed (i.e., having a diverse European background) white informants who, along with their parents, have lived in St. Louis their entire lives, were chosen and divided ten apiece into demographic cells reflecting social class (upper, middle, lower), age (below 20, 20–40, 40–60, and 60–80), and gender. Thus 240 respondents were used (none was related to any of the others), each of whom responded to a lengthy questionnaire.

The Data

A large number of linguistic features were surveyed in this study, only some of which, as table 8.1 shows, actually revealed variation with respect to the several independent demographic variables of the informants.

Table 8.1
Proportion of Investigated Items Depicting Variation

Number of Items Investigated		Independent Variables			Items Showing No Variation
		SEC	Context	Gender	Age	
Phonology:	46	52%	52%	2%	30%	48%
Morph./Syn.:	110	64%	NA	55%	64%	36%
Lexicon:	96	77%	NA	61%	77%	23%

As table 8.1 makes clear, all four independent variables proved fruitful in isolating the causes of linguistic variation in St. Louis. Although a detailed analysis of each sound, morphological and syntactic form, and lexical item investigated would require far more space than can be afforded here, several general patterns emerged from the data. First, however, a sample of the kinds of data collected and conclusions reached (all comparisons in the following list are to Kurath 1949, Atwood 1953, or Kurath and McDavid 1982, as appropriate):

1. All St. Louisans prefer [w] rather than [hw] in *wh-* words (*which, wheel,* etc.), a dialect feature associated with the Midlands and South.

2. Most St. Louisans use the voiced interdental fricative—a Northern feature—rather than its voiceless counterpart—a Midlands feature—in *with* and *without,* though both occur frequently.

3. The Midlands' intrusive [r] in such words as *wash* and *Washington* occurs throughout St. Louis, but more frequently as one descends the socioeconomic scale and the index of contextual formality.[6]

4. Both the Northern and North Midlands' [s] and the Southern and South Midlands' [z] occur in *grease* and *greasy*—the former among the members of the upper class and in formal contexts, the latter among the members of the lower class and in informal contexts.

5. Southern and Midlands' [ɔ] predominates in *log, fog, on,* and so forth.

6. There is no distinction made among St. Louisans in the famous *Mary-marry-merry* trilogy, a feature usually associated with the Midlands.

7. The vast majority of St. Louisans say [ruf] rather than [rʊf], which is considered a Southern pronunciation.

8. The schwa predominates as the stressed vowel in *because* (as opposed to [ɔ]), which is a Northern feature. Many St. Louisans also use non-Northern [ɔ], however.

9. The Northern and North Midlands' [u] is usually favored in *due, Tuesday,* and other similar words; in *coupon,* however, lies the exception to the rule: [ju] is favored.

10. *Creek* is usually pronounced by St. Louisans as Southern and South Midlands' [krik], especially among the upper class and among speakers under the age of 60. Northern and North Midlands' [krɪk] occurs only about one-tenth as often, and then only among the middle and especially lower classes.

11. Most St. Louisans prefer Northern *dove* as the past tense of *to dive,* although *dived* occurs with increasing frequency as one descends the socioeconomic scale, as one hears males rather than females speak, and as speakers advance in age.

12. Northern *hadn't ought* occurs slightly less frequently than general *oughtn't.*

13. *Wants off* is more typical in St. Louis than *wants to get off,* especially among members of the lower class and speakers over the age of 40. *Wants off,* of course, is a Midlands term.

14. It is more often quarter *to* the hour—a Northern and Southern particle—for St. Louisans, although that is true mainly of the upper and middle classes and speakers under the age of 60. Most of the rest of the speakers use Midlands' *till,* with *of* occurring occasionally, especially among members of the upper class.

15. St. Louisans both wait *for* and *on* people—the latter, Midlands term common as one descends the socioeconomic scale or listens to speakers aged 40 to 60, the former, general term common elsewhere.

16. Northern and North Midlands' *corn on the cob* occurs almost exclu-

sively in the Gateway City; *sweet corn* occurs only very infrequently.

17. The vast majority of all St. Louisans eat the Northern and North Midlands' *string bean*, though *green bean* occurs about one-fourth of the time among the lower class and seems to be increasing in frequency among the young.

18. Cherries have *pits* in St. Louis, but peaches have *seeds*; cherry eaters use a primarily Northern term, peach eaters a primarily Southern and Midlands term.

19. The Southern and South Midlands' *shucks* is much more common in St. Louis than *husks* to describe the outer covering on an ear of corn.

20. *Chipmunk*—a Northern and North Midlands term—is used universally in St. Louis; *ground squirrel* does not occur.

21. With similar universality, *bucket* occurs in the Gateway City rather than *pail*, and *bucket* is associated with the South and South Midlands.

22. The Northern (paper) *bag* occurs almost exclusively among all St. Louisans; *sack* shows up only very infrequently.

23. St. Louis window coverings are usually called the Southern and South Midlands' *blinds*.

24. Children who intentionally miss school in St. Louis *play hookey*—a Northern and North Midlands term, though babies *crawl*—a term usually traced to the South and Midlands.

25. Finally, babies lie in *baby buggies*—a Midlands term—and do not use *prams* or any other such vehicle.

Given a corpus of data just as varied as these 25 examples but ten times larger, one could easily surmise that the language of St. Louis is a hopeless amalgam of Northern, Southern, and North and South Midlands speech traits. Yet when a comprehensive survey of the entire corpus of data is made, several distinct patterns do begin to emerge. Consider, for example, that St. Louisans perceive some pronunciations as "more correct" or "more standard" than others, as attested by the variation according to contextual formality; and in each instance there is a corresponding pattern of variation according to the socioeconomic class of the speaker. Conclusions such as these are perhaps to be expected (cf. the similar findings of Labov 1966, Wolfram 1969, and Trudgill 1974), but it is interesting to note further that whenever there is variation according to the age of the informant, the usage of increasingly older speakers seems to parallel a decline in social class and contextual formality. Put another way, the older a Gateway City speaker gets, the more his or her stylistic ideals seem to diverge from "standard" English.

Regarding the morphological forms, two patterns identical to the ones noted above emerge: first, there is a frequent correlation between decreased socioeconomic status and increased use of nonstandard conjugations; second, an increase in age also typically parallels an increase in the use of such conjugations, and especially so for speakers between the ages of 60 and 80. And when there is variation according to the gender of the speakers, males far more often than females tend to use the nonstandard forms (cf. the conclusions of Labov 1972a: 243; Trudgill 1974: 93–94; and Wolfram and Shuy 1974: 93–94).

Furthermore, a number of more minor patterns can be noted that follow closely the findings of Atwood in his *Survey of Verb Forms in the Eastern United States* (1953). To begin, the preterite and past participle forms of verbs often level to a single construction, especially among the members of the lower class (thus, for example, *broke, done, drank, drunk, drove, rid, rode, seen, shrunk, swelled, swum,* and *wore* all occur frequently), and this construction is usually the standard preterite of the verb in question (cf. Atwood 1953: 43). Moreover, some preterites and participles of verbs ending in -*t* level to the present indicative tense (*fit,* which appears to be the standard in St. Louis, as well as *knit* and *sweat;* cf. Atwood 1953: 44). And many uninflected forms (e.g., *come, give,* and *run*) "have more or less currency in popular but not in cultured speech" (44). Atwood also lists the following verbs as "popular" favorites that are "extensive in the noncultured types but relatively uncommon among the cultured" (41), a contention that my data strongly support: *bit* 'bitten', *broke* 'broken', *done* 'did', *drug* 'dragged', *kneeled* 'knelt', *rode* 'ridden', *rung* 'rang', *seen* 'saw', *swelled* 'swollen', *tore* 'torn', and *wore* 'worn'. Finally, *hadn't ought,* which Atwood says is sometimes used in cultured speech, and *dasn't, here's your clothes,* and *laid* 'lay', which he says are often used by as many as one-half of the cultured speakers (1953: 41), also occur in similar proportions in my data.

A consideration of syntactic forms and lexical items is a bit more problematic, for they are not typically regarded as standard or nonstandard except in particular geographic areas, and thus do not lend themselves to easy analysis. Yet the data show a surprisingly high percentage of patterns parallel to the socioeconomic class, gender, and age of the speaker, so some attempt at explanation is clearly necessary. When we compare all of the forms in my data that are favored by a majority of the speakers to those that have been linked to one or more of the major dialect areas in the United States by Kurath's *Word Geography* (1949) or Atwood's *Survey of Verb Forms* (1953), we again find the North and North Midland represented much more heavily than the South and South Midland areas (46% versus 23%, or 2:1; if the pronunciation items are included and compared to Kurath and McDavid's *Pronunciation of English,* the overall percentile comparison jumps to 51 versus 15, or better than 3:1).

A comparison of my data with other bodies of data allows still further conclusions to be drawn. The *Word Geography of Missouri* (Faries 1967), for example, investigated 68 of the same morphological, syntactic, and lexical items that I used in my study;[7]—and although the results of the two bodies of research are often identical (e.g., the indices of usage for terms such as *privy, faucet, creek, cornbread, doughnut, hotcakes, firefly, lightning bug, hard maple, porch,* and *stoop*) or at least similar (e.g., for terms such as *front room* and *living room, bucket* and *pail, pancakes, cottage cheese, skunk, sugar maple, skip school,* and *belly buster*), one is also struck by the large number of discrepancies. Almost all St. Louisans want *off* the bus when they get sick *to* the stomach whereas other Missourians want *to get off* the bus when they get sick *at* the stomach. Similarly, most St. Louisans either use or recall using the *seesaw* at the playground, but elsewhere in Missouri *teeter totter* is preferred; and though most St. Louis horses *neigh,* apparently only a few neigh in other parts of the state. Moreover, St. Louisans tend to *shell* their *string beans* and perhaps serve them with *corn on the cob* whereas residents of other parts of the state usually *hull* their *green beans* and almost never serve anything but *sweet corn.* Finally, while *chipmunks* and *dragonflies* are commonplace in the Gateway City, they are known by other names almost everywhere else in Missouri. Both St. Louis and Missouri may be located squarely in the North Midland dialect area, but St. Louis definitely has more of a North/North Midland orientation, and the state as a whole is more heavily South/South Midland.

Other comparisons of the language of St. Louis with known dialectal patterns in Missouri as well as in Illinois can be made in a more general way. More than a generation ago, Dakin (1971), for example, although working only east of the Mississippi River, projected that much of Missouri and certainly the entire city of St. Louis would fall into a dialectal area that could perhaps best be characterized as a "transitional region" lying south of the North Midland isogloss and north of the South Midland isogloss. In this region both North Midland and South Midland linguistic forms predominate, often with coexistence in the same speech community and even the same speaker, and sometimes with no discernible preference between them. Subsequent investigation by Donald Lance (1974a, 1974b, 1975, 1977) has confirmed Dakin's suspicions about Missouri and St. Louis; Lance calls the transitional region "ambiguously midland" (1974a: 9–10; see map 12.3, regions 5–6).

Although the Gateway City clearly falls within the bounds of this transitional area, I have already determined that St. Louisans generally seem to favor Northern and North Midland rather than Southern and

South Midland linguistic forms. This conclusion fits nicely with the findings of Frazer (1973, 1978a, 1979), who, following Marckwardt (1957), confirmed the existence of a "speech island" that surrounds the St. Louis area and in which, as Frazer (1979: 186) says, "the vocabulary and pronunciation are Northern and North Midland, contrasting sharply with the regional [South Midland] speech of the surrounding area." The approximate boundaries of this speech island, which, according to Frazer (1979: 192n1), includes all or part of seven counties in Illinois and eight in Missouri—including St. Louis County—are depicted in map 8.1.

Finally, a comparison of the language of St. Louis with the known dialectal patterns of the eastern United States—a comparison that requires a rather extensive correlation of all the linguistic forms gathered in my study that were also investigated by Kurath (1949), Atwood (1953), and Kurath and McDavid (1982), and which were found to have isogloss boundaries placing them in at least one of the five major dialect areas of the United States—also yields interesting results. The first step in such a comparison is to list all of the variant linguistic forms of the present study that have been linked to at least one major dialect area in the eastern states. Second, a tally must be made of the quantity of items

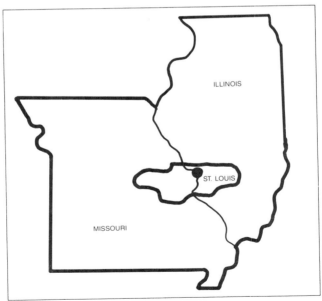

Map 8.1. Approximate boundaries of the Northern/North Midland speech island surrounding St. Louis (after Frazer 1979: 192n1).

linked to each of these areas for each demographic group of informants (all those who are upper class, all those aged 20 to 40, and so on). This is a straightforward process requiring only that percentile indices of usage be converted to coefficients and placed adjacent to the dialect area(s) with which the linguistic forms they are associated have been matched. When this has been accomplished for all the items in a given portion of the survey (e.g., phonology), the coefficients of the representative dialect areas are added, the end result being one usage index for each area or combination of areas (South, South + Midlands, and so on). To reduce these indices to only five—one for each major dialect area—five formulas are used that were first developed by Donald Lance and Rachel Faries and used successfully by Johnson (1976). I have modified the formulas slightly for the present study. They are as follows (as reported by Johnson 1976: 69, with my modifications occurring in square brackets):

1. Midlands Index = M + NM + SM + 2/3 (N + M) + 2/3 (S + M) + 1/2 (N + NM) + 1/2 (S + SM) [+ 1/3 "general use"]
2. Northern Index = N + 1/2 (N + S) + 1/3 (N + M) + 1/2 (N + NM) [+ 1/3 "general use"]
3. Southern Index = S + 1/2 (N + S) + 1/3 (S + M) + 1/2 (S + SM) [+ 1/3 "general use"]
4. North Midland Index = NM + 1/2 M + 1/3 (N + M) + 1/3 (S + M) + 1/2 (N + NM) + 1/2 (S + NM) [+ 1/6 "general use"]
5. South Midland Index = SM + 1/2 M + 1/3 (N + M) + 1/3 (S + M) + 1/2 (S + SM) + 1/2 (N + SM) [+ 1/6 "general use"]

In addition to these five indices, I have also calculated values for "urban" forms and "St. Louis only" forms.[8]

The sum of these seven values represents the total possible regional affiliations of any major portion of the survey for any given demographic group of informants. To ascertain what percentage of that group's language is traceable to a specific dialect area, one need only divide the indices of that area into the total. The affiliations of St. Louis phonology, morphology/syntax, and lexicon with the major dialect areas of the eastern United States are presented in tables 8.2, 8.3, and 8.4, respectively.

These tables provide the clearest evidence yet for the claim that I have been making throughout this chapter—that although it is a Midlands city, St. Louis strongly favors the North and North Midlands dialect areas rather than the South and South Midlands. Indeed, with regard to the morphological/syntactic and lexical items (shown in tables 8.3 and 8.4), the Northern area outweighs even the Midlands in most demographic groups, and when combined with the North Mid-

Table 8.2
The Affiliations of St. Louis Phonology with the Major
Dialect Areas of the Eastern United States (%)

Demographic Group[a]

Dialect Area	UC	MC	LC	In	Mid	For	Male[b]	Fem[b]	<30[b]	<40[b]	30–60[b]	40–60[b]	<60[b]	>60[b]	All
Mid.	25	30	29	30	31	31	35	35	28	34	29	36	35	22	28
North	16	19	16	16	19	18	17	17	18	20	17	22	16	16	17
South	14	13	14	13	12	11	13	13	9	8	9	10	10	8	13
N Mid.	22	19	21	20	20	21	24	24	22	27	23	18	28	26	21
S Mid.	15	12	15	15	13	12	11	12	11	10	11	13	11	11	13
Urban[b]	6	5	4	4	4	5	NA	NA	13	NA	12	1	NA	18	5
St. L.[b]	1	2	2	2	2	1	NA	NA	NA	NA	NA	NA	NA	NA	2

[a] Names of demographic groups are abbreviated as follows:

UC = upper class   Mid = midformal context   < = less than
MC = middle class   For = formal context   > = greater than
LC = lower class   Male = male gender   numbers = age
In = informal context   Fem = female gender   All = combined total for all respondents

[b] Figures for this demographic group or dialect area are based on extremely limited data.

Table 8.3
Affiliations of St. Louis Morphology and Syntax
with the Major Dialect Areas of the Eastern United States (%)

Demographic Group[a]

Dialect Area	UC	MC	LC	Male	Fem	<20	20–40	40–60	>60	All
Mid.	18	23	31	26	22	20	22	25	26	24
North	36	28	21	27	30	32	29	26	25	28
South	8	12	13	12	10	9	11	13	13	11
N Mid.	13	12	7	9	13	12	12	11	8	11
S Mid.	4	6	14	10	5	5	7	8	12	8
Urban	21	18	14	16	20	20	19	18	15	18

[a] For key to abbreviations used in the naming of the various demographic groups, see first note to table 8.2.

Table 8.4
Affiliations of St. Louis Lexicon
with the Major Dialect Areas of the Eastern United States (%)

Demographic Group[a]

Dialect Area	UC	MC	LC	Male	Fem	<20	20–40	40–60	>60	All
Mid.	23	25	23	24	22	23	23	24	25	24
North	31	27	26	27	29	30	29	28	26	28
South	12	13	15	14	13	12	13	13	14	13
N Mid.	21	20	20	20	21	21	20	20	19	20
S Mid.	13	15	16	15	15	14	15	15	16	15

[a] For key to abbreviations used in the naming of the various demographic groups, see first note to table 8.2.

lands, typically accounts for 40 to 50% of the total linguistic forms used (compared to a combined total of only 15 to 30% from the South and South Midlands). Furthermore, and again reinforcing an earlier conclusion, linguistic usage in St. Louis is not typically balanced among the several demographic groups sampled: when variation occurs, members of the upper class, females, and young informants tend to use Northern and North Midland forms; members of the lower class, males, and elderly informants, however, tend to use Southern and South Midland forms (Lance and Slemmons 1976 have reached a similar conclusion concerning the independent variable of age). Precisely why these patterns occur as they do is too complex a topic for treatment here, though I have dealt with it elsewhere (see Murray 1987b); suffice it merely to say that such choices are often the result of St. Louisans' perceptions of which other speech communities in Missouri use the same forms.

Conclusion

St. Louis, Missouri has proven to be an extremely fruitful topic for study: the phonology, morphology, syntax, and lexicon of the Gateway City—far from being homogeneous entities—can now clearly be labeled primarily Northern and North Midland, though of course Southern and South Midland forms also persist because of the city's settlement history and geographical location. But however many questions this study has answered, it has also raised and left unanswered some new ones. What, for example, of the linguistic forms uncovered in St. Louis but for which no other research exists (such as the pronunciation of *sundae* discussed in n7)? Does the way English is taught in the elementary and secondary schools reveal a bias for Northern and North Midland and against Southern and South Midland forms? (If so, how are teachers recruited from outside the St. Louis area inculcated with these attitudes?) Will the general linguistic patterns and attitudes of the Gateway City continue to persist relatively unchanged over the coming generations, or will the former be modified to accommodate new versions of the latter? These questions and others like them can serve as the focus of the next study on the language of St. Louis—a topic that will undoubtedly need to be returned to often if it is ever to be described and explained completely.

9

Sound Change and Gender in a Working-Class Community

ROBIN HERNDOBLER

STUDIES OF GENDER as a variable affecting linguistic change are by now commonplace enough. We know that in many societies men and women use different linguistic forms; we also know that in many societies women are on the cutting edge of language change in some respects, while they remain more conservative than men in others. What we do not understand well enough, it seems to me, is what I call in this chapter the psychosexual motivation in language variation: why do women use one variant more often than men? Why are women in advance of many sound changes? Recently, feminist scholars have begun to study gender variation more intensively, but largely in an ethnographic framework (Thorne, Kramarae, and Henley 1983). In this chapter, I will bring their emphases to the problem of sound change, examining three phonetic variables in the speech of a sample of working-class white men and women—largely of Italian, German, and Polish extraction—on Chicago's "East Side."

In the late 1970s I surveyed the speech of this community on the southeast side of Chicago, interviewing 82 informants from three- and four-generation families who had lived continuously in the community. All interviews lasted from one to four hours and included formal questionnaires, readings, word lists, and free conversation. Because I found the informants through extensive personal contacts formed through ten years' residence in the community, most of these conversations were informal and relaxed. Since the interviews covered several generations of family members, they also produced anecdotes which illuminated the psychosexual and social implications of various speech forms.

The East Side is an unusually stable community even now, with many families living there for five and more generations since the area

137

was developed in the last century. It is a geographic island bounded by the Calumet River, Lake Michigan, and the Indiana state line; one must literally cross a bridge over the river to enter the community. Moreover, it is a sociological island: mostly working-class, all white, generally grounded in traditional working-class values of hard work, thrift, clear definition of gender roles. Few residents attend college, even fewer graduate, and, until recently, many did not complete high school.[1]

However, because the area has been surrounded for years by heavy industry, until recently most people found work that provided a good living without advanced training. Work and recreation have taken place within the community, and residents have little contact with the rest of the city to the north, which many view with suspicion, sometimes disdain. Family remains the primary value for most East Side residents; the divorce rate is still very low. Such social continuity provides a ready laboratory to observe language change or the lack of it without the degree of outside influence and population flux characteristic of most urban communities.

Sex roles and beliefs on the East Side are similar to those in other working-class communities. Traditionally, working-class women have not had careers and have only worked when they had to because money was short. On the East Side both the men and the women believe that woman's place is in the home, that man must be the provider. Among the people I interviewed there, only one first-generation woman had a career (as a music teacher), and she was a spinster. All the others worked only when necessary. Even the three second-generation women with careers (two as elementary school teachers and one as a beautician) share the beliefs of their noncareer sisters, that woman's first duty is to her family, and that her career must take second or third place. The beliefs about the roles of men and women expressed by the informants in this survey are apparently common to working-class people (LeMasters 1975). Even after all the changes in ideas about women's roles, most of the women and all of the men maintain traditional notions regarding appropriate behavior and work for men and women.

Both the men and women in this study also believe that women are more tender, fragile creatures who need protection, and that masculine occupations are unfit for women, who belong in a protected environment. When asked to comment on women moving into traditionally masculine work, nearly every informant, including most of those in the third generation, scoffed, insisting that office work and the like would be more appropriate. And, indeed, most of the women in this survey have worked only as cleaning women, office workers, or sales personnel. When the men in this study were asked to comment on women in mills and factories these days, they all insisted, "she gets whatever happens and has it coming for being where she doesn't belong."

All these influences create a need in working-class women to observe the standard in speech, to uphold the position of culture-bearer in which they and their husbands place them. But there is more. At work, blue-collar men are oppressed by educated, well-dressed, well-spoken white collar authority. At home, blue-collar women are oppressed by the traditional division of labor their husbands insist upon. In study after study, these women bemoan their lot, stating that working-class marriage is unfair to their sex and gives the man more freedom and less responsibility, even less work (Komarovsky 1962: 178–204; Lemasters 1975: 82–91).

These insights from sociological studies are echoed by many women in this survey. While they would not trade places with their men and do not envy their lot in what is obviously a hard, work-a-day world, the women do recognize the inequities in the traditional agreement. One first-generation Italian woman talked with great feeling about the restrictions she experienced as a young girl, never allowed to go to parties, visit friends, go on trips, or do any of the things most middle-class girls took for granted, even in her day. This arrangement changed little after she was married. Both she and her husband talked at length, in separate interviews, of the many activities which kept him out constantly while she was at home raising their children. (Oddly enough, although her husband acknowledged that this arrangement was unfair, he still insisted that women belong in the home and men must be free to do as they please.)

The linguistic variables in this study include /æ/, often tensed and raised; /a/, also tensed and raised; and substitution of /t/ and /d/ for the corresponding interdental fricatives. Some difference in the level of awareness of these variables is apparent in the anecdotal evidence from the interviews themselves. The vowel shifts are largely unconscious and uncontrolled, while /t/ ~ /d/ substitution is conscious and even stigmatized. Both /t/ and /d/ are generally regarded as masculine and especially old-country by the community. They are particularly associated with the Polish, who serve as the local symbol for the immigrant population. SG, for example, a second-generation German woman married to a Pole, remarked in answer to a language question, "Polacks—you can't teach no Polack how to talk." When pressed to be specific, she responded, "Dese, dem, and dose."

I will examine /t/ ~ /d/ substitution first, because of its place in the consciousness of the speech community. (Throughout this discussion, wherever frequencies and indices are mentioned, in the text as well as in the tables, it should be remembered that all phonetic transcriptions represent an impressionistic, not an instrumental measure. Because the interviews were taped on site, with no control over background noise, instrumental measure was not possible for this study.[2])

/t/ ~ /d/ Substitution

The substitution of stops for the English interdental fricatives (hereafter, collectively, *th*) is a well-known foreign language interference phenomenon. Its presence in this community can be assumed to originate with the community's immigrant history. The first generation in the sample is largely of immigrant parentage (4 of 6 males; 14 of the 18 women), and many of them are bilingual in English and German or Italian.

The first generation reflects this phonological immigrant heritage. All of the first-generation men show evidence of /t/ ~ /d/ substitution but one, that one the only upper middle class male (unusual for this community) in the sample. Overall, the indices for /t/ (23.3) and /d/ (193) for the first-generation men are higher than for any other group in the sample (see tables 9.1 and 9.2 for all /t/ and /d/ indices, including those referenced in this discussion).

Evidence for /t/ ~ /d/ substitution can also be found among the first-generation women. However, first generation women's respective /t/ ~ /d/ figures of 3.5 and 21.9 are obviously much lower than those just

Table 9.1
Indices for the Use of /t/ for /θ/:
Free Conversation (Style A)

Informant	Generation			Total
	1	*2*	*3*	
Males	23.3	17.4	12.0	16.5
Females	3.5	2.4	4.9	4.8
LMC	8.9	12.0	4.7	9.7
MC	0.0	1.6	8.5	4.3
LMC Males	28.0	24.2	10.7	20.5
LMC Females	4.3	3.8	5.4	4.6
MC Males	0.0	4.0	13.6	8.9
MC Females	0.0	0.3	3.4	1.4
Total	8.9	8.1	7.5	

Table 9.2
Indices for the Use of /d/ for /ð/:
Free Conversation (Style A)

Informant	Generation			Total
	1	2	3	
Males	193.0	166.9	188.7	152.5
Females	21.9	14.4	30.8	23.1
LMC	83.7	83.3[a]	64.2	75.0
MC	0.3	52.1[b]	67.2	49.7
LMC Males	231.6	174.3[c]	124.3	173.5[d]
LMC Females	26.8	22.6	33.9	28.5
MC Males	0.0	152.0[e]	112.0	112.9[f]
MC Females	0.3	2.2	22.4	9.0
Total	68.5	71.6	63.1	

[a] Several of these figures are skewed by the background and index of one informant, LT. A retired Coast Guard skipper who is now a working partner in his brother-in-law's lucrative manufacturing firm, LT has definitely arrived in the middle class. Yet he comes from lower-middle-class parents by way of the rough life of a riverboat pilot. His extremely masculine speech includes /d/ index of 456, third highest in the survey, and cultivated in conscious defiance of his wife, daughter, and mother-in-law. If LT were ranked LMC rather than MC, this figure would rise from 83.3 to 106.7.

[b] If LT were ranked LMC rather than MC, this figure would fall to 1.7!

[c] If LT were demoted to LMC, this figure would go up to 214.6.

[d] If LT were LMC, this figure would be 189.2.

[e] LT is responsible for this index, which would be 0 without him.

[f] Excluding LT, this figure would drop to 70.0.

cited for the men, despite the prevalence of immigrant parentage and bilingualism among both groups. Even in this generation, /t/ ~ /d/ substitution has moved from a purely linguistic phenomenon to a gender-related variable, apparently one with a masculine identification.

This trend continues in the second generation, where women have a much lower /t/ index (2.4) and /d/ index (14.4) than do the men (17.4 and 166.9) of the same generation. Only 3 of the 17 second-generation women had /t/ ~ /d/ scores approaching those of the men.

An additional dimension of second-generation women's /t/ ~ /d/ usage is illustrated by the case of SG, quoted above on "Polack" speech. This woman, whom I have known personally for over twenty years, prides herself on being correct and careful in her speech, condemns /d/ and /t/ as nonstandard and careless, but in fact has the most frequent substitution of /d/ for *th* in her generation. Since she eliminates /d/ and /t/ in the reading and word list, she is obviously aware of the stigma attached to such pronunciations and, in a formal situation, has enough control to eliminate them. Women, again, are subject to the same foreign language interference as the men, but because these nonstandard pronunciations (/d/ and /t/) come so quickly to be identified with masculinity, the incidence of such forms in their speech is reduced.

One reason for this difference is the discourse world the women live in. First, in general, they have less difficulty handling school, at least to begin with. Then, as they marry and begin raising children, a major portion of their time is spent in conversation with the children, with other housewives, with business people, with doctors, lawyers, anyone with whom the family may have dealings, for on the East Side, it is the women who handle family affairs, especially when they involve talking or making phone calls or social arrangements. Working-class women tend to do the verbal work of the family (Fishman 1983). Moreover, child care is largely in the hands of the mothers, particularly with younger children; they most often supervise school work, an activity which gives them more concern for standards and more contact with the middle-class values of the schools (Komarovsky 1962).

In most of the families in this study, this pattern holds true. As one second-generation man put it, "Women are conscious of the importance of good speech because they are mostly responsible for the upbringing of the children. I'm not home all day, and I'm not very good with the kids, anyway. Most men work in shops or factories or mills where it's noisy and hard to talk. And who are they gonna talk to anyway—their machine, the line? So they get into the way of being quiet and they're not used to talking as much as women. When a bunch of men talk, they mostly bullshit, anyway. Women talk more, they talk faster, and they talk better." In general, this opinion is shared by most of the informants in this study, and by most working-class people who have participated in various studies (Komarovsky 1962: 51–53; LeMasters 1975: 119–48). And, while recent research suggests that traditional perceptions about the frequency and style of the speech of men and women must be questioned, the ideas people hold continue to influence both thought and behavior as well as speech, as we shall see (Fishman 1983; McConnell-Ginet 1983; West and Zimmerman 1983).

A further dimension of second-generation usage is presented by the case of IS, a male of 29, and his sister ID, 31. IS had the highest figure for /d/ among the second-generation males, nearly five times greater than the figures for his parents. Though a high-school graduate with a year of college, he works as a police officer on the vice squad, an occupation which obviously encourages tough speech and behavior. As a former student and good friend of mine, he felt quite at home during the interview—it is his personal style to be himself wherever he is. His sister and his father are both concerned for correct speech in a way he is not, the sister because it is part of her role as a woman, the father, because he has made many speeches as a well-known community organizer on the East Side who has worked to improve his pronunciation and control of standard English and greatly admires good speakers. This experience makes him unique among the informants in this survey and accounts for his low percent of /d/-*th* substitution and infrequent use of non-standard verb forms, only three in a four-hour interview.

Even though his father has modified his speech towards the standard, IS maintains the nonstandard variety called for by his sex, his peer group on the job and in the neighborhood, and his sense of himself as a virile figure in the world of men, as do men in similar studies (cf. Labov 1972a: 263–71). During the interview he talked at length about his relationships with the prostitutes he has come to know well working on the vice squad, and he commented that they are "wonderful girls," all of them, all, that is, but the "dykes" who don't know that the police are merely trying to do a job and often fight back during an arrest and cause a lot of trouble. He has no use for "queers" of either sex and is vehement in condemning them. For him, as for all the men in this study, the lowest form of human is a homosexual, who undermines the "normal" sex roles so essential to the concept of masculinity subscribed to on the East Side.

ID's use of /d/ was mid-frequency for her generation, and she used only one nonstandard past participle and one *youse* during the entire interview. She is obviously aware of standard usage and largely in control of it, even in her relatively casual speech; she has moved some distance from the speech of her parents, both Italians, both of whom replace *th* four times more often than their daughter does.

In her interview, ID revealed the conflict most of these working-class women experience—the men they love and in some ways admire still adhere to a code of behavior which many of them find more and more unacceptable. These younger, working-class women are beginning to make decisions for themselves and to think, tentatively, about being more independent. While this only daughter in a patriarchal family still says women should be subservient to their husbands, she acts in quite another way. Her speech, standard for a working-class woman with only a high school education, reflects the decision she has made in regard to the use of those nonstandard forms identified as peculiarly masculine. On the whole, she rejects them, just as she is beginning to reject the values and life style grudgingly accepted by her mother. And it is clear that most of the first- and second-generation women also reject such forms. Thus, the rejection of masculine, nonstandard speech by the women parallels the rejection of middle-class, standard speech by the men.

What happens in the third generation is just as interesting. Many third generation females use *more* nonstandard forms. The female third generation's overall /t/ index (4.9) and /d/ index (30.8) is clearly higher than those of the second generation (2.4;14.4), and, for that matter, at least slightly higher than those for the first-generation women (3.5; 21.9). Through the comments and anecdotes of these informants, it is possible to construct a picture in which the third generation's use of language can be connected to the identification of its members with the masculine or feminine role. Obviously, if third-generation men and boys use a large number of nonstandard forms in their casual speech, then they must perceive and agree with the community judgment regarding the significance of these forms. The fact that even middle-class boys have high frequencies of *dese, dem,* and *dose* and the like is understandable—they are identifying with the speech of their peer group, which demands adherence to the collective norm, generally nonstandard speech in a mostly working-class community (they are even overcompensating—among third-generation males, the overall /t/ score is even higher for the middle class (13.6) than for the lower middle class (10.7)). But how to explain the frequent use of such forms in the speech of third-generation females? Three case histories shed light on this question.

One of the families in the survey provided an interesting array of relationships in which the psychosexual identifications of the mother and daughter typified a pattern that runs through several other families. The parents in this family took two older boys from their family of four on a two-week camping trip, leaving the two younger girls, Mary (then 6) and Terry (then 3) with their grandmother. The two little girls were quite happy until mom and dad returned, when Terry screamed and cried and refused to have anything to do with them. She threw a bar of soap at her mother, who became furious and refused to have anything to do with the child, but the father gently explained that she was too young to go and that he would take her on such an expedition as soon as she was old enough. After a few minutes, he had the child happily in his arms.

Needless to say, I was eager to interview these girls, and finally Terry was persuaded to cooperate. Terry ended by giving a full hour and a half to the interview, and her conversation proved instructive.

First, Terry introduced herself as a tomboy who loves sports and is an all-star on the girls' softball team. Her grades in school are low to average; she likes math and hates English. She is not interested in boys or marriage, though she admits she may change as she grows older. Most interesting, however, was her notion that she is her father's favorite child. Her favorite activity, is, of course, fishing with her dad. A large girl, strong and muscular, Terry is obviously a girl athlete.

Terry's relationship with her mother has not been as satisfying, so she has modeled herself more after her father than her mother. (Meanwhile, her sister has adopted the [perceived] traditionally feminine role.) Terry's speech reflects her identification with her father, for she has the second most frequent /d/ substitution among the girls, the third highest /t/ substitution (an even more masculine form), and a substantial number of other nonstandard forms in her conversation.

Two other case histories further reveal how a young girl's masculine identification influences her speech. The 16-year-old daughter of SB, wife of a successful lawyer, is equally interesting. Gerry is the oldest of three children, the only girl and an avowed tomboy and sports addict. She describes herself as "completely" independent, needing no one, anxious for the day when she can move out of her parents' home and have her own apartment. Both her mother and father see her as more independent than their 14-year-old son, and both commented on the nonstandard character of her speech, which they believe is "worse" than the boy's, and for which they reprimand her, though both agree it does no good.

Gerry's speech does reflect a masculine identification. Her /d/ substitution is fourth highest in her group and more than three times as high as the closest middle-class girl, and she is the only middle-class female in the third generation to use /t/ for *th*. As a lawyer, Gerry's father obviously works in a fairly aggressive profession, but since she does not like school and has no intention of going to college or entering any profession (whereas both her brothers plan to be dentists), her masculine identification probably derives from her peer group, reported to be a bit rowdy by another teenager who attends the same school.

As a final example, consider these female twins, eight years old, very good friends. They get along remarkably well—they were the only children that young who did not have to be reprimanded once during the entire interview. Yet they are very different. Mary Beth, the feminine twin, prefers dolls and quiet games, has a few friends, and is shy, quiet, and retiring compared to her sister. Karen, the more talkative, outgoing, and aggressive, plays catcher on the little girls' softball team and has a host of friends, many of them boys whom she regularly fights and beats. Karen's speech reflects her masculine identification; she has the highest use of /d/ in her generation, more than twice that of the nearest informant. Her sister never replaced *th* with /d/ or /t/, a remarkable demonstration. (Both girls use nearly the same number of nonstandard verbs and other stigmatized morphological features.)

The issue seems fairly clear in these three examples—to the degree that the girls identify with the masculine world, their speech reflects that identification in its use of nonstandard forms associated with men. This pattern repeats in the lives of several other young girls, but does not occur with any of the four grown women in the third-generation (ages 23, 25, 29, and 30). Two are elementary school teachers and college graduates. All have very low indices for every nonstandard form. It is, of course, impossible to know if any of these young women used the masculine-identified forms as children, but the low incidence of such forms in the speech of most second-generation females (surely they can't all have talked like ladies when they were young) does suggest that at least some of the girls will outgrow the masculine forms.

The situation of the boys is similar. The young man of 17 who has the highest use of /d/ in his generation is solidly middle-class, an honor student who plans to major in business administration in college and eventually "make a lot of money and live in an upper-middle-class neighborhood." For now, he is happy on the East Side, has many friends, participates in sports, and works in his parents' store, but his direction is up and out of his working-class neighborhood. He uses no nonstandard grammatical or morphological forms, yet has a very high percentage of both /d/ and /t/, obviously because in his peer group these forms are "required." It is also obvious that if he is to move at will in the corporate world, he will have to modify his linguistic performance (cf. Milroy 1987).

Similar stories could be written for his four other young middle-class peers. But the point seems clear. Certain working-class, nonstandard forms identified as more generally masculine are picked up by young male members of the middle class in search of masculinity as defined by their current peer group, then by females of both classes who have identified with certain behaviors and speech forms as masculine but desirable for one reason or another. Thus, these youngsters reveal certain self-concepts in their linguistic choices, while the second-generation women avoid these masculine forms; eventually, the third-generation girls will follow suit.

The "Northern Cities" Vowel Shift (/æ/ Raising/Fronting)

Urban women across the country are leading the way in a major shift in the articulation of specific vowel sounds, two of which are particularly interesting in this study, /æ/ (popularly designated short *a* as in *bad*, which as it shifts position approaches short *e* as in *bed*), and /a/ (popularly identified as short *o* as in *pot*). Various researchers (Labov in New York, Shuy and Fasold in Detroit, and Callary in northern Illinois) have correlated vowel position with social class, age, ethnicity, and gender. In Ireland, Milroy has made similar connections. In northern Illinois this shift is being led by white, working-class females and sometimes young males. It occurs strictly in urban areas and is found most frequently in major cities, where it appears to be an emerging prestige pronunciation (Callary 1975). Unlike the other linguistic forms discussed in this chapter, shifting vowel sounds are rarely moderated by conscious control and therefore provide interesting opportunities to correlate speech choice with psychosexual identification.

To chart the various positions of /æ/, I used a ranking which distinguished three categories of sound into which a specific token of /æ/ could fall for each speaker: not raised, raised to medium position (m), raised to high position (h). The values of /æ/ were charted for both height and frequency (measured impressionistically) for each speaker, male and female, in all three generations, and in two styles, A and C, free conversation and reading respectively. An index was calculated to indicate each speaker's percentage of raised variants, high and mid, and their preference for the high- or mid- raised form. Thus an informant with an index of 71.4h raises /æ/ 71.4% of the time and prefers the high variant. The figures for the grandmothers, mothers, and daughters who participated in the study can be seen in table 9.3, which also indicates each female's age and social class. Even though this analysis is impressionistic, the resulting figures are striking, as table 9.3 shows.

The average for the men in all generations is only 7.7, compared to 36.5 for the women (Style A). This confirms the supposition that on the East Side, as elsewhere, women lead in raising /æ/. When the figures for the generations are examined, an even more striking division appears.

Table 9.3
Percentage of Raised Variants of /æ/

Free Conversation of Selected Categories of Informants (Style A)

Informant	Generation			Total
	1	2	3	
Males	0.0	11.8	8.6	7.7
Females	7.9	63.2	44.1	36.5
LMC Males	0.0	12.4	3.3	
LMC Females	4.7	62.5	40.5	LMC = 26.4
MC Males	0.0	10.6	14.9	
MC Females	28.5	64.4	56.4	MC = 29.8
Total	6.1	44.7	31.1	

Story Reading of Selected Categories of Informants (Style C)

Informant	Generation			Total
	1	2	3	
Males	1.1	3.1	3.1	2.5
Females	8.8	62.4	50.0	39.2
LMC Males	1.3	3.8	0.0	
LMC Females	2.3	60.1	54.4	LMC = 28.4
MC Males	0.0	2.0	7.7	
MC Females	44.9	65.4	24.1	MC = 36.1
Total	7.0	45.2	32.4	

First-generation men have no incidence of /æ/ raising to either degree. First-generation women have an average of 7.9, but when table 9.4, which gives individual figures, is examined, it is clear that this index results from the figures for only 5 of 20 first-generation women, the remainder having no raising in either degree. Reasons for this breakdown can be considered after examining the figures for second-generation women.

These are much higher, showing an average for the group of 63.2, the highest of any group in the survey. Thus, it is apparent that second-generation females are leading in the percentage of raised variants; and when the values for /æ/— height and frequency—are studied in individual women, it is also obvious that these speakers consistently use the highest values of /æ/. Examination of the relationships between the women in this survey who are kinfolk will reveal some of the reasons for the high incidence of this form in the second generation.

The five women in the first generation who had some raised /æ/ can be separated into two groups (see table 9.4, "First" column): MH (12.8%), JD (7.3%) and ZB (7.7%), all relatively low indices; however, MO (77.7%) and DB (52.7%) are both very high, especially for their

Table 9.4
Percentage of Raised /æ/ in the Free Conversation (Style A)
of Individual Informants, Preference for High-
or Mid-Raised Variants, Age, and Social Class

Women

Name	First Age	Class	Index	Name	Second Age	Class	Index	Name	Third Age	Class	Index
B	95	LMC	0.0	SK	30	LMC	64.3h	KB	15	MC	51.6m
ZB	72	UMC	7.7m	Mrs. B	55	LMC	54.5m	KD	17	LMC	40.6m
BH	68	LMC	0.0	JC	48	MC	72.6h	TO	8	LMC	0.0
EF	73	LMC	0.0	SB	34	MC	83.8h	DO	7	LMC	56.3m
MR	79	MC	0.0	TR	30	LMC	68.3h	MBJ	8	LMC	63.6m
AM	78	LMC	0.0	LE	52	LMC	53.8m	KJ	8	LMC	29.0m
MG	66	LMC	0.0	LB	50	MC	83.2h	LW	15	LMC	40.0m
FG	74	LMC	0.0	LP	45	LMC	49.2m	GS	17	LMC	9.1m
EO	76	LMC	0.0	MT	30	MC	76.7h	ReS	16	LMC	62.5h
MO	53	MC	77.7h	VI	50	MC	21.4m	BW	24	LMC	59.2m
LD	74	LMC	0.0	MM	51	MC	43.8m	LZ	16	LMC	6.1m
AO	82	LMC	0.0	PJ	33	LMC	87.8h	CK	29	LMC	55.0m
JK	70	LMC	0.0	MW	38	LMC	84.4h	MT	12	MC	69.0h
DB	67	LMC	52.7m	FS	55	LMC	86.2h	JP	14	LMC	55.0m
JD	55	LMC	7.3m	SZ	46	LMC	81.4h	PB	18	MC	31.9m
MH	75	LMC	12.8m	SD	44	LMC	59.4m	BH	18	LMC	35.0m
BW	66	LMC	0.0	Miss B	65	LMC	0.0	JC	18	MC	73.1h
LH	70	LMC	0.0					DE	23	LMC	65.7m

Men

Name	First Age	Class	Index	Name	Second Age	Class	Index	Name	Third Age	Class	Index
AK	71	LMC	0.0	JO	38	LMC	28.6m	CI	17	MC	0.0
AD	76	LMC	0.0	RW	39	LMC	0.0	KO	14	MC	16.7m
JB	74	UMC	0.0	CB	59	LMC	0.0	RW	17	LMC	20.0m
JD	60	LMC	0.0	JC	52	MC	0.0	RgS	17	LMC	0.0
HH	70	LMC	0.0	EE	60	LMC	0.0	RnS	11	LMC	0.0
FH	81	LMC	0.0	LT	38	MC	22.2m	AT	8	MC	20.0m
				HB	35	MC	9.7m	CB	14	MC	9.1m
				RH	42	LMC	0.0	JB	15	MC	28.6m
				JD	27	LMC	45.8m	JH	16	LMC	0.0
								EB	24	LMC	0.0
								DR	8	LMC	0.0

Table 9.5

Percentage of Raised /æ/ in the Free Conversation (Style A)
of Grandmothers, Mothers, and Daughters, with the Preference
of Each for High- or Mid-Raised Variants and Her Age and Social Class

Grandmothers				Mothers				Daughters			
Name	Age	Class	Index	Name	Age	Class	Index	Name	Age	Class	Index
ZB	72	UMC	7.7m	SB	34	MC	83.8h	KB	15	MC	51.6m
EF	73	LMC	0.0	LE	52	LMC	53.8m	DE	23	LMC	65.7m
								DH	30	LMC	44.1m
AM	78	LMC	0.0	MM	38	MC	43.8m	CK	29	LMC	55.0m
MO	53	MC	77.7h	PJ	33	LMC	87.8h	KJ	8	LMC	29.0m
								MBJ	8	LMC	63.6m
AO	82	LMC	0.0	FS	55	LMC	86.8h	GS	17	LMC	9.1m
								RES	16	LMC	62.5h
JK	70	LMC	0.0	SZ	36	LMC	81.4h	LZ	16	LMC	6.1m
								BW	24	LMC	59.2h
DB	67	LMC	52.7m	LP	45	LMC	49.2m	JF	14	LMC	45.4m
JD	55	LMC	7.3m	TR	30	LMC	68.3h				
MH	75	LMC	12.8m	LB	50	MC	88.2h	PB	18	MC	31.9m
LH	70	LMC	0.0	SD	44	LMC	59.4m	KD	17	LMC	40.6m
HG	66	LMC	0.0	MT	30	MC	76.7h	MT	23	MC	69.0h
LD	74	LMC	0.0	JC	48	MC	72.6h	JC	18	MC	73.1h
AW	65	LMC	0.0	MW	38	LMC	84.4h	LW	15	LMC	40.0m

generation, in which raising is rare. All five of these women had a daughter in the survey, and all but one of the daughters have indices well over 60 (see table 9.5), which suggests that some of the mothers may have picked up the form from their daughters. However, DB's daughter, DO, has an index of 49%, a bit lower than her mother's. MO's daughter, PJ, has an index of nearly 88%, second highest in the survey but still not much higher than that of her mother, though she prefers the high variant, her mother, the mid. One might speculate that these two first-generation women learned to raise /æ/ independently of their daughters, and indeed, there is evidence to support that hypothesis in the backgrounds of these informants.

Operating on a suspicion that this form has been taken as citified and sophisticated in the psyches of urban women (a theory supported by Callary's findings), I examined the histories of these two women to see if there was any common factor in their backgrounds that separated them from the rest of the first-generation females. Both MO and DB had worked for some years in South Shore (the upper-middle-class community north of the East Side) in the late 1930s and early 1940s. MO had been a sales person in an elegant dress shop on 71st Street, the main shopping area for the community, and DB had been a maid about a dozen blocks from the shop. None of the other first-generation women had ever worked off the East Side, and none had any extended connection to South Shore.

In that period and for some years after, South Shore was a prestigious, professional community with a fairly high level of education and a fair amount of money. The community was approximately 35 to 40% Jewish[2] and remained so until nearly all the white residents were replaced in the late 1960s and early 1970s by a rapid influx of blacks.

When DB described her experiences in South Shore, she singled out two groups as having been very good to her, the black maids with whom she worked, and the Jewish women who lived in the apartment hotel where she was a maid. Similarly, MO described herself as the only gentile "girl" ever to work at Seder's, but said all the saleswomen loved her and accepted her as one of their own. When she left after several years, they were all sad to see her go.

MO is part of the first generation in her family born in this country. She is 53, lively, friendly, and Italian, with an expressive style and high energy. In her speech, MO sounds more like a Jewish woman from New York than an Italian-American born and raised on the East Side. While the analysis that follows is frankly speculative, it does reveal a plausible origin for the raised /æ/ in the speech of these two older East Side women. And if their unusually intimate association with South Shore does account for their acquisition of the form, it is conceivable as well that South Shore has influenced some of the younger women who also use it.

South Shore, separated from the East Side by South Chicago and the Bush, both working-class millgate neighborhoods (Hunter 1974; Kornblum 1974), was the only middle-class neighborhood near the East Side. It served as a reference point for East Side residents, particularly women, who have traditionally looked up to the community as a charming and gracious place to live. East Side women often shopped there or patronized its doctors, dentists, and the like, of whom there has always been a shortage in their own community. In fact, the East Side had few shops, none stylish, and no bank or major shopping center until well into the 1960s, so residents sometimes, albeit reluctantly, had to leave the community for particular needs. Moreover, many supervisors and foremen from the mills and plants on the East Side lived in South Shore, thought of by some as the neighborhood to which one moved to upgrade their style of life.

East Side men, the majority solidly working-class in values and ideals, would not be particularly impressed with such an effort. Indeed, there is a deep tradition, among both men and women of the East Side, that the "real people," those worth the most, remain in the community even after their financial circumstances improve, while the values of those who succeed and leave are derided. For most residents, the East Side is the best of all possible worlds. But women who remain there often look wistfully at the gracious ambience of South Shore, with its wide, tree-lined streets, spacious lawns surrounding large, elegant homes, and clean air.

And while the speech of Chicago's Jewish population has not been examined, Labov's work in New York defined raised /æ/ as distinctively Jewish and Italian (Labov 1972b) and it is certainly characteristic of first-generation Jews heard on the streets of Chicago. All this suggests that it may have been as prevalent in the speech of South Shore Jews in the 1940s and 1950s as it is today in the Jewish population of a northern suburb like Skokie, where many former residents of South Shore now live.[3] Thus, South Shore becomes one plausible source for the raised /æ/ now found in the speech of East Side women.[4]

Of course, the men, who are not as impressed with middle-class values, would be less influenced by the speech of South Shore or any other middle-class community, an indifference reflected in their continuing use of nonstandard constructions. When the men's figures for raised /æ/ are examined, they prove to be predictably low, 11.8% for the second generation, 8.6% for the third. Clearly, wherever it originates, /æ/ raising is regarded as feminine by men and women.

The subliminal nature of this variable is emphasized by the finding that in no generation is there indication of much style shifting (middle-class females of the first and third generations remain exceptions, but their style shifting goes in opposite directions!). Most speakers, especially those in the lower middle class, remain almost completely unconscious of relatively subtle changes in vowels, changes which have never been identified by the schools or other "authorities" as nonstandard and stigmatized, vowels which, in fact, are used by those very authorities themselves. Further, the lack of LMC style shifting in the use of raised /æ/ suggests that, while this form does connote femininity, it does not symbolize standard or prestigious use in the "school" sense. Instead, it represents a level of culture more than social class, beginning in the women's perception of the form as sophisticated and urban, cosmopolitan rather than provincial, like South Shore instead of the East Side.

Fronted /a/

The history and sociology of fronted /a/ are less clear except that the forward movement of this sound is also new. /a/ is the sound of popularly designated short *o* as in *pot*; fronted, it moves towards /æ/, as in *pat*, though it never quite reaches that position. (Fronted /a/ is also nasalized and tensed. Both nasality and tenseness have been correlates with masculine identity [Fischer 1964]). Table 9.6 indicates the impressionistically-measured percentages for fronting in this study. The first generation uses fronted /a/ 12.7% of the time. The second generation increases frequency to 57.6%, but that of the third drops to 41.9%. The figures for women (34.2%) and clearly working-class informants (34.5%) are a bit lower than those for men (43.9%) and the middle-class (46.3%), suggesting that the variant may be associated more with men, perhaps even more with middle-class values. This perception of the sound as masculine and middle-class is especially new, since the form belongs to working-class informants among first-generation males. Some facts about first-generation women may explain how this putative shift in the social evaluation of the sound has occurred.

Table 9.6
Percentage of Fronted Variants of /ɑ/

Free Conversation of Selected Categories of Informants (Style A)

Informant	Generation			Total
	1	*2*	*3*	
Males	19.2	66.4	41.1	43.9
Females	10.8	53.3	42.5	34.2
LMC Males	23.0	68.1	36.6	
LMC Females	7.0	56.2	39.9	LMC = 34.5
MC Males	0.0	61.5	46.5	
MC Females	37.7	49.5	50.8	MC = 46.3
Total	12.7	57.6	41.9	

Story Reading of Selected Categories of Informants (Style C)

Informant	Generation			Total
	1	*2*	*3*	
Males	6.0	17.4	15.8	9.2
Females	0.0	8.7	12.7	15.1
Total	7.1	20.9	18.6	

(LMC = 13.8; MC = 12.2)

When the indices for individual first-generation females are connected with their work experiences and their attitudes toward the position of women and men, an interesting common thread can be seen. All of the five first-generation women who use fronted /a/ (ZB, DB, JD, MO, and AB) are either middle-class or have been independent of men for some period in their lives. In the interviews, all spoke positively about more independence for women. Although MO and AB may have picked up the form from their daughters, it does seem there is some link between feelings about sexuality and the fronting of /a/, for none of the first-generation women who lack this speech form expressed attitudes quite like those of the three women discussed here. In fact, most women on the East Side in all generations regard "Women's Lib" as improper and misguided.

One might speculate that fronted /a/ begins as masculine and is picked up by women who admire certain behaviors popularly identified as masculine—independence in work, thinking, attitude, certainly the ability to control one's life and freely to pursue one's interests. But at least one question arises: why do women who reject the most obviously masculine forms, /d/, /t/, etc., then reverse their position on the fronting of /a/? The answer may be that women will only pick up a form from men that has not been consciously identified as masculine and working-class. Throughout this study women have consistently avoided items overtly stigmatized as nonstandard just as men have often deliberately used them. Clearly, these working-class women and their middle-class sisters are concerned with attaining and maintaining standards of speech that both enhance their femininity and give them the perceived marks of culture and education as well as social mobility.

Some of the same factors operate in the lives of the second-generation women. All of them who have a high percentage of fronted /a/ work or have attended college and have expressed strong views about women's need for independence. They believe women must find their own identities as distinct individuals and not depend completely on their husbands for fulfillment. In the third generation, this pattern recurs, except that the youngest informants have little or no fronted /a/. Of course, it is unlikely that little girls would be concerned with masculine independence, although they are sometimes concerned with masculine toughness. And it is clear that fronted /a/ will persist, for the third generation's figures for this feature are strong for both men and women.

The figures for style-shifting present subtle variations. If a form is becoming prestigious, its use should increase in the formal styles; if it is not prestigious, its frequency should drop as informants consciously correct according to their perceived ideas of standard usage. This is exactly what happens in all three generations of men for this form. On the other hand, the women use the fronted variety more than the men in the formal segment of the interview, indicating that they perceive the form from a different angle than do the men. For men, the reading signified school and all that is anti-masculine, and many of them were visibly embarrassed as they read, complaining about their poor ability whether they had been successful or failed students. (Even the two lawyers read poorly.)

Traditionally, among working-class people, school has not been thought necessary for girls, but important for the boys, and this double standard is only beginning to fade, for many of the informants expressed similar attitudes. For the women, however, school and education symbolize independence and the freedom to explore new possibilities and opportunities. One third-generation female teenager was extremely unhappy because her parents simply refused to support her in college although they had sent both her brothers to expensive private schools and never complained. Such a situation is not unusual on the East Side. Many of the older women voiced great disappointment, even bitterness, over lost opportunities because they had not been allowed to pursue advanced schooling.

For many women, education and the opportunity to have a career, perhaps even a profession, symbolize freedom and independence, those wonderful masculine prerogatives so long denied them in the working class. Thus, a phonetic form that suggests masculinity but does not connote nonstandard usage and masculine toughness may also be associated in the minds of some women with school, leading to the higher number of women who used fronted /a/ in the reading. And, while the specifics controlling fronted /a/ are not as clear as those controlling raised /æ/, it is clear that all the vowels in urban speech are shifting around a good bit (cf. Labov 1992), and that these shifts can be correlated with certain sociological patterns. Some linguists believe that we are witnessing the emergence of a new urban dialect in Illinois (Callary 1973).

The results of this survey also suggest that a part of this new dialect may be an increasing separation and distinction between the speech of men and women. A number of studies of industrial workers in the last thirty years have indicated an increasing psychosocial separation of the sexes, and have found that men at work are becoming increasingly hierarchical, hostile, and vulgar in their relationships with each other, whereas women are moving in the opposite direction and are becoming increasingly egalitarian, cooperative, and friendly among themselves (Meisner 1976). Perhaps this increasing separation of the sexes in the working class lends some of the impetus to the increasingly divergent character of their speech. Although the sexes have always been more separate in the working class and have maintained more distinct life styles and role models, this separation does seem to have intensified.

Obviously, the marked increase in years of education between the first and second generations in this study is partly responsible for some of the changes documented here, but just as obviously, the concerns of female informants have intensified that shift. Moreover, the psychosexual identification of the young people in this survey is a powerful factor in their linguistic choices. The clear separation of gender roles among working people provides a concrete symbol against which the young measure themselves, and it appears that their judgments call for increasing separation, though of a new kind (Gilligan 1982). Although no second-generation woman in this study would have considered remaining unmarried or viewed the single life as an opportunity for self-fulfillment, women and girls of the third generation regard marriage as only one of many options available to them, and their choice of speech forms, revealing as it does dual concerns for correctness *and* power, emphasizes an expanding awareness of multiple possibilities.

Finally, attitudes about gender roles reveal themselves in language choice. East Side working-class men feel oppressed by middle-class values, which they reject in speech deliberately nonstandard, rough, even vulgar. East Side women feel oppressed by men and adopt the linguistic norms of the hated middle class, partly as a move upwards, partly as a rejection of masculine domination. To the degree that these women feel empowered in a personal position in the world, they adopt forms as yet identified only subliminally as masculine. Obviously, the preferred speech form further empowers, further expands (or contracts) the idea of the self, and so on. Where all this will lead remains unclear, but it is clear that any analysis of gender-linked speech forms must take into account a great many variables.

10

Yankee Words in Chicago Black Speech

MICHAEL I. MILLER

Population, Sampling, and Data Collection

SEVERAL PROCESSES CONTROL the structure and dynamics of Chicago's African-American speech. These include adaptation of an urban vernacular specific to Chicago's culture and stratification along at least three interrelated social dimensions. This chapter reports on a survey designed to investigate one of these processes and formulate hypotheses about how Chicago's middle-class black speech is currently changing. The focus of the investigation is a list of 46 semantic fields used by the Linguistic Atlas of the United States and Canada and by Lee Pederson for his intensive analysis of Chicago's vocabulary in 1964 (Pederson 1971).

Pederson used face-to-face interviews, in the tradition of Jules Gillieron. In contrast, my students and I asked people to fill out a Regional Vocabulary Checklist based on Pederson's work and developed from a technique pioneered in the Midwest by Alva M. Davis (1948). Davis's checklist technique harks back to the father of dialectology, Georg Wenker, relying on self-reports and depending on sheer volume of reponse to the checklist as opposed to direct observation *sur place* to achieve reliability. As with all self-reports, one intuitively doubts checklist reliability; on the other hand, in Michigan, Indiana, and northern Illinois, Davis's clear delineation of isoglosses, later confirmed by direct observation, demonstrates the usefulness of the checklist approach, particularly as a supplement to direct observation. (The method used by Davis and for this survey consequently displays the strengths—and weaknesses—of Wenker's work [see Virginia

McDavid 1956: 1–4]). I have described checklist details elsewhere, including more specific limitations on reliability (Miller 1986, 1987).

We collected usage and frequency data for about 1,000 words from just under 200 respondents. The data provide a quick snapshot of the Yankee vocabulary in Chicago's middle-class African-American community a quarter century after Pederson's original study. Pederson originally targeted 240 words as elements of the regional (i.e., Inland Northern) vocabulary. The tables in this paper indicate their geographical origin in linguistic atlas terms, their frequency of use in our sample, and their classification as dominant, common, uncommon, or rare. The "list" column in the tables gives the item and choice numbers from the checklist: for example, 14.2 indicates the second choice for question 14. Table 10.1 summarizes our sample.

Our informants included 116 blacks, 66 whites, another 11 Asians and Hispanics, and 5 people who did not indicate race. The average educational level for both blacks and whites is high, and the age range is low, so the sample does not represent a cross-section of either the black or white communities in Chicago. The sample specifically ex-

Table 10.1
Sample Characteristics

Characteristic	Black Subsample	White Subsample	Total Sample	Total N
Black	100%	0%	59%	116
White	0%	100%	33%	66
Other	0%	0%	6%	11
Unknown	0%	0%	3%	5
Male	30%	45%	36%	71
Female	70%	55%	61%	121
Unknown				6
Native	68%	77%	69%	136
Non-Native	32%	23%	29%	58
Unknown			2%	4
Worldly	70%	85%	72%	142
Insular	29%	15%	23%	45
Unkown	1%		6%	11
Total %	64%	36%	100%	
Total N	116	66		198
Mean Age	28.35	34.14	30.46	189
(SD)	9.51	15.83	12.53	
Mean Education	13.51	14.05	13.75	184
(SD)	2.14	3.54	2.70	

cludes such stereotypical Chicagoans as middle-aged working-class white ethnics or poorly educated blacks with little income. Among blacks this sample also under-represents males. Our sample therefore differs radically from the samples of black speech commonly used by many investigators. However, the sample does represent the younger, college-educated middle classes of both groups. These groups are often identified as the catalysts of rapid change (cf. Labov 1972a), so we think this sample can provide useful clues about current developments. Furthermore, investigating the vocabulary of these groups provides a corrective to studies that concentrate merely on phonology or grammar and that present all blacks as poor, uneducated, rural or ghettoized, and illiterate.

Dominant Regional Words

Our central goal was to discover basic facts about the frequency of use, social distribution, obsolescence, and replacement of a core regional word stock. The top layer of this core appears in a list of dominant words, identified by Pederson in 1964 and reproduced in table 10.2.

The frequency data show that most of these words have maintained their dominant status in the last 25 years in both black and white speech. The top seven words on the list occur in the speech of nearly the entire sample with no significant difference between black and white speech. This lack of difference is sometimes surprising, as in the case of *wishbone*, where we might have expected more instances of the Southern term *pulley bone*. But for 19 of the 31 words on this list—or about two-thirds—black and white speech do not differ.

Assuming that our sample is reliable, the last seven words on the list (*baby buggy* to *shivaree*) have lost currency in the last 25 years, occurring now in less than 50% of middle-class usage. Technological and cultural change coupled with the Northern or North Midland regional identification of several of these words probably accounts for their shift in status. *Baby buggy*, for example, has given way to *stroller*; *pig sty* is primarily limited to metaphorical senses. The sudden abandonment of a classic Mississippi Valley marker like *shivaree* may seem startling, but this word has always been an upper- or lower-class white term, so it is not surprising that the middle class of both races would hardly know it.

Eleven of the dominant or formerly dominant regional words differ significantly in black and white speech. Two major types of differences between black and white speech occur. For example, as table 10.3

Table 10.2
Dominant Regional Words

No.	Item	List	Frequency (N = 198)	Geog. Dist.	Black Speech (N = 116)	White Speech (N = 66)
I. Dominant Words						
238.	wishbone	29.1	189	N, NM	112	66
75.	faucet (1)	11.1	188	N	109	65
86.	garbage	9.1	187		110	63
111.	horseshoes	26.1	183		109	62
54.	corn bread	31.1	182		110	61
65.	doughnut	32.1	177		104	61
57.	cottage cheese	35.1	173		104	57
22.	bucket (1)	7.1	164	NM, SM, S	90	62
67.	dragonfly	42.1	162	N, NM	90	60
83.	front porch	1.2	160		99	51
93.	gutters	3.2	158		87	59
120.	kerosene	22.1	153	N	95	50
94.	harmonica	15.2	150		87	54
114.	husks	39.1	145	N, NM	77	59
181.	siding	2.2	141		83	49
212.	string beans	38.1	141	N, NM	97	37
153.	quilt	23.1	134		84	42
148.	pit (1)	36.1	128	N	60	59
240.	worms	41.1	127		70	47
85.	frying pan	10.1	126		56	61
138.	pail (2)	8.1	120	N	69	45
32.	burlap	14.1	116	N, NM	62	48
58.	creek	25.1	116		57	52
77.	faucet (3)	13.1	103		48	46
II. Common Words						
3.	baby buggy	45.1	93	NM, SM	67	44
224.	teeter-totter	21.1	89	N	23	60
101.	headcheese	33.1	70	SM	33	34
237.	white bread	30.1	69	N, NM	37	29
214.	sty	5.2	60	N	34	21
III. Uncommon Words						
206.	stone (2)	37.1	38		8	27
IV. Rare Words						
178.	shivaree	46.1	7	NM, SM, S	1	5

Note: Black speech plus white speech do not always equal totals because of informants marked "other" or "unknown."

Table 10.3
Gutters by Race

Item	Black (1.00)	White (2.00)	Total N	Percentage
Gutters (2.00)	76.3	89.4	146	81.1
Other (7.00)	23.7	10.6	34	18.9
Total N	114	66	180	
Percentage	63.3	36.7		100.0

Chi-Square	D.F.	Significance	Min E.F.	Cells with E.F. < 5
3.85183	1	.0497	12.467	None
4.66640	1	.0308	(Before Yates Correction)	

Numbers of Missing Observations: 2

shows, the term *gutters* for the horizontal open piping used to drain a roof is the usual Chicago term for both racial castes, as opposed to the Yankee term *eaves troughs*.

Almost 90% of the white sample uses *gutters*. Blacks do too. But nearly 25% of the black sample uses a variety of other words for the same thing—most commonly drain pipe but including even the Yankee folk term *eaves trough*. This relatively minor difference in frequency illustrates a typical pattern. White speech is unified around a single term long identified with local speech. To designate the same thing or idea, blacks include variants from several different dialect areas and from more general, national usage.

Table 10.4 illustrates a second and different pattern of differences between black and white speech. This pattern also helps explain the loss of currency of a formerly dominant but geographically limited word.

Table 10.4
Teeter-Totter by Race

Item	Black (1.00)	White (2.00)	Total N	Percentage
Teeter-totter (1.00)	20.4	90.9	83	46.4
Seesaw (4.00)	79.6	9.1	96	53.6
Total N	113	66	179	
Percentage	63.1	36.9		100.0

Chi-Square	D.F.	Significance	Min E.F.	Cells with E.F. < 5
80.59022	1	.0000	30.603	None
83.40326	1	.0000	(Before Yates Correction)	

Number of Missing Observations: 3

The Yankee term *teeter-totter* and its variants *teeter* or *teeters* are still used by 91% of the white subsample. Blacks, however, commonly use *seesaw*, a more general, national term. Segregated schooling probably created and perpetuates this sharp difference between black and white speech.

The decline in currency for *head cheese* and *stone* 'peach seed' are also due partly to black-white speech differences. Though *head cheese*, the thing, is less common than it once was, 50% of the white sample continue to use this term. Blacks, on the other hand, prefer *hog-head cheese*, a slight variant but a distinctively Southern term. *Souse* is also a common term among blacks, but not whites. For the seed of a peach, blacks prefer *seed* or *pit* and hardly use *stone* at all; whites use *stone* or *pit* and seldom or never use *seed*. In sum, several Yankee and North Midland words, once dominant in middle-class Inland Northern speech, have lost ground to Southern and general-currency terms.

On the other hand, middle-class Chicago blacks have also adopted a number of Yankee words, such as *wishbone, faucet, dragonfly, husks, string beans, cherry pit, pail,* and *burlap* in spite of perfectly good Southern and South Midland variants that their grandparents and great-grandparents must have known and used. Though there are differences between black and white speech for several of these, the Northern word has gained currency in black speech. The most dramatic example is *string beans*, a classic Northern and North Midland marker currently under pressure from *green beans*, the term preferred by frozen-food packagers. Younger, middle-class whites are adopting the national marketing term, just as their ancestors adopted *cottage cheese* under the same sort of pressure a few generations ago. Younger middle-class Chicago blacks use the regional Yankee word.

Minor Regional Patterns

In addition to these changes in the dominant, core vocabulary, several minor patterns influence the structure of middle-class speech, particularly the absence of influence from foreign languages on black speech.

Pederson identified 15 words influenced by bilingualism and acculturated at different levels. Table 10.5 lists these.

Pederson classed terms like *Weissbrot* as poorly acculturated because its phonemic structure was unmodified and it occurred only in the German subculture. He classed *Schmierkäse* and *smetlak* as highly

Table 10.5
Impact of Foreign Languages

No. Item	List	Frequency	Black Speech	White Speech
I. Dominant Words				
94. harmonica	15.2	150	87	54
II. Common Words				
194. sour milk	34.3	77	48	24[a]
89. green beans	38.2	38	10	23[a]
IV. Rare or Obsolete Words				
178. shivaree	46.1	7	1	6
217. Sulze	33.6	3	0	3
231. Weissbrot	30.7	2	0	2
166. Schmierkäse	35.2	1	0	1
220. sylteflesk	33.8	1	0	1
14. Bibbelkäse	35.4	0	0	0
37. charicari	46.3	0	0	0
53. cook-cheese	35.5	0	0	0
107. hog stable	5.12	0	0	0
190. smetlak	35.6	0	0	0
216. sulc	33.9	0	0	0
219. sylte	33.7	0	0	0

Note: Black speech plus white speech do not always equal the total frequency because of informants classified "other" (i.e., Asian or Hispanic).
[a] Black speech and white speech differ significantly.

acculturated because the first is widespread in German settlement areas and both occur outside their originating subcultures, including black speech. Pederson classed *cook-cheese, hog stable, harmonica, sour milk,* and *green beans* as tenuously related to the German subculture of typical Midwestern cities. In current, middle-class Chicago speech most of these terms have become obsolete. Except for English words reinforced by foreign cognates, like *harmonica, sour milk,* and *green beans,* the few borrowed words that remain current occur exclusively in white speech and with low frequency.

Pederson recognized the marginal status of several words in table 10.5 and included them in another list, shown in table 10.6, of disappearing words.

Wheat bread 'bread made from wheat flour' is the only word on his original list that has belied his prediction. Pederson misclassified this word (as "disappearing" rather than merely "low frequency") because he had no way of anticipating the sudden interest in health foods of the last ten years. On the other hand, when our informants checked off

Table 10.6
Disappearing Words

No.	Item	List	Frequency	Geog. Dist.	Black Speech (percentage)	White Speech (percentage)
II. Common Words						
232.	wheat bread	30.3	79		52	23
IV. Rare or Obsolete Words						
234.	whiffletree	17.2	11	N	6	4
42.	clump	44.6	7		1	6
164.	rock fence	6.10	7	SM	5	2
154.	quoits	26.2	6	N	2	3
70.	drywall fence	6.7	5		3	1
81.	floor bed	24.6	4		2	2
82.	fried cake	32.2	4	N	1	2
39.	clabber	34.7	3	SM	3	3
46.	coal oil	22.3	3	NM	2	0
73.	facerboards	2.4	3		2	1
105.	hog pen	5.11	3		3	0
209.	stoneboat	18.3	3	N	2	1
217.	Sulze	33.6	3		0	3
45.	coal hod	20.5	2	N	1	1
87.	glow worm	43.5	2		1	1
155.	rain pipe	3.4	2		2	0
157.	rainworm	41.4	2	NM	1	0
215.	sugar bush	44.7	2	N	2	0
231.	Weissbrot	30.7	2		0	1
5.	bakery bread	30.4	1		0	1
142.	perambulator	45.5	1		0	1
166.	Schmierkäse	35.2	1	NM, SM	0	1
198.	spider	10.3	1	N	1	0
218.	swill	9.3	1	N	0	0
220.	sylteflesk	33.8	1		0	1
14.	Bibbelkäse	35.4	0		0	0
53.	cook-cheese	35.5	0		0	0
104.	hog barn	5.7	0		0	0
107.	hog stable	5.12	0		0	0
156.	rain trough	3.5	0		0	0
162.	riverlet	25.6	0		0	0
168.	gee horse	21.5	0		0	0
184.	sinker	32.3	0		0	0
216.	sulc	33.9	0		0	0

wheat bread they probably meant 'whole wheat bread', not the older distinction between 'bread made from wheat flour' as opposed to 'bread made from corn meal.' So Pederson was correct with respect to the meaning, if not the form. Nearly all the remaining words on Pederson's list are either disappearing or have disappeared in middle-class speech, with little difference between blacks and whites. An additional 86 words (about one-third of the older regional vocabulary) do not occur at all or occur in less than 5% of the sample, in either black or white speech. Most of these rare words are properly considered obsolete or obsolescent.

In addition to disappearing words, Pederson identified a list of 17 incipient words, that is, words he thought would increase in currency in Chicago because they appeared primarily in younger speech. Table 10.7 reproduces this list. Most of these words are either Midland, Southern or general currency terms. None of these words is yet dominant, but the Southern word *earthworm* and the commercialized Yankee folk term *comforter* have spread in the last generation. *Earthworm* is more common in black than white speech. (Since total frequencies are low, this table indicates proportions to clarify relationships between the two subsamples.)

Pederson also studied another list of 36 Yankee words which he used to construct an index to the relative acculturation of his sample. The interest of the list today (in addition to the idea of using it to create an index) is that all 36 words are well-known New England terms once dominant in Chicago speech. Table 10.8 lists these 36 words in 28

Table 10.7
Incipient Words

No.	Item	List	Frequency	Geog. Dist.	Black Speech (percentage)	White Speech (percentage)
9.	barn pen	5.10	0		0	0
190.	smetlak	35.6	0		0	0
2.	arbor	44.5	1		1	0
26.	bunch	4.13	1		1	0
102.	heart	36.4	3		3	0
159.	redworms	41.5	3	SM	0	5
55.	cornmeal bread	31.3	6		3	2
122.	landing	1.6	7		3	5
126.	loaf of bread	30.6	9		5	3
197.	spicket (2)	13.9	9	NM, SM, S	1	2
123.	light bread	30.5	10	SM, S	9	0
121.	lamp oil	22.4	14	NM, SM	5	6
61.	curdled milk	34.5	15		8	7
135.	orchard	44.4	19	SM	10	6
13.	bed roll	24.4	20		8	10
71.	earthworm	41.3	52	S	39	10
52.	comforter	23.2	55	N	28	22

Table 10.8
Status of Yankee Dialect Terms in Chicago Middle-Class Speech

	Frequency	*Percent*	*RHCD Usage Note*
I. Dominant Words			
faucet or tap (sink)	196	99.0	None
pig sty or pen[a]	168	84.8	None
kerosene	153	77.3	None
pit (cherry)[a]	128	64.6	U.S.
pail (tin)	120	60.6	None
faucet (outdoor)	103	52.0	None
II. Common Words			
teeter(s), teeter-totter[a, b]	91	46.0	None
pit (peach)[a]	82	41.4	U.S.
faucet or tap (barrel)[a]	75	37.9	None
chipmunk[a]	58	29.3	None
comforter[a]	55	27.8	U.S.
firefly[a]	54	27.3	None
stone wall[a]	49	24.7	No Entry
III. Uncommon Words			
pail (wooden)[a]	27	13.6	None
whippletree or whiffletree	27	13.6	None
coal scuttle or hod[c]	26	13.1	None
bossie	25	12.6	U.S.
brook	21	10.6	None
stoop[a]	12	6.1	U.S.
IV. Rare or Obsolete Words			
quoits	6	3.0	None
curds	5	2.5	None
fried cake	4	2.0	None
drag	3	1.5	None
stoneboat	3	1.5	No Entry
sugar bush	2	1.0	U.S. Canada
angleworm	1	0.5	None
johnnycake	1	0.5	U.S.
spider	1	0.5	None
swill	1	0.5	None
darning needle	0	0	U.S. Dial.

[a] Indicated terms show significant differences between black and white speech.

[b] No entry for *teeter-totter,* but the entry for *teeterboard* adds "also called teeter-totter."

[c] No entry for *coal hod; hod* 2. = "a coal scuttle."

groups and classifies the words using Pederson's four-way system. The table also adds information about black-white speech patterns and about the usage notes applied to these words by the *Random House College Dictionary.*

Thirteen of these 28 Yankee words, or nearly half, remain part of the dominant or common lexicons of middle-class Chicagoans. The remainder have become uncommon, rare, or obsolete. Differences between black and white speech show up particularly among the seven common words, although as we have seen, blacks often prefer Southern, South Midland, or general currency words.

Perhaps of most interest to lexicographers, the *RHCD* provides a restrictive usage note for only one of these items, *darning needle*, though why this one is singled out over other equally "dialectal" words like *sugar bush, johnnycake,* or *spider* is unclear. The *RHCD* does not enter the "dialectal" words *stoneboat, coal hod,* or *stone wall,* perhaps because the latter two are compounds and *stoneboat* is rare outside New England. But the *RHCD* also does not lemmatize the commonly used word *teeter-totter.* As Sydney Landau has admitted, "dictionaries have had an indifferent record in reporting regional usages" (1984: 177). On the other hand, silence is sometimes golden (cf. Zgusta 1971: 291).

In addition to the 240 words in Pederson's original vocabulary, informants wrote in another 52 words, listed in table 10.9.

Some of these attest shifts in meaning. For example, *nightcrawlers* is now used for any worm used for bait. Other written-in words further attest the influence of Southern and Midland speech, like *snap beans* and *nicker.* Still others attest the continuing attenuation of the underlying Yankee vocabulary, such as *bunch of trees* for the classic Yankee marker *sugar bush. Buttermilk* 'thick, sour milk', the most common written-in form, reflects both a change in culture and a central methodological problem with postal questionnaires and checklists. *Buttermilk* is a completely different thing from what Southerners used to call *clabber* and Yankees knew as *lobbered milk.* The informants, not recognizing any of the proposed terms, and not familiar with *buttermilk,* offered the nearest equivalent. Confusions caused by the checklist technique probably account for several of the written-in forms—such as *squirrel* 'chipmunk', *water hose* and *hose* 'faucet', *handles* 'shafts', and so on. However, these "inappropriate forms" and problematic responses also turn up in face-to-face interviews, so their appearances here is not fatal.

Several written-in forms provide invaluable evidence for the lexicographer and dialectologist. *Potato sack,* for example, and the

Table 10.9
Written-In Words

Word	List	Freq.	Word	List	Freq.
buttermilk	34	11	sprinkler	13	1
nightcrawlers	41	7	tap	13	1
snap beans	38	6	trees	44	1
bag	14	5	water faucet	13	1
sack	14	5	water outlet	13	1
squirrel	40	4	water valve	13	1
water hose	13	4	compost	9	1
hose	13	3	corn pone	31	1
blanket	23	2	cover	23	1
bunch of trees	44	2	cruller	32	1
coal bin	20	2	doctor fly	42	1
duffle bag	14	2	fence	1	1
handles	16	2	fly	42	1
hay stack	4	2	griddle	10	1
potato sack	14	2	here cow	27	1
aluminum siding	2	1	hog head south	33	1
bagel	32	1	hose faucet	13	1
bars	16	1	lagoon	25	1
basinette	45	1	lightning bug	43	1
box spring	24	1	maple trees	44	1
pump	13	1	moo moo	27	1
reins	16	1	mouthpiece	15	1
rubber hose	13	1	nicker	28	1
scraps	9	1	pan	10	1
skins	39	1	pound cake	32	1
sleeping bag	24	1	pram	45	1

variety of terms for an outdoor water faucet will be useful for future investigation. A classic portmanteau is *doctor fly*, a previously unattested form, combining elements from *dragonfly* and *snake doctor*. Another previously unattested portmanteau is *hog head south*, combining *hoghead* and *souse* with a phonemic change implying folk etymology. These unattested written-in forms suggest the rich lode waiting for investigators willing to extend the investigation beyond phonology and grammar.

Vocabulary Change

Within the 46 semantic areas surveyed, there appear to be no differences between middle-class black and white speech that suggest anything like diglossia. The dominant words used by the middle class as a whole seldom differ between blacks and whites and have not differed for a generation or more.

Words classed as common, however, often differ between the two racial castes. Usually, African Americans use a Southern or Midland term while whites use a Yankee word. But two patterns emerge. In one, whites use a single, old local word while blacks use more than one different word for the same thing, as in the *gutters* example. In the second pattern, whites use one word while blacks favor a single different word, as with *teeter-totter* and *seesaw*. The third possibility—blacks using a single word while white speech has fragmented among several choices—is rare but nevertheless occurs in the case of *string beans* versus *green beans*. All of these differences are differences in frequency; none are categorical. They reinforce the general trend in Chicago usage to replace older Northern and North Midland words with words of general currency. A minor pattern is the steady introduction and spread of Southern and South Midland words like *light bread*. When the Southern term has become general national currency, as in the case of *seesaw*, it tends to replace the older Yankee word.

Compared to white speech, the speech of American blacks is and apparently always has been conservative, a phenomenon Hans Kurath identified forty years ago (Kurath 1949: 6). Therefore, to point to innovations in white speech or conservatism in black speech as evidence of sharp cultural differences seems naive. On the contrary, a remarkable feature of Chicago's black culture is the sharp stratification emerging as middle-class blacks assume different social roles while poor people become even poorer and more isolated in impacted ghettoes (cf. Wilson 1987). The poorest, most poorly educated, and most isolated groups no doubt speak differently from the middle class. But their speech is not black speech.

A follow-up to this study will add to what we know about how Chicago's vocabulary is currently changing. For the moment, however, this brief survey includes more data from more informants than any previous survey of Chicago speech and can serve to supplement the baseline established by the atlas and by Pederson's 1964 survey.

III

Geographical Studies

11

Positive *anymore* in the Midwest

THOMAS E. MURRAY

IN ALL VARIETIES of English, the adverb *anymore* is most frequently found at the end of negative clauses such as the following:[1]

1. The doctor says that I probably shouldn't eat chocolate anymore.
2. The bus doesn't stop at this corner anymore.
3. Why don't you play softball anymore?
4. John and Chris hardly call me at all anymore.
5. He says he doesn't do it anymore, but I know he must be lying.

In these sentences and others like them, which are everywhere considered to be standard English,[2] negative *anymore* appears to refer to some kind of change from the past to the present—either to an event that used to occur but no longer does, or to something that was characteristic of the past but no longer is. In addition to these negative, clause-final usages of *anymore*, however, some varieties of English also accept the adverb in various positions in positive clauses:

6. Do you fish anymore?
7. He used to take naps on the couch, but he sprawls out in that new lounge chair anymore.
8. In college basketball anymore, any team seems to be able to beat any other team on any given night.
9. [Does the heat really get to you?] Huh! Anymore it sure does.
10. Pantyhose are so expensive anymore that I just try to get a good suntan and forget about it.
11. [Do you always use that many coupons when you shop?] Anymore I do.
12. The only thing anymore about politicians is they're all crooked.
13. Well, anymore people just don't save their money like they used to.
14. Anymore those things are completely useless.

15. Anymore do you ever go to church, or have you turned into a heathen?
16. I wonder whether you could get a part to fit that anymore?
17. Do you ever wonder anymore about things like life after death?
18. Is it the same anymore as it used to be?
19. What's the worst thing anymore about your job?
20. [Do you eat red meat?] Anymore.

In these kinds of sentences, variously regarded as standard or nonstandard by Americans, positive *anymore* seems to take on the meaning 'nowadays', 'these days', or 'presently', and refers to an activity or situation that was not formerly true, but has come to be characteristic of the present.

Thus exist the two broad categories of *anymore* usage, negative and positive. And as Walt Wolfram and Donna Christian say in their book *Appalachian Speech* (1976: 105), "speakers who come from regions where *anymore* is used only in negative contexts may find the use of positive *anymore* rather obtrusive, [though] native speakers of varieties where positive *anymore* is current tend not to view it as a socially diagnostic linguistic feature."

What I would like to do in this chapter is focus on the various positive uses of *anymore* in the Midwest to discover where they are accepted and/or used and where they are perceived as odd or unusual. More specifically, I pose the following questions: (1) Can any of the conclusions of the many earlier studies of positive *anymore* (see Background, below) be further validated with a more recent and enlarged sample of data? (2) Since positive *anymore* can appear in different kinds of clauses as well as in various positions in those clauses (as illustrated by the sample sentences above), is it then reasonable to assume that these many variable uses probably do not have equal acceptance throughout the Midwest? If so, what precisely are these patterns of usage? And (3) How can the various patterns of usage of positive *anymore* be best explained, using either traditional dialectological methods, more recent advances in sociolinguistic theory, or both?

Background

Although three generations of linguists have attempted to unravel the mysteries of positive *anymore* in the United States[3]—mysteries that center on the construction's origins, precise meaning, and breadth of usage—no study or combination of studies to date answers completely the questions I pose in this chapter. This is not to suggest that the projects of these other researchers were flawed in serious ways, but that their goals were different or that their work needs to be updated. Some restricted their investigations to a single state (e.g., Hindle 1975, Pennsylvania; Youmans 1986, Missouri); some had so few informants that their conclusions are incomplete and speculative at best (e.g., Cassidy et al. 1985, which uses only 110 informants for the entire United States); some did not investigate the various possibilities for syntactic placement of positive *anymore* (e.g., Hagerty 1986 makes no distinction between clause-initial, clause-medial, and clause-final occurrences, or between conditionals, imperatives, and interrogatives); and many were done in the 1930s and 1940s (see n2).

Still, these other studies do have much to offer in terms of methods, general conclusions, and what might be called the sociolinguistic nature of positive *anymore*. For example, Youmans (1986: 64) has shown that fill-in-the-blank surveys "cannot be used to draw negative conclusions" (i.e., because the filling in of the blank with an acceptable synonym for the construction being tested does not exclude the possibility that the respondent also uses the construction itself). Moreover, Hindle and Sag (1973: 105) found that many respondents to written surveys show a "bias to give sentences a lower rating than they deserve," which bias is frequently rooted in stylistic reasons having nothing to do with the object of the survey (e.g., as when an informant objects to a test sentence concerning positive *anymore* because *anymore* is not followed by a comma or is spelled as one word rather than two). Regarding general conclusions, most linguists now accept as facts that positive *anymore* is a phenomenon which continues to spread outward from the Midlands dialect region, that it is concentrated most heavily in areas which were settled heavily by Scotch-Irish populations, and that its use is not governed by socioeconomic status, gender, or age (see, e.g., Hindle 1975, Youmans 1986). And as for the sociolinguistic nature of positive *anymore*, a number of researchers (e.g., Labov 1972a: 309, Hindle 1975: 22–23, Youmans 1986: 71) have noted that positive *anymore* seems to hold a special place among syntactic regionalisms in that people can be unaware of its existence all around them until they are made to notice it. In fact, some informants, only moments after using the construction, innocently deny that it is a part of their speech.

Methods

Armed with the accumulated knowledge of all the previous investigations into positive *anymore*, I set out to discover exactly what kinds of usage and attitudinal patterns existed in the Midwest.[4] The surveys that I conducted spanned just over three-and-a-half years—from September 1984 to April 1988—and included the following kinds of data-gathering:[5] (1) 4,011 students who had lived their entire lives in the Midwest and who then attended one of 41 colleges or universities in the Midwest (including all those in the Big Eight and Big Ten Conferences as well as 23 smaller schools) were polled by questionnaire; (2) My students and I conducted 2,179 personal interviews; (3) 7,236 questionnaires were mailed to Midwestern residents. 4,915 were returned with the information requested; (4) My students and I analyzed approximately 650 hours of surreptitiously-collected tape recordings made throughout the Midwest. The recordings yielded 1,156 occurences of *anymore*; and (5) 300 student projects (most from Ohio, and all containing 20 to 50 pages of conversational transcripts) in the Folklore Archives of the Department of English at The Ohio State University were analyzed, yielding 876 occurences of *anymore*. Both the questionnaires and the personal interviews—once the necessary demographic information such as age, gender, race, education, occupation, and so forth had been collected[6]—were structured in part as a series of questions about the sample sentences numbered 1–20 above. Respondents were asked to read each of those sentences to themselves, then answer the following questions:[7]

> a. When you say this sentence to yourself, does it sound okay, or do you think there's something "wrong" with it?[8] If you think there's something wrong with it, circle the wrong part.
> b. Do you think you would ever use such a sentence? If not, why? If so, in your written or oral communication? If not, what would you think if you saw or heard someone else use it?

These questions as well as the sample sentences were embedded in a much longer questionnaire concerning other linguistic as well as cultural matters, so the informants' curiosity about why they should be asked specifically about positive *anymore* was kept to a minimum.

Although not entirely planned, the demographic diversity of the respondents—with the exception of distribution of race—was quite good: as map 11.1 shows, all of the Midwestern states were represented nearly equally, the only ones having disproportionately high numbers of respondents being Ohio (where most of my students were from) and Missouri (where almost one-half of the surreptitiously-collected tapes were recorded); all three major social classes (as indicated by education, occupation, income, and location of home) and four major age groups (under 20, 20–40, 40–60, and 60–80) were well represented, as were both genders; and the number of informants who had done a mini-

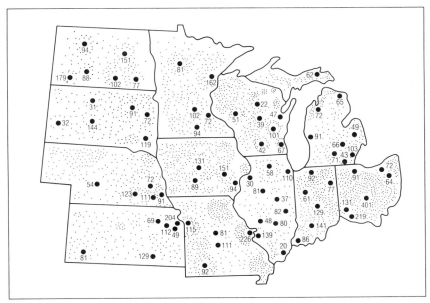

Map 11.1. Approximate location of informants.

mum of traveling and living away from the home area was quite high (all others were eliminated). In all, of 13,137 respondents, 10,019 were judged acceptable for inclusion in the study; they were proportioned as indicated in table 11.1.

Analysis of Data

Responses to the two survey questions were tallied into the following twelve categories for each of the twenty sample sentences: (1) sounds okay; (2) something "wrong" with it; (3) circled *anymore*; (4) circled some other part of the sentence; (5) would use such a sentence; (6) wouldn't use such a sentence; (7) wouldn't use such a sentence because of the presence of *anymore*; (8) wouldn't use such a sentence for any other reason; (9) would use such a sentence in oral communication; (10) would use such a sentence in written communication; (11) if heard or saw someone else use it, reaction would be positive or neutral; and (12) if heard or saw someone else use it, reaction would be negative.

Initially, all of the categories of responses for each sample sentence were listed in tabular form opposite the various demographic groups of respondents; however, such a presentation merely confirmed one of

Table 11.1
Demographic Distribution of Informants

Demographic Category	Number of Respondents
Upper social class	2,304
Middle social class	5,310
Lower social class	2,405
Under age 20	3,215
Aged 20–40	2,804
Aged 40–60	2,301
Aged 60–80	1,699
Males	4,609
Females	5,410
Whites	9,117
Blacks	902
Ohio residents	1,281
Michigan residents	792
Wisconsin residents	761
Minnesota residents	736
North Dakota residents	813
South Dakota residents	768
Nebraska residents	699
Kansas residents	781
Missouri residents	1,019
Iowa residents	782
Illinois residents	780
Indiana residents	807

the previously mentioned conclusions of other researchers—that is, that the use of *anymore* is not governed by such traditional demographic factors as social class, gender, and age.[9] Thus instead of giving a quantitative presentation of results, I will give a pictorial one. From the data collected, I drew a series of maps—one for all of the sample sentences numbered 1 through 5 above (i.e., the sentences containing negative *anymore*), and representative maps for sentences numbered 6 through 20 (i.e., those with positive *anymore*)—that depict the answers to question (a) without regard to any of the respondents' demographic characteristics except geographic location. Ten maps (11.1–11.10) represent each of the resulting geographic patterns.

Several conclusions emerge from a close analysis of these maps. First, we can note that another of the previously mentioned conclusions of earlier investigators has been confirmed, though with a much larger data sample: positive *anymore*, in one or more of its forms, is well entrenched throughout most of the Midlands dialect area, and particularly in those regions known to have been traveled and settled heavily

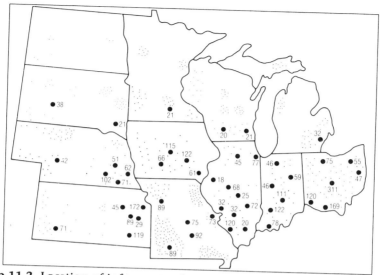

Map 11.2. Location of informants who use positive *anymore* in "He used to take naps on the couch, but he sprawls out in that new lounge chair anymore." Also approximate location for those who use "In college basketball anymore, any team seems . . . ." and "Pantyhose are so expensive anymore that . . . ."

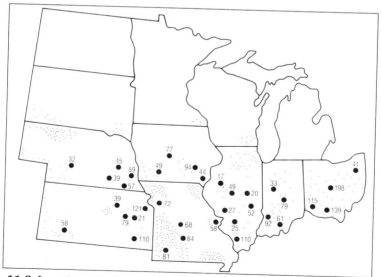

Map 11.3. Location of informants who use positive *anymore* in "[Does the heat really get to you?] Huh! Anymore it sure does." Also approximate location for those who answer a question [Do you ———?] with "Anymore I do."

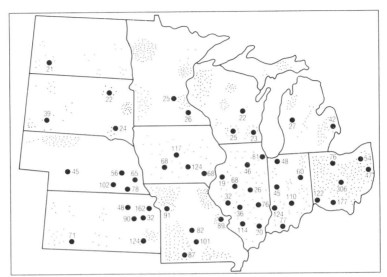

Map 11.4. Location of informants who use positive *anymore* in "The only thing anymore about politicians is they're all crooked."

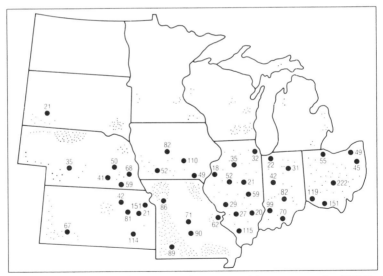

Map 11.5. Location of informants who use positive *anymore* in "Well, anymore people just don't save their money like they used to."

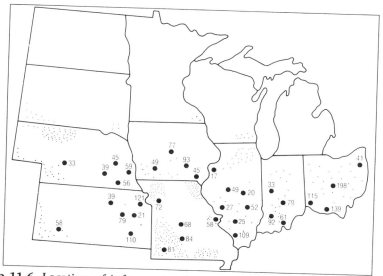

Map 11.6. Location of informants who use positive *anymore* in "Anymore those things are completely useless."

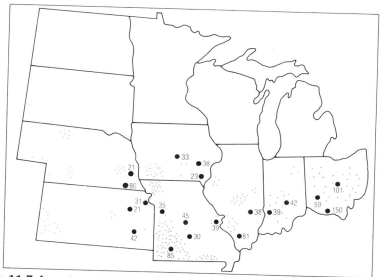

Map 11.7. Location of informants who use positive *anymore* in "Anymore do you ever go to church, or have you turned into a heathen?"

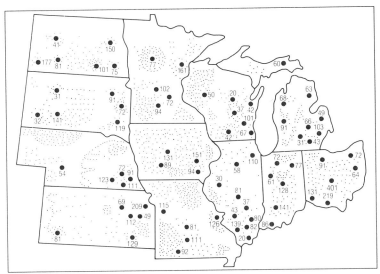

Map 11.8. Location of informants who use positive *anymore* in "Do you ever wonder anymore about things like life after death?" Also approximate location for those who use "I wonder whether you could get a part to fit that anymore?"

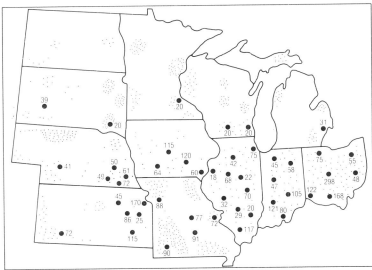

Map 11.9. Location of informants who use positive *anymore* in "What's the worst thing anymore about your job?" Also approximate location for "Is it the same anymore as it used to be?"

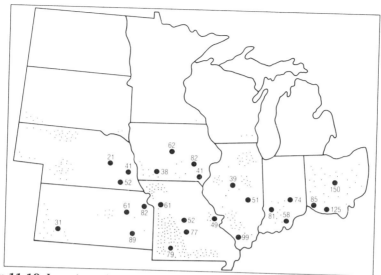

Map 11.10. Location of informants who use positive *anymore* in "[Do you eat red meat?] Anymore."

by Scotch-Irish immigrants and their descendants (especially Ohio, which borders Appalachia, and the Ozarks of southern Missouri; but also the Ohio, Missouri, and central-Mississippi Valleys). Perhaps more significantly, the patterns in many of these maps suggest a "wave model" effect[10] in that progressively less dense concentrations of positive *anymore* occur as one moves farther away from these Scotch-Irish areas. This effect confirms that these areas must have been—and even, for some of the rarer usages, must continue to be—the locus of positive *anymore*.

A second conclusion lies in the various forms of positive *anymore* having unequal acceptance throughout the Midwest: all forms are evidently not considered equal in the minds of all users; but, again, those regions most heavily settled or traveled by the Scotch-Irish tend to have the highest levels of acceptance for even those usages of the construction that other parts of the Midwest reject as nonstandard. Perhaps surprisingly, this seems to be true even in larger cities such as Indianapolis, St. Louis, Kansas City, Columbus, and so on—cities that may be considered cultural centers, and hence as having higher "standards of correctness" than the surrounding rural areas (which supports the observation that positive *anymore* has little or no sociolinguistic significance).

Finally, if both of our earlier conclusions are correct—that is, if the various forms of positive *anymore* both follow the wave model and have unequal rates of acceptance across the Midwest—the result should be a kind of implicational scale of usage[11] for Midwestern speakers. Such is exactly the case: of those 89% of the respondents in my surveys who did not find all of the sentences containing positive *anymore* acceptable, nearly three-fourths (73%) showed a pattern of preference as indicated in table 11.2. In other words, judgments of "acceptable" for any given sentence (or complete category of sentences) also imply judgments of acceptability for all those sentences that rank above it in the table; and, conversely, a speaker finding any given sentence (or, again, any complete category of sentences) *un*acceptable would also find all of the sentences below it unacceptable.[12]

As mentioned earlier, other researchers have already established that positive *anymore* has little or no sociolinguistic significance. Further evidence of this benignity can be found in the responses to the remaining question in the surveys. First, people to whom any of the forms of the construction "sound okay" have no qualms about using them, both in their oral and in their written discourse; and, conversely,

Table 11.2

Implicational Pattern of Sample *anymore* Sentences

Sentence Rank[a]	Sentence Number[b]	Percent of Informants Judging Sentence Acceptable[c]
1	1–5	99+
2	6, 16, 17	96–98
3	18	58
4	8, 12	51
5	7, 10, 19	43
6	13	37
7	9, 11, 14	34
8	20	28
9	15	11

[a] Each rank may apply to a single sentence or to a category of sentences. Sentences were placed in the same category because their rankings by informants were nearly indistinguishable. Had they not been placed in the same category, the implicational scale effect would have been lost.

[b] These numbers correspond to the numbers of the sentences given in the introduction of this chapter.

[c] These figures include informants who used the construction either in the surreptitiously-collected data or in the transcripts from students' folklore projects.

people to whom any of the forms of the construction sound wrong or strange do not use them at all. Second, and even more telling, speaker-attitudes to the various forms of positive *anymore* are nearly all either positive or neutral; regardless of whether they themselves use the form in question, hardly anyone (fewer than 8% of those queried) perceives use of the "nonstandard" forms as negative.

Conclusion

Positive *anymore* occupies a special position in the Midwest. Geographic patterns of its use show unquestionably that it is a linguistic feature (or perhaps, in its various syntactic usages, a series of linguistic features) that has spread and continues to spread outward from those regions known to have been settled most heavily by eighteenth-century Scotch-Irish immigrants and their descendants—especially Appalachia and the Ozarks, but also including the Ohio, Missouri, and central-Mississippi Valleys. More interesting, perhaps, is that patterns of its usage in its various forms suggest an implicational scale effect: most regions that accept and use increasingly rarer forms also accept and use all of the more common ones; and those regions not using the common forms do not use the rarer forms, either. Furthermore, a lack of sociolinguistic patterning suggests that the users of positive *anymore* regard it not as a marker of nonstandard or ungrammatical speech, but merely as a syntactic construction to be incorporated into one's vocabulary. One cannot help wondering whether its current pattern of use will continue to spread, and how far, and whether it will eventually be accorded a place of dignity in the standard version of the language. Certainly such a vision is not too farfetched, given that a substantial number of people already seem to have incorporated it into their written language.

Other questions, equally interesting—and more important, perhaps—also persist. It would be interesting, for example, to know how positive *anymore* is dealt with in the elementary, middle, and high schools across the Midwest: some of the respondents in my surveys are teachers—several with masters degrees—and if they perceive the construction as "okay," are we to assume that they teach it, or at least sanction its use by not correcting it? Should it even be corrected, existing as it does in a sort of noncommittal sociolinguistic limbo? Perhaps the rest of us—those who have studied the language and learned that it is a feature of Appalachian and Ozarkian speech (and how much does that color our attitudes toward it?)—should cease viewing it as "nonstandard"? These kinds of questions and others like them cannot be answered now, of course; only time will tell what the best approach to positive *anymore* is. And whatever our answers would be, we must remember that responsibility for the ultimate fate of the construction will lie first and foremost in the mouths of the people who use it.

12

Some Dialect Features in the Speech of Missouri Germans

DONALD M. LANCE

THIS CHAPTER TREATS language shift as well as dialectology. In it, I will explore the nature and source of the English dialect of the last generation of Missouri Germans to have much command over the German language. Primary data come from interviews of 33 Missouri residents of German ancestry born between 1890 and 1925, selected from a pool of more than 100 tapes in the collection of the Missouri Oral History and Folklore Project at the University of Missouri-Columbia.[1] Thus the findings apply to the first generation of this century, but not necessarily to generations born after 1925. The primary criterion for the selection of informants for the Oral History Project was that they or their families still practiced some Old World customs; the primary criterion for the selection of interviews for this language study was that the individuals had to have spoken German as children, and might still have spoken German at the time of the interview. The locations of the informants are indicated by dots on map 12.1.

The first German-speaking immigrants in Missouri came to Bollinger, Cape Girardeau, and Wayne Counties in southeast Missouri in 1798–1800, while the area was still a French possession (Gerlach 1976). The German settlements in Missouri that are familiar to most people, however, are those established by immigrations in the 1830s and 1840s into a 10-county area extending about 80 miles from St. Louis down the Mississippi River to Perry County and 100 miles up the Missouri River to Jefferson City, as shown in map 12.1.[2] I will refer to these 10 counties as "the German area." Substantial German settlements can be found in many other sections of the state as well, but no other areas have as great a concentration as these 10 counties. (Gerlach 1976, Schroeder 1979, Lance 1986).

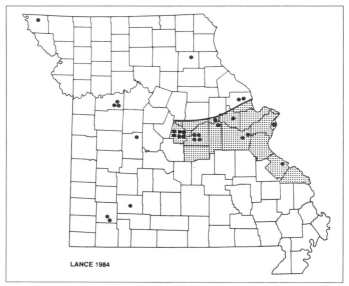

Map 12.1. Area of strong German settlement.

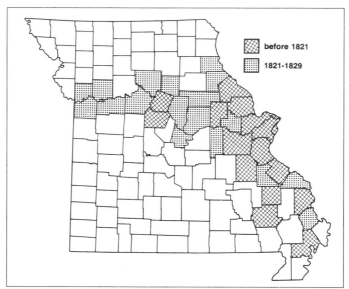

Map 12.2. Counties organized in 1821–1830.

The earliest American settlers in Missouri came via western Virginia and western North Carolina, through the Cumberland Gap into Kentucky, later into southern Ohio, Indiana, and Illinois, and in the 1780s into the Mississippi and Missouri River valleys of Illinois and Missouri (Faries 1967: 28; Gerlach 1976: 16–18; Rafferty 1981: 36–37). These were Southerners and South Midlanders. The Southerners were descendants of slave-holding old stock Virginians and Carolinians. The South Midlanders, many of them Ulster Scots, were descendants of Virginians and Carolinians who had originally settled in the western portions of these states. As the Southerners migrated to new territories, they searched for large tracts of land suitable for growing cotton, tobacco, and hemp, whereas the South Midlanders moved in family groups and settled in smaller self-sufficient communities (Faries 1967; Gerlach 1976; McDavid 1958: 500–508). By 1830, when German immigration began on a large scale, Americans had settled along the Mississippi River as far north as Hannibal and along the Missouri River as far west as present-day Kansas City. Map 12.2 shows the areas that had been settled by 1830.

The settlement history outlined above indicates that the original dialect of the German area was a combination of Southern and South Midland. One would expect then that as the Germans shifted to English they would adopt a Southern or South Midland dialect.

When Roger Shuy (1962) was mapping dialect items in a study for the North-Central portion of the Linguistic Atlas of the United States and Canada, he found pockets of Northern pronunciations and vocabulary items in the part of Illinois opposite St. Louis, an area with many German immigrants.[3] In recent years, Timothy Frazer has focused on this area, but has expanded his base to include not only data from the Atlas files but also data from Missouri and Illinois informants in the files of the Dictionary of American Regional English. Using traditional procedures of regional dialectology, Frazer (1979) presents convincing evidence that the German settlement areas in both Illinois and Missouri constitute a distinct Northern speech island in a predominantly South Midland dialect area.

In an attempt to determine how and why the Germans were able to establish a Northern speech island in an otherwise South Midland area, Frazer analyzed some early census data. The original settlers in this part of Illinois, like those across the River in Missouri, were Southerners. For example, in the 1850 census, only 7% of the American-born adults in Monroe County, Illinois, were from Northern states (New York, Massachusetts), with another 7% each from Pennsylvania and Ohio.

Thirty-three percent were born in Illinois, however, which in the early years would indicate Southern parentage, while a combined 30% originated in Virginia, North Carolina, Kentucky, or Tennessee (Frazer 1979: 189).

Although Southerners had initially settled the counties into which the Germans had immigrated, the foreign immigrants tended to establish their own communities, with their own schools, newspapers, and other institutions, interacting with their American neighbors for economic rather than personal reasons. But there were differences among these neighbors. Frazer found that the Northern settlers were generally much better educated and much better off financially than the Southerners. Also, Northerners tended to live in the cities, whereas Southerners lived in rural areas. Not only were the (urban) businessmen more likely to be Northerners, but the school teachers also tended to come from outside, as shown in table 12.1. Frazer also found suggestions in historical accounts that both the Yankees and the Germans considered the Southerners to be socially inferior and their dialect to be less pleasant (Frazer 1979: 188–92).

In the remainder of this chapter, I will use vocabulary data from a dissertation study of Missouri and pronunciation data from the Oral History interviews to test Frazer's claim that there is a Northern speech island surrounded by South Midland dialect in east-central Missouri.

In 1967 Rachel Faries surveyed the state in a doctoral dissertation and found that dialect patterns follow settlement history rather well.[4] The Bootheel, in the southeast, settled mostly by plantation owners, has clear evidence of Coastal Southern dialect influence. The Ozark Highlands were found to be an extension of the South Midland dialects of the mountainous areas of Kentucky and Tennessee. In the north-central part of the state, in an area known locally as "Little Dixie," terms of combined Southern and South Midland dialects were very common.

Table 12.1
Place of Birth of School Teachers
in Madison County, Illinois, in 1870

Northern states	14
Pennsylvania and Ohio	13
Southern states	7
Illinois	7
Missouri	1
Germany	1
Switzerland	1
Total	62

The northern and western plains were found to be strongly North Midland. Most parts of these plains areas were settled after the Civil War, when primary settlement was coming from Midwestern states rather than the South—in part because the "Iron Clad Oath" forbade the immigration of admitted supporters of the Confederacy. But the 10-county German area, much like the German settlement area of Illinois in Frazer's study, was found to have a relatively high incidence of Northern and North Midland terms.

The regional dialect divisions that dialectologists traditionally use were established by Atlas studies of New England and the Middle and South Atlantic States in the 1930s and 1940s (Kurath et al. 1939, Kurath 1949, Kurath and McDavid 1982, Atwood 1953). Later studies have shown that the dialect divisions found in the Eastern states could still be clearly discerned as settlers migrated west of the Appalachians (Allen 1973–76, Marckwardt 1957, Dakin 1971, Wood 1963). These divisions are shown in map 12.3.

Faries's dissertation is based on a questionnaire study of all counties of the state except St. Louis city. The questionnaire consisted of 120 vocabulary items that Kurath had found to have fairly clear regional distribution in the Eastern states (Kurath 1949). Table 12.2 lists 14 items that Faries found to be significantly stronger in the German area than elsewhere. The first two columns indicate the number of informants who said they used a particular word and the number of informants in the entire state who said they used it. Only 50 informants were interviewed in these 10 counties, constituting 7% of the 700 informants interviewed in the entire state; thus, it is of interest to see whether more than 7% of the instances of a particular dialect item occurs in these counties. The third column indicates how often a

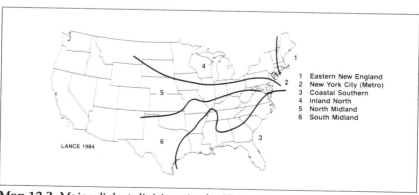

Map 12.3. Major dialect divisions in the United States.

Table 12.2

Dialect Items with Frequent Occurrence in German Settlement Area

	Numbers of Occurrence		Percentages	
	German	Entire	Occurrences	Speakers
Dialect Item[a]	Area	State	of Item	in Area (50)
cruller (doughnut) (N, NM)	6	15	38	12
smear case (M)	19	94	20	38
smear cheese (M)	10	15	67	20
bite (between meals) (N)	11	60	18	22
sick to the stomach (N)	13	41	32	26
sick in the stomach (S, NM)	7	39	18	14
quarter to eleven (N, S)	26	152	17	52
school leaves out (NM)	8	11	73	16
lowlands (river bottom) (N, S)	15	84	18	30
sheep buck (ram) (NM)	19	40	48	38
pavement (sidewalk) (NM)	8	32	25	16
angleworm (N)	5	28	18	10
earthworm (S, N, urban)	11	53	21	22
groomsman (best man) (S, M)	14	75	19	28
Total	172	740	23	

[a] Regional abbreviations: N = Northern; S = Southern; NM = North Midland; SM = South Midland; and M = Midland.

particular item occurs in the area (column 1 divided by column 2) and the fourth column indicates what percentage of the speakers in the 10-county area used the term (column 1 divided by 50).

Thirteen of the 14 items in table 12.2 have a clearly Northern dialectal bias; no others in Faries's study had a strong presence in the German area. Not even one item is of primarily Southern or South Midland usage. Interestingly, Kurath lists 9 of these 14 terms as being in common use in southeastern Pennsylvania: *cruller, smear case, smear cheese, sick in/to the stomach, school leaves out, lowlands, sheep buck, pavement.* Two of the others (*bite, angleworm*) are Northern, one (*quarter to eleven*) was common in western Pennsylvania, and the remaining two are in somewhat general use. It is also interesting that three of the terms in table 12.2—constituting over one-fourth of the occurrence total (48/172)—are definitely loan translations: *smear case/smear cheese,* (from German *Schmierkäse*), *sheep buck* (from German *Schafbock*). Kurath found that the dialect item *smear case/smear cheese,* prevalent in the Pennsylvania German area, had spread (with anglicized pronunciation and spelling) into non-German areas throughout North Midland dialects and into western Virginia and West Virginia (Kurath 1949: 71).

Thus, though these cheese terms are loan translations, they could also have been brought to Missouri by South Midlanders from Virginia.[5] The typical South Midland term for this generation—*clabber cheese*—occurs 130 times in Missouri, in no particular pattern, and the general term— *cottage cheese*—is used throughout the state. Both *clabber cheese* and *cottage cheese* occurred in the German area as well. The only dialect term for cottage cheese that shows a definite regional tendency in Missouri is the Rhineland loan translation.

Other terms listed in table 12.2 are also possible loan translations from German (e.g., *bite*) or English forms that developed as a result of interference from German (e.g., *school leaves out*, from the German *lassen*, translated as "leave" or "let"). Thus, one cannot be absolutely sure whether the vocabulary items used by Frazer and by Faries in classifying German settlement areas as North Midland were terms translated directly from German into English, terms favored by early school teachers and editors from the North, or terms used by North Midland neighbors with whom the Missouri and Illinois Germans interacted. Because the number of items in table 12.2 is relatively small, and because there are various possible sources for the terms, one cannot feel confident in drawing firm conclusions based solely or primarily on the basis of these vocabulary items.

In determining the dialectal classification of a particular area, dialectologists usually use not only vocabulary items but also verb forms, syntactic constructions, and pronunciation. Perhaps the least ambiguous aspect of dialect is pronunciation; it is the determining factor in what is popularly called "regional accent." In his study of German areas in Illinois and Missouri, Frazer selected six vowel sounds: those in *ground, due, time, cough, him, them* (Frazer 1978: 40). He was particularly interested in the typical South Midland pronunciations of these six vowels: fronted /au/ in *ground*, [dju] for *due*, diphthong flattening (or a long monophthong) in *time*, diphthong in *cough*, glides in *him* and *them*.

In the interviews used for the present study there were relatively few instances of South Midland pronunciations. None of the 33 interviewees used the last three features in Frazer's list. Only 3 of the 33 Missouri Germans produced a fronted /au/—a farmer from Northwest Missouri, a teacher (female) from Lincoln County, and a minister who grew up in St. Louis and spent his adult years in Lincoln County—but only the farmer had fronted the vowel enough for his dialect to sound "Southern." Flattening of the /ai/ diphthong was found in the speech of 8 of the 33 speakers, but in all instances, it occurred either in the pronoun *I* or in a word with weakened stress; in no instances did simplification of this vowel occur in a stressed word, the typical South Midland feature. Thus with the exception of one individual in the northwest corner of the state, none of the Missouri Germans in this study had adopted these 5 features of South Midland speech.

The remaining vowel nucleus—the one in *new*—is analyzed here along with a consonant that has similar regional classification in the United States—the initial consonant sound in *wheat*. In most of New England and in both Southern and South Midland speech, the [h-] is pronounced in *wheat*, and *new* has the [ju] diphthong. The typical North Midland pronunciations are [wit] and [nu]; these pronunciations are also becoming dominant in Inland North areas (Kurath and McDavid 1982: 113, 174, 178). Frazer found islands of North Midland [nu] in German areas of Illinois and Missouri, surrounded by South Midland [nju], but he did not discuss the /hw/ cluster in the references cited here. Because the present study is based on rather short passages, only a few instances of words with [ju] and /hw/ occur in the data: six speakers used the South Midland [ju] pronunciation, all but one in counties with strong German population;[6] three used the North Midland [u] pronunciation, one in the German counties and two outside them. Thus, the Missouri Germans in this sample appear to prefer the South Midland [ju] pronunciation; however, Missouri Germans both inside and outside the area appeared to prefer the North Midland [wit], with six of these inside the area using initial [w-] and three using [hw-], and five of the others using [w-] and three using [hw-]. See table 12.3.

The Missouri Germans' choices of the pronunciations for words like *new* and *wheat* suggest an inconsistency in their preference for North Midland versus South Midland usage. But these two sounds can also demonstrate consistent attention to factors other than settlement and migration patterns. Radio and television announcers are usually careful to say [njuz] (the pronunciation common in New England, Southern, South Midland dialects) but the advertisements for bread and toilet tissue almost always have speakers who say [wɑit] (Inland North and North Midland pronunciations); thus these Missouri Germans adopted the pronunciations favored by Walter Cronkite and Mr. Whipple.

Even though the preceding paragraphs have raised some serious

Table 12.3
Use of [ju] and /hw/

	SM [ju]	NM [u]	SM [hw]	NM [w]
Inside the German area (20)	5	1	3	6
Outside the German area (13)	1	2	3	5

questions about their having specifically adopted the North Midland dialect, no doubt remains that the Illinois and Missouri Germans do constitute a non-Southern island within an otherwise South Midland area—at least for the generations represented in the surveys that serve as sources of data for this study. What accounts for the island? Questions about vocabulary items in table 12.2 suggested that loan translations or other first-language influences may be sources of usages that are often classified as North Midland in the dialect surveys. Can that be the case with phonology too?

Transcriptions of the 33 interviews revealed a number of direct carryovers from German phonology. Five were systematically tabulated: substitution of [t,d] for *th* (*dese tings*), devoicing of final consonants (*happent* = *happened*), use of the tongue position of the German long [ɒː] in the pronunciation of English [a] (farther back in the mouth), and the use of mid-level off-glides in the /ai/ and /au/ diphthongs (i.e., /ae/, /ao/). Table 12.4 summarizes the evidence of carryover of German accent into the English of the informants in this sample.

The most common feature of German accent is the pronunciation of the two diphthongs, and next the devoicing of final consonants. The only accent feature that appears less often in the German settlement areas than elsewhere is the low back /a/.

The [t,d] substitutions seem to persist in many ethnic dialects, even in the speech of German- and Italian-Americans whose parents and grandparents were essentially monolingual English speakers. Seven of the informants had both [t,d] substitution and final-consonant devoicing, three had [t,d] but not devoicing, and five had devoicing but not [t,d].

Evidence of German influence in the vowels is more subtle. In German the difference between long [ɒː] and short [a] is not simply vowel length; the tongue position for the long vowel is considerably farther back in the mouth. Ten of the 33 people in this study maintained the German long [ɒː] tongue position for words like *hot* and *father.* This variant is also common in other American dialects, but not in the Midwest, nor in southeastern Pennsylvania; it is common throughout coastal Southern dialects and occurs sporadically in eastern

Table 12.4
Features of German Accent

Location	[t, d]		Devoicing		[ɒː]		[ae]		[ao]	
	#	%	#	%	#	%	#	%	#	%
German Area (20)	7	35	7	35	3	15	16	80	14	70
Others (13)	3	23	5	38	7	54	8	62	8	62

New England and South Midland dialects, none of which are likely sources for the phonology of Missouri Germans. The /ai/ and /au/ diphthongs likewise reflect German phonology, having [-e] and [-o] off-glides rather than the expected high vowels. These mid variants also occur in Eastern dialects, but with different regional distribution: [-o] occurs occasionally in eastern New England and along the Southern coast, and [-e] occurs sporadically in all of New England and frequently in the inland South (Kurath and McDavid 1982). The frequency with which Missouri Germans use the mid off-glide suggests that the source of this articulation is carryover from German rather than imitation of existing dialects of English.

In addition, a few instances of other stereotypical features of German accent occur in the data, such as failure to distinguish between the vowels of *bet* and *bat* (two individuals) and interchanging of /v/ and /w/ (three individuals); all five instances of these two features occurred within the German area. In addition to carrying over the German off-glide in the two diphthongs, a number of speakers in this sample tended to pronounce /i/ and /e/ without the off-glides that are natural to English, producing them more like the German monophthongs /i/ and /e/.

Speakers within the German areas had more carryover of German phonology than did those who lived in Anglo-dominant areas (3.0 German features per speaker versus 2.3 elsewhere). The strongest accent was found in a carpenter and his wife living in a rural town in Cole County west of Jefferson City; their parents were also born in that community. Those who had adjusted most completely to English were in some sense "farther away" from areas popularly known as German settlements—two informants in Lincoln County, which was rather strongly South-South Midland in Faries's study; the informant in far northwest Missouri; the informant in the center of the Ozark Plateau in a county with strong Southern settlement history; and two who were employed in urban settings in Jefferson City and Springfield where contact with individuals identified as "Missouri Germans" would have been minimal.

The data in this study on Missourians of German ancestry suggest several patterns. Those who live in areas known as "German areas," such as the Missouri Rhineland west of St. Louis or in the city of Concordia, have maintained traces of German heritage in their speech for up to three generations after their ancestors immigrated. Those who did not live in such areas were more likely to anglicize completely and adapt to English phonology. It must be kept in mind, however, that these findings refer to the generations of Missourians born between 1890 and 1925; younger generations, particularly university students, rarely manifest these features of foreign accent. In all cases where vestiges of German influence were found outside the German area, the informants lived in small German enclaves. Thus the data in this study suggest that the Northern or North Midland islands found by dialectologists in otherwise Southern areas may be attributable in part to German influence on the English of the speakers. It would be interesting to see to what extent the speech of German or other European ethnic groups played a role in Atlas studies in Pennsylvania and Ohio in defining the North Midland dialect.

13

Regional Speech Variation in Wisconsin

CRAIG M. CARVER

WHILE MAPPING THE Upper North for *American Regional Dialects: A Word Geography* (Carver 1987: 67–71, maps 3.7–8), I unexpectedly discovered that a boundary divided Wisconsin into eastern and western sections (see map 13.1). This map was based on 62 isoglosses or word distributions from the fieldwork collected for the Dictionary of American Regional English (DARE). The results of earlier fieldwork done in Wisconsin, the Wisconsin English Language Survey (WELS), also archived at the DARE offices, gave me the unique opportunity of corroborating or discounting the existence of such a boundary.

In the late 1940s Frederic Cassidy and Audrey R. Duckert developed a fieldwork questionnaire (see Cassidy 1953) intended for use in the preparation of the American Dialect Society's dictionary, later realized as DARE. This questionnaire consisted of about 1,900 questions and was used as a checklist in the WELS survey. Each question was printed on a 4 x 6 slip of paper bound together in pads of 100 questions each. Two of these pads at a time were sent by mail to informants in 52 selected Wisconsin communities, one informant per community. In addition to these 52 informants, who were assigned code numbers 1 through 52, there were 11 auxiliary informants. The results, as Cassidy put it, "were even fuller and more various than had been anticipated" (Cassidy 1953: 8n7).

Because of the enormous number of responses garnered from the WELS checklist, many of which were "oncers," it was not practical to create a database from all of them. Instead I selected those questions that seemed most interesting, especially if the question elicited several different responses that might show regionality within the state. Accordingly I selected 165 questions eliciting some 2,700 different responses.

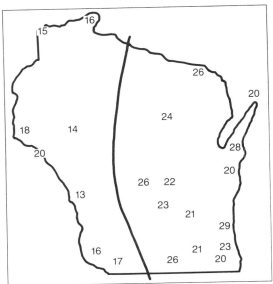

Map 13.1. Upper North dialect layer in Wisconsin (from map 3.7, *American Regional Dialects*).

To analyze the data, I developed a computer program written in Pascal. The program, which runs on an IBM PC, is tailor-made for the data, though it could easily be modified for other data sets and geographies. It is menu driven—the operations that the user wishes to perform are selected from a menu of options—and it is fully interactive. It offers four broad categories of operations: (1) data input and error testing; (2) mapping of specific isoglosses, including contrast maps, automatic mapping and regionality testing; (3) social statistics, including social maps and summaries; and (4) generalizations of isoglosses or "count maps."

The East-West Boundary

At least twelve complementary distributions hint at the east-west division in Wisconsin. But the most compelling evidence for this division and its primary importance in the linguistic geography of Wisconsin is that the most common isoglosses in the WELS data are distributed over the eastern half of the state. When taken together they form an eastern "layer" (see Carver 1987: 16–19 for a definition of "layer"). Map 13.2 shows this layer as a "count map" or "participation map" of 32 individual isoglosses. (This method counts the number of words that each informant used in this sample, in this case 32 responses. See Carver 1987: 14–16.) Because these maps were generated using characters instead of graphics, letters are used to symbolize double-digit numbers. (See the appendix for a conversion table.) A sharp drop in the numbers shows the approximate boundary of this layer.

Not surprisingly there is a contrasting western layer, as suggested by map 13.3, which composites 22 isoglosses. The Western Wisconsin speech region is in part the record left by settlers from the Mississippi Valley and Lower North. Migrating up the Mississippi and St. Croix rivers into Wisconsin and Minnesota, they mixed with settlers from the Northeast, especially New England, and established towns and farms along or inland from the river.

The Western layer boundary overlaps much of the Eastern layer, but this is to be expected since dialect boundaries are rarely sharp dividing lines. If there is a "line" at all it is a very wide one, as suggested in map 13.4, which combines the boundaries from the eastern and western maps with the boundary from the Upper North layer (map 13.1). Despite its breadth, which is actually a relatively sharp transition,

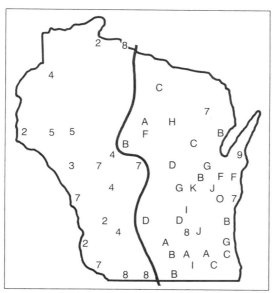

Map 13.2. Eastern layer (32 isoglosses).

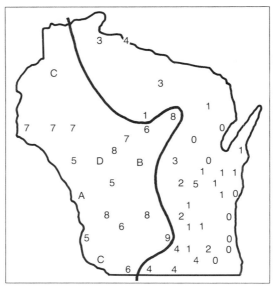

Map 13.3. Western layer (22 isoglosses).

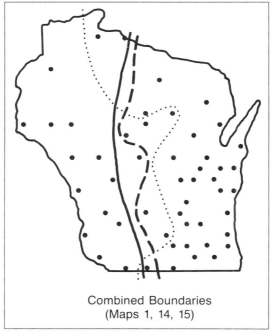

Combined Boundaries
(Maps 1, 14, 15)

Map 13.4. Combined boundaries (maps 13.1, 13.2, and 13.3).

the East-West dialect boundary is very real, as will become even clearer as we consider the eastern subregions.

Eastern Subregions

There are four sets of isoglosses that indicate subregions of Eastern Wisconsin. The most clearly defined of these is a set of 21 isoglosses that cluster in the southeastern section of the state, composited in map 13.5. (This region is also negatively outlined in map 13.7.)

There are contrasting isoglosses within the Eastern region, hinting at two subregions, one that hugs the Lake Michigan coast and another inland. These subregions are more clearly defined by separate sets of isoglosses composited in maps 13.6 and 13.7. The Inland East layer (map 13.6) contrasts with the Coastal layer (map 13.7).

Finally, the northeastern section is defined by a handful of word distributions composited in map 13.8.

When all isoglosses of eastern Wisconsin and its subregions are combined (map 13.9), it becomes clear that the boundary running south and north dividing the state into Eastern and Western regions is the major dialect feature in Wisconsin linguistic geography.

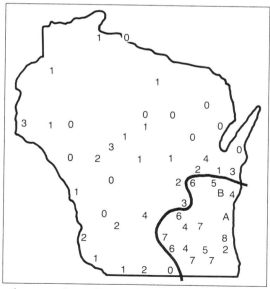

Map 13.5. Southeastern layer (21 isoglosses).

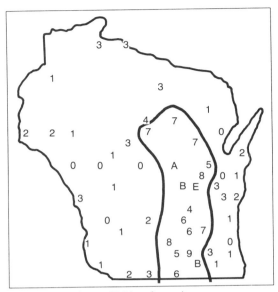

Map 13.6. Inland Eastern layer (26 isoglosses).

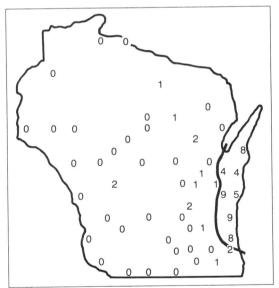

Map 13.7. Coastal layer (18 isoglosses).

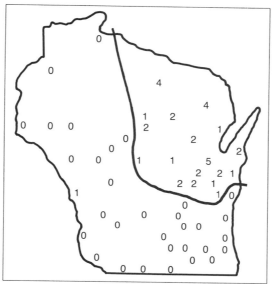

Map 13.8. Northeastern layer (8 isoglosses).

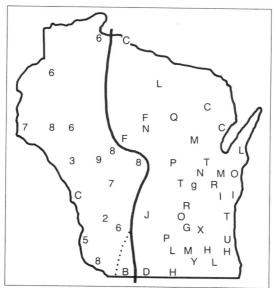

Map 13.9. Combined Eastern layers (101 isoglosses).

As part of the great westward expansion in the 1830s, settlers from New England and New York, and to a lesser extent, from Pennsylvania, flooded into southeastern Wisconsin. This tide of settlement peaked in the 1850s, defining the linguistic landscape, notably the southeastern section of the state.

Not surprisingly, then, the Eastern lexicon and its subvarieties share many words with New England and its Upper Northern settlement region. The Eastern layer area shares *curd* 'thickened sour milk' and *soda* or *soda water* (or *pop*) with New England, and *whippletree* or *whiffletree* 'the pivoting crossbar on a horse-drawn wagon to which the traces are fastened', *marsh hay, clunker* 'an old, rundown car'; and *hay mow* 'a barn loft for storing hay' with the North. With Pennsylvania and the Lower North, it shares *filled doughnut.*

Inland Eastern's *gentleman cow* 'a bull' and *cinch* or *cinch strap* 'the harness band that goes around a horse's abdomen' are also New England and Northern terms. The Northeastern Wisconsin layer shares *fodder corn* 'feed corn' and *muck* 'heavy, sticky soil' with New England and its derivative areas. The Southeast has *husk* 'the covering of a nut, hull', *murphies* 'potatoes', and *cattle pass* 'cattle crossing' in common with the Upper North, and shares *rainstick* 'umbrella' primarily with the Lower North. In common with the Upper North, the Coastal region of Wisconsin has *belly-strap* 'the harness band that goes around a horse's abdomen', *bee* 'a meeting or social gathering to accomplish coopera- tively a particular task', *swamp hay* and *grub ax* 'a mattock'. It also has the Lower Northern forms *gee horse* 'the horse on the driver's right hand', *haw horse* 'the horse on the left hand', and *spongy* 'of root vegetables: pulpy, pithy'.

Two factors that contributed to the linguistic division of Wisconsin were the early heavy settlement of the eastern part of the state, especially the southeast, together with an influx in the 1830s and 1840s of German settlers who tended to stay on smaller holdings in the east toward the lakeshore areas. This east-west split was further emphasized by the immigration of large numbers of Norwegians, who favored the southern interior and western parts of the state. The sparse settlement in the infertile central sand plains further separated the two regions from each other (see Finley 1976: 220–59).

A handful of words with German origins is almost exclusive to the Eastern regions as defined by the WELS data. *Kraut* 'cabbage' and *thick milk* 'thick, sour milk' are part of the Eastern layer lexicon, while *speck* 'bacon' and *berliner* 'a deep fried, filled pastry' are part of the Coastal lexicon. The Western layer's *making hay* 'storing hay' may also be a German calque.

Because the WELS questions form the basis of the DARE question-naire, it is relatively easy to compare the local isoglosses with the national results. Except for a handful of words, however, such as the German expressions noted above, it is difficult to describe the differences—historical or cultural among the Wisconsin regional lexicons. Unlike the different lexicons of the major United States regions, such as the North and the South, the systematic differences in Wisconsin are relatively minute and difficult to detect.

The influence of Southern regional English on Wisconsin speech, for example, is real enough, if admittedly slight. This influence, however, is not confined to any one of the Wisconsin regions. The Western Wisconsin layer (map 13.3) has *branch* 'a stream' and *long handles* 'long underwear', both of which DARE clearly shows to be Southern regionalisms. *Male animal* 'bull' is also a Western layer term from the South according to DARE, though Kurath (1949) also notes that it is a New England expression.

The Eastern layers also show in their lexicon's Southern influence. The Southeastern layer (map 13.5) has *soup hound* 'a mongrel'. DARE's 22 informants who gave this as a response to the questions "What do you call a dog of mixed breed?" and "What joking or uncomplimentary words do you have for dogs?" are almost all in the Southern United States except one in central west Wisconsin. *Mattock* from the Coastal layer (map 13.7) is shown in DARE to be a primarily southern Appalachian term.

Most of the words in this study, however, are standard colloquial expressions used virtually everywhere, even though they pattern according to Wisconsin's speech regions. But the isoglosses used to discover geographical patterns do not have to be dialectal and quaint. The choice of words favored by speakers in a particular area, even if they are known elsewhere, is also a valid criterion for defining regional speech.

The South-North Boundary

Map 13.10 combines 30 southern Wisconsin isoglosses. This layer covers the lower half of the state except the Coastal region. When combined with the Southeastern layer, the boundary dividing the southern portion of the state becomes even clearer (map 13.11).

The Southern layer lexicon also shares several regionalisms with New England and the Upper North, including *tainted* or *tinted milk*

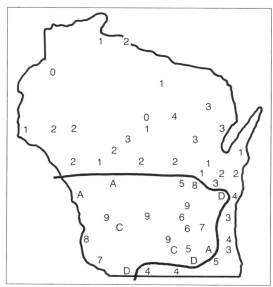

Map 13.10. Southern layer (30 isoglosses).

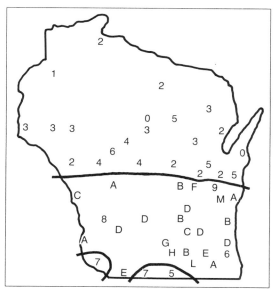

Map 13.11. Combined Southern layers (53 isoglosses) (maps 13.5, 13.10).

'milk having the flavor of the weeds that a cow has grazed on', *exchange work* 'work done for someone in exchange for similar work', *curdled milk* 'thick, sour milk', and *it's snowing down south* 'a warning to a woman that her slip is showing'. *Baby buggy* is shared with the Inland North.

The northern portion of the state remained virtually unsettled into the 1880s. It was during that decade that lumbering attracted significant numbers of settlers to the dense forests and infertile soil of the northern highlands, setting it off linguistically from the south.

Only a handful of words, composited in map 13.12, defines the northern region. Map 13.13 adds the Northeastern isoglosses to it.

The northwest is also a subregion, but has virtually no isoglosses of its own in this data sample. It is attested negatively by the relative absence of isoglosses, indicated by the relatively small numbers in map 13.14, which conflates all of the eastern and southern layers.

Map 13.15 does the same thing for the Northeastern region, by combining all of the western and southern isoglosses, and map 13.16 shows the Southeastern region by combining all of the western and northern isoglosses.

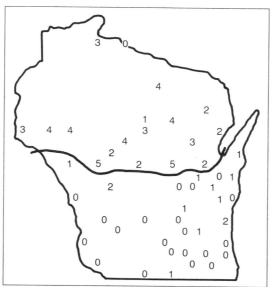

Map 13.12. Northern layer (10 isoglosses).

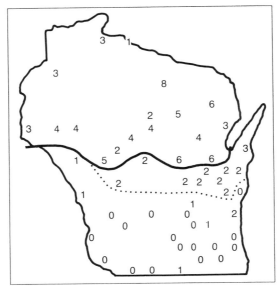

Map 13.13. Combined Northern layers (17 isoglosses) (maps 13.8, 13.12).

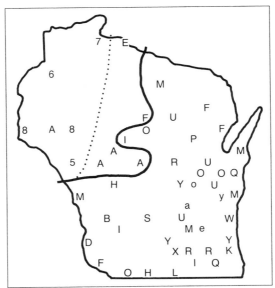

Map 13.14. Combined map (maps 13.9, 13.11: 131 isoglosses); negative evidence for a Northwestern region.

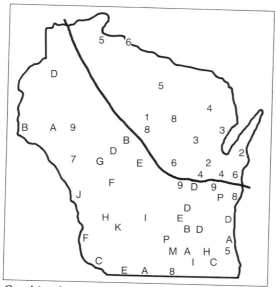

Map 13.15. Combined map (maps 13.3, 13.11: 73 isoglosses); negative evidence for a Northeastern region.

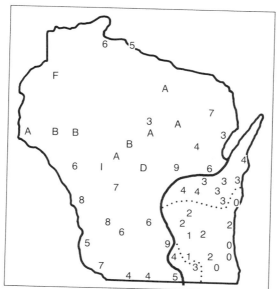

Map 13.16. Combined map (maps 13.3, 13.13: 39 isoglosses); negative evidence for a Southeastern region.

The Southwest

The earliest major settlement of Wisconsin was in the southwest corner of the state after 1822, when settlers from Kentucky, Tennessee, southwestern Missouri, and southern Illinois moved there to work the lead mines. In the next decade they were joined by immigrants from Cornwall, England. This enclave of Upper Southern speakers and their influence on the language, like the influence of the Northwestern Wisconsin region, is measured primarily by negative evidence. That is, this corner of the state has little participation in the lexicons of the other layers, as seen in map (13.17), which combines the eastern and western isoglosses.

Generalized Boundaries

It is clear by now that, except for the interior complexity of the Eastern region, Wisconsin's linguistic pie is cut into four quarters. This is apparent when the boundaries of maps 13.14–13.17 are combined (see map 13.18). Map 13.19, which takes into account the first order East-West boundary, gives a simplified general view of the speech regions of Wisconsin.

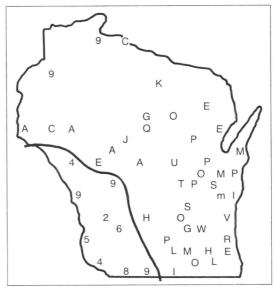

Map 13.17. Combined map (maps 13.9, 13.13: 111 isoglosses); negative evidence for a Southwestern region.

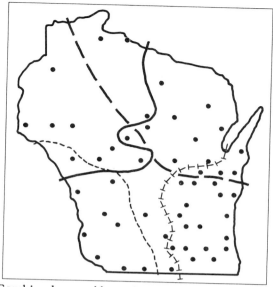

Map 13.18. Combined general boundaries (maps 13.14–13.17).

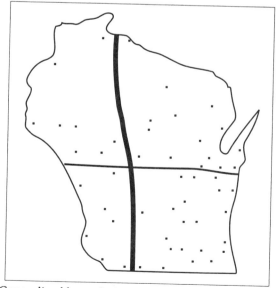

Map 13.19. Generalized boundaries.

Appendix
Letter/Number Conversion Table for Count Maps
(The numbers on the right of each column represent numbers of isoglosses.)

A = 10	a = 36
B = 11	b = 37
C = 12	c = 38
D = 13	d = 39
E = 14	e = 40
F = 15	f = 41
G = 16	g = 42
H = 17	h = 43
I = 18	i = 44
J = 19	j = 45
K = 20	k = 46
L = 21	l = 47
M = 22	m = 48
N = 23	n = 49
O = 24	o = 50
P = 25	p = 51
Q = 26	q = 52
R = 27	r = 53
S = 28	s = 54
T = 29	t = 55
U = 30	u = 56
V = 31	v = 57
W = 32	w = 58
X = 33	x = 59
Y = 34	y = 60
Z = 35	z = 61

14

"Kentuck" English in Wisconsin's Cutover Region

DONALD LARMOUTH and MARJORIE REMSING

THE CUTOVER REGION in northern Wisconsin is the home of migrants from eastern Kentucky who have preserved many "Kentuck" features in their speech for more than 90 years. For the most part, these features do not appear elsewhere in Wisconsin, although Cassidy's 1940 field records for the Linguistic Atlas of the North Central States (LANCS) cite a few similar features, mostly in some southwestern counties. However, a very similar cluster of features appears in the eastern Kentucky LANCS materials collected by McDavid in the mid-1950s, and others appear in Wentworth (1944) and McDavid and McDavid (1973). The Atlas records and the more recently collected data reported here clearly reflect the settlement history of the cutover region and the relative isolation of the Kentuck population.

Settlement History of the Cutover Region

Before describing the features that characterize their dialect, it may be helpful to review the settlement history which brought migrants from Kentucky to the cutover region in northern Wisconsin around the turn of the century. The "cutover region" is an informal term which describes an area in northern and northeastern Wisconsin which was "cut over" by the softwood lumbering industry that flourished in the Great Lakes in the latter part of the nineteenth century. The removal of the big pine timber left the region open for second growth hardwoods as well as pines and other coniferous trees, changing both the ecology and the economic significance of the region, which now is included within Marinette, Forest, and Langlade counties and encompasses a large forest management area, the Nicolet National Forest.

Census data from 1900 and 1905 show that the "Kentucks" came directly from Kentucky to northeastern Wisconsin, settling first in Langlade County and later in Forest County (see table 14.1). They were followed by other Kentucky migrants between 1910 and 1920, locating in such communities as Antigo, Elton, Langlade, Lily, and Hollister in Langlade County, Alvin, Argonne, Crandon, and Laona in Forest County, and Fence in Marinette County, as well as several rural townships, where many of their descendants remain (see map 14.1). A few of their descendants also live in Florence County. Their primary motivation for moving into the region appears to be the opportunity to work in the lumbering industry, and the 1900 and 1905 census data bear this out (see table 14.2). Because the area was heavily wooded, it was also attractive to poor settlers because of the ready supply of wood

Table 14.1
1900 and 1905 Census Data:
Kentuck Settlement in Wisconsin's Cutover Region

	1900	1905
Kentuck Men of Forest County		
Married adult males	3	70
Single adult males	2	90
Born in Kentucky	5	166
One or more parents born in Kentucky	5	165
Kentuck Women of Forest County		
Married adult females	3	71
Single adult females	1	19
Born in Kentucky	4	89
One or more parents born in Kentucky	4	90
Kentuck Men of Langlade County		
Married adult males	77	105
Single adult males	78	61
Born in Kentucky	148	157
One or more parents born in Kentucky	136	154
Kentuck Women of Langlade County		
Married adult females	69	96
Single adult females	16	21
Born in Kentucky	76	112
One or more parents born in Kentucky	80	114

Note: In these census data, "adult males" are those who list employment, while "adult females" are at least 13 years old and not in school. This latter designation reflects the early age at which many Kentuck women married.

Map 14.1. "Kentuck" communities in the cutover region.

for buildings and fences (Smith 1929: 77). There was also a desire on the part of some to avoid the dangers of working in the clay and coal mines of eastern Kentucky, according to several informants. Many Kentucks settled on stump lands sold off cheaply by the departing big pine lumber companies, who promoted it for settlement even though the soil was poor and water sources were uncertain (Kane 1954: 237). *Northern Wisconsin: A Guide Book to Aid the Homeseeker*, a popular publication of the Wisconsin State Board of Immigration, promoted the cutover region as ideal for "the farmer without means" but with "a sound, healthy body" and "the willingness to do hard manual labor." This publication also says that crops like Kentucky bluegrass, tobacco, and "Yankee" pumpkins were being grown in the region (78, 86).

Table 14.2
1900 and 1905 Census Data:
Employment of Kentuck Men in Wisconsin's Cutover Region

	1900	1905
Employment in Forest County		
Farming	15	48
Farm laborers	30	21
Lumbering and day laborers	103	74
Other	7	18
Employment in Langlade County		
Farming	1	17
Farm laborers	2	6
Lumbering and day laborers	1	142
Other	1	4

Letters to Henry Casson, Wisconsin secretary of state in 1897, indicate that county boards of immigration also wrote letters to friends and relatives of local residents, encouraging them to settle in northern Wisconsin (cf. letter to Walter Lyon, 1899). It was commonplace for young men to arrive first, then return to Kentucky to bring their families (or to find a wife). As a result, many extended families eventually settled in the cutover region.

Most of the land was actually not very suitable for farming, but the Soo Line and Chicago and Northwestern railroads had been built through the area in the 1880s, and this made it possible to develop a new hardwood lumbering industry, which prospered between 1910 and 1920 and attracted many more Kentucks to the region (Elliott 1978: 16, 19). Sawmills sprang up along the railroad tracks because it was too expensive to ship hardwood logs without cutting them into lumber. (Besides, hardwood logs could not be floated downriver like the big pine logs in the great river drives—they would sink!) Small, mostly temporary settlements also developed along the railroads, and older people living in the area today still refer to section numbers to describe their family homesteads.

Poor land management, drought, forest fires, and a declining economy closed many local sawmills by the mid-1930s (Elliott 1978: 16, 21), and even though many Kentuck families had settled on marginal farmland, some had already turned to moonshining after Prohibition was enacted and did a brisk trade in illegal whiskey to augment the meager income from their crops; indeed, Crandon became known as "the moonshining capital of the north," and local residents can still recall seeing piles of whiskey barrels at the railroad depot. Others tell of a steady flow of trucks arriving from Green Bay with sugar and grain and leaving with cases of medicine bottles filled with bootleg whiskey. Several have said that they would have starved if it hadn't been for moonshine, which sounds like a romantic story, but they say it with conviction, and it was virtually the only "cash crop" in the area (see "Moonshine Legend Colors Crandon History"). However, as the Great Depression worsened in the 1930s, the state of Wisconsin began the Northern Wisconsin Settler Relocation Project to move some of the poorer and more isolated families to more suitable land—even to the Matanuska Valley in Alaska. This project continued from 1934 until 1940.

Seasonal work in the woods has remained important in the local economy to the present day. The Conner Forest Industries lumber mill in Laona, which just recently closed, was at one time the largest hardwood lumber mill in the world, producing a million board feet a month. Even today, lumbering crews may work in the woods for six to eight months at a time (Pantzer 1974: 10). Many of the descendants of the original Kentuck settlers remain largely isolated in the Nicolet National Forest and small rural communities, and barter or the direct exchange of labor for goods continues, even though Saturday "trade days" in Crandon are a thing of the past. One informant said that he had recently purchased a used car with a combination of cash, labor, and unspecified goods. Rumors of involvement with organized crime during the bootlegging days and stories of overzealous game wardens who "turned up missing" have added to a general reputation for shiftlessness, "clannishness," and suspicion of outsiders (Pantzer 1974: 9; Van Goethem n.d.: 94). Today, many people in Marinette, Antigo, and other nearby communities regard the Kentucks as unreliable and even dangerous poachers, moonshiners, and "violators." Very good moonshine whiskey is still made, deer are still poached (many locals say with some pride that they were raised on venison and cornbread), and working in the woods still supplements marginal incomes from on-and-off work in sawmills, bowling-pin and particle-board factories, and fishing resorts. Economic decline has forced many younger Kentucks to leave the region, and this has broken down traditional extended families (Pantzer 1974: 12–13), although some have begun to return as retirees (Van Goethem n.d.: 107). It is striking to note the similarities of accounts of life in the cutover region and the McDavids' description of circumstances in eastern Kentucky (McDavid and McDavid 1973; see also B. G. Packer papers), and it goes far toward explaining why the Kentucks have not assimilated very easily into the surrounding population.

Counties and Communities of Origin in Kentucky

In order to make productive use of LANCS records, it was necessary to identify the counties of origin for the Kentucks in the cutover region. Some informants could identify counties of origin or remembered communities that still exist in Kentucky, such as Beattyville, Olive Hill, Morehead, and Cracker's Neck. Others mentioned communities which were not on current maps, but Rennick's *Kentucky Place Names* (1984) proved to be very helpful in locating these communities of origin, especially obsolete townsites such as Stark in Elliott County.

So far, seven counties of origin have been identified for the Kentucks of the cutover region—Carter, Elliott, Jackson, Lee, Lewis, Rowan, and Wolfe—all of which are located in eastern Kentucky. Because LANCS records did not include all of the counties of origin, we decided to add the contiguous eastern Kentucky counties to the list to increase the chances of finding relevant connections. Bath, Boyd, Breathitt, Clay, Estill, Fleming, Greenup, Laurel, Lawrence, Madison, Magoffin, Mason, Menifee, Morgan, Owsley, Powell, and Rockcastle were thus included in the search of LANCS field records (see map 14.2).

LANCS Records for Wisconsin

If genuine Kentuck features were to be correctly identified in this study, it was necessary to examine LANCS field records for Wisconsin as well as Kentucky. Cassidy's 1940 field work for LANCS covered most Wisconsin counties but did not include the Kentuck communities in the northeast. However, Harold Allen has pointed out (personal communication) that there were Kentuck migrants living in southeastern Minnesota and probably in southwestern Wisconsin. An examination of LANCS records for those counties turned up a number of relevant features in such southwestern counties as Grant, Pepin, St. Croix, Iowa, and Trempealeau, as well as some in Dane, Green, Juneau, and even Douglas County in the northwest, which reflect what Allen described as an upriver settlement pattern as well as an attraction to the lead mining district in Wisconsin. LANCS field records from these and other Wisconsin counties helped to sort out genuine Kentuck features from other features which were at first presumed to be distinctive in the cutover region but turned out to have had much wider distribution in Wisconsin a half-century ago than they do now.

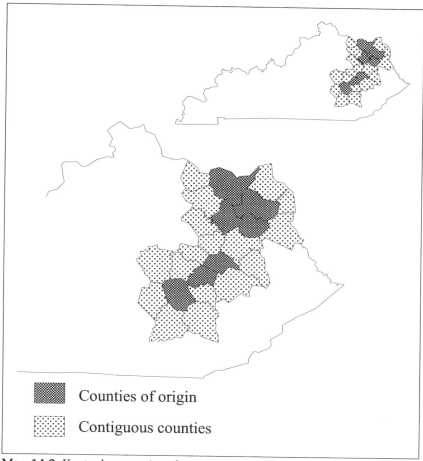

Map 14.2. Kentucky counties of origin and contiguous counties.

Fieldwork in the Cutover Region

The relative isolation of the Kentucks in the cutover region made dialect fieldwork difficult in some ways, as many individuals were reluctant to be interviewed, and it was necessary to arrange some interviews through intermediaries. However, we were able to complete a total of ten interviews and picked up more fragmentary material from another ten individuals. All but three informants would be classified as Type I, and only two fragmentary interviews took place with female informants (one interview was interrupted by an angry husband, who ordered the [female] fieldworker out of the house). Of these, eight were older individuals (ages 62 to 75); the others were middle-aged (ages 37 to 56). Several individuals were willing to be interviewed but were afraid that tape-recordings might somehow be used against them, possibly in court. Other informants were more accommodating, but it soon became clear that the only successful interview technique would be casual conversation, rather than a structured questionnaire with circumlocutions and reading samples. The informants were unwilling to read a text or respond to questions which resembled a quiz. Our interview material therefore consists largely of narratives of varying lengths describing area history and family life and reminiscences of fishing, hunting, logging, farming, and moonshining. This means that it is largely a matter of luck that items appear which can be checked in the LANCS records, although in some ways we can perhaps be more confident that the material is representative of local speech, especially in more extended narrative segments (see table 14.3).

"Kentuck" Phonological Features

Residents of the cutover region have retained several phonological features which reflect their eastern Kentucky origins as well as their subsequent isolation in northeastern Wisconsin and do not correspond to speech patterns characteristic of the larger region. We examined their distribution in LANCS records collected elsewhere in Wisconsin, and then looked at LANCS records from the eastern Kentucky counties of origin and contiguous counties to determine which ones actually reflected the settlement history of the cutover region.

Intrusive [-t] in *once* and *twice* (LANCS 2, items 6 and 7) was recorded among older Type I residents of the cutover region. There are several citations in the LANCS field records collected elsewhere in Wisconsin, but mostly in the southwestern counties (Grant, St. Croix, and Trempealeau) and in central Wisconsin (Green, Outagamie, and Prairie du Chien). Intrusive [-t] also turns up in several eastern Kentucky counties in the LANCS records—in two of the seven counties of origin (Carter and Lewis) and five of the 17 contiguous counties (Bath, Estill, Mason, Menifee, and Owsley).

Absence of [l] before final consonants, as in *help* (LANCS 39, item 6), was also found in the cutover region. This feature is not widespread elsewhere in Wisconsin (there is only one LANCS citation, in Portage County), but it shows up in one of the counties of origin (Lewis) and five of the contiguous counties (Bath, Estill, Mason, Menifee, and Owsley). Pronunciation with a very weak [l] was also recorded in the cutover region, and this appears in the LANCS records from Carter County, which is also a county of origin in eastern Kentucky. Other examples of [l]-less forms are *light bulb, golf, gulf, pulp,* and *wolves,* which are not in the LANCS inventory.

In the cutover region, schwa [ə] replaces [ow] in final position, as in *meadow* (LANCS 24, item 2) and *widow* (LANCS 49, item 3). This feature appears in three other counties in Wisconsin (Grant, Green, and Iowa). It is also extensively cited in the LANCS records for eastern Kentucky, appearing in two of the counties of origin (Carter and Lewis) and four of the contiguous counties (Bath, Estill, Mason, and Owsley). Another variant for these items which was recorded in the cutover region was the retroflex vowel [ɚ] as in [mɛdɚ] and [wɪdɚ], which does not appear in the LANCS records elsewhere in Wisconsin but is recorded in two of the eastern Kentucky counties (Breathitt and Menifee). Wisconsin LANCS records show a somewhat wider distribution for a variant pronunciation of *tomorrow* (LANCS 4, item 4), which usually has a clear [ow] in Wisconsin but has schwa [ə] in the cutover region and several Wisconsin counties, again mostly in the southwest (Grant, Iowa, Portage, St. Croix, and Trempealeau), and scattered elsewhere (Bayfield, Fond du Lac, and Kenosha). This item also appears with schwa in two of the counties of origin (Carter, Lewis) and five of the contiguous counties (Bath, Estill, Mason, Menifee, and Owsley).

Another feature recorded in the cutover region is a fronted monophthong [aː], which replaces the typical diphthong [ɑy], as in *wife* (LANCS 49, item 2). This item shows no monophthongal citations elsewhere in Wisconsin, but it appears in the LANCS records for one of the counties of origin (Carter) and three of the contiguous counties (Bath, Estill, Owsley). Another variant of *wife* with a fronted vowel and a high and very weak off-glide [aɪ] was also recorded in the cutover region. Like the fronted monophthong [aː], it also appears nowhere else in the LANCS records for Wisconsin, but appears in one of the counties of origin (Lewis) and two of the contiguous counties (Mason and Menifee). Many other examples of these forms appear in the cutover region but are not part of the LANCS inventory, such as *life, light, swipe,* and *skinnin' knives.* The feature is a dead giveaway which is often remarked and parodied by other people when they describe the Kentucks.

Another dead giveaway is an inserted off-glide in *can't* (LANCS 45, item 3), as in "from cain't see to cain't see"—an expression used to describe the dawn to dark winter work schedule in the logging camps.

Table 14.3
Appearance of Kentuck Variants for the [ay] Diphthong
in a Typical Narrative Discourse

Speech Event #	Duration (seconds)	Topic	Appearance of [ay][a]	Variants		
				[ay]	[aː]	[aɪ]
1	6	family background (Q/A)	2	2	0	0
3	10	family background (Q/A)	2	2	0	0
4	16	family background (Q/A)	3	3	0	0
5	3	family background (Q/A)	1	1	0	0
7	8	family background (Q/A)	1	0	0	1
8	15	children	3	0	0	3
9	8	going back to Kentucky	1	0	0	1
12	13	going back to Kentucky	2	0	1	1
14	15	going back to Kentucky	3	3	0	0
15	23	Lewis County	1	0	1	0
16	67	jobs in cutover region	8	1	2	5
17	35	back to Kentucky	4	0	2	2
20	62	returning to Crandon	8	1	1	6
23	25	foods at home	2	0	1	1
26	10	use of lard	1	1	0	0
27	25	making soap	3	0	0	3
28	10	Kentuck Day in Crandon	1	0	0	1
29	35	Old Kentuck's history	1	0	0	1
31	25	schools and schooling	2	0	2	0
32	22	Conner (school and job)	1	0	0	1
33	19	companies	1	0	0	1
34	8	family reunion	3	0	0	3
35	45	relatives	7	0	6	1
36	17	relatives coming to Crandon	1	1	0	0
37	22	Canada and Alaska	4	1	1	2
38	12	trip to Kentucky	1	1	0	0
39	24	visit by parents	3	1	0	2
40	75	neighborhood historian	8	0	5	3
41	53	change in county line	7	5	0	2
42	19	seeing deer on the road	1	0	0	1
43	106	hit deer in road; aftermath	20	1	12	7
45	13	other Crandon informants	1	0	0	1
46	15	"Poke" nickname	3	0	1	2
47	12	other Kentucky folk	1	0	0	1
48	15	death of a neighbor	3	2	0	1
Totals			114	26	35	53

[a] Lexical items cited: *alive, all right, behind, by, died, driving, finally, five, guy, heights, I, Irish, July, knives, life, like, lye, might, mile, mind, mines, my, nice, night, Ohio, Oneida, retire, Rhinelander, right, side, ties, time, try, why, wife.*

McDavid records a similar expression—"kin to cain't"—with the same meaning. Cassidy found this inserted off-glide in two other Wisconsin counties (Dane and Kenosha), and McDavid recorded it in *can't* in two of the eastern Kentucky counties of origin (Carter and Lewis) and six of the contiguous counties (Bath, Breathitt, Estill, Mason, Menifee, and Owsley). The same off-glide appears with [æ] elsewhere, as in *aunt, branch* 'creek', *half, last,* and *past.*

Yet another feature of Kentuck speech in the cutover region is a clear rounded off-glide in words like *hog, log,* and *dog,* among others. This feature appears in the Wisconsin records (LANCS 29, item 2), but only in Green County, while McDavid recorded it several times in eastern Kentucky—in two of the counties of origin (Carter and Lewis) and six of the contiguous counties (Bath, Breathitt, Estill, Mason, Menifee, and Owsley). Other examples in Wisconsin include *off and on, hauled, Wausau, lost, all right, call,* and *daughter,* among many others.

Variant pronunciations of *chimney* were also recorded in the cutover region, both [tʃɪmlɪ] and [tʃɪmblɪ] (LANCS 6, item 7). The pronunciation [tʃɪmlɪ] appears in five other counties in Wisconsin, three in the southwest (Pepin, St. Croix, and Trempealeau) and two others (Douglas and Kenosha), while [tʃɪmblɪ] appears in two southwestern counties (Iowa and Grant) and in the city of Wausau in central Wisconsin. These two pronunciations also appear frequently in the LANCS records for eastern Kentucky: [tʃɪmlɪ] is cited in two of the counties of origin (Carter and Lewis) and five contiguous counties (Bath, Breathitt, Estill, Menifee, and Owsley); [tʃɪmblɪ] is also cited in Owsley County.

The replacement of final unstressed [ɚ] by schwa [ə], as in *father* (LANCS 49, item 4) was often cited in the cutover region, but the LANCS records elsewhere in Wisconsin do not cite schwa in this item. In eastern Kentucky, however, it appears in two of the counties of origin (Carter and Lewis, as usual) and three of the contiguous counties (Bath, Menifee, and Owsley). The item is missing in the notes from Breathitt County, and the retroflex [ɚ] is cited in other counties, including Estill and Mason.

These examples show that the LANCS field records often cite other appearances of features in the cutover region elsewhere in Wisconsin, though usually in the southwestern counties where there were other migrants from Kentucky. In some other instances, however, the LANCS records help to identify some features which were thought to be distinctive in Kentuck speech but turned out to be widespread elsewhere in Wisconsin (at least in 1940, if not now). This suggests that the Kentucks also preserve some archaic pronunciations. For instance, four different variants for *minnows* (LANCS 47, item 5) were recorded in the cutover region, including [mɪnowz], [mɪnɪz], [mɪnɚz], and [mɪnəz]. Since [mɪnowz] is widespread in Wisconsin, it seemed obvious that these other pronunciations were typical of the Kentucks and might all reflect eastern Kentucky origins. But the situation was a little more complex than that. It turns out that only the pronunciations [mɪnəz] and [mɪnɚz] actually show up in eastern Kentucky: [mɪnɚz] with the retroflex unstressed vowel is not cited elsewhere in Wisconsin, but is recorded in three of the contiguous counties in eastern Kentucky (Estill, Menifee, and Owsley); [mɪnəz] with the schwa appears in three Wisconsin counties (Grant, Green, and Portage) and in the city of Wausau and also is recorded in two of the counties of origin (Carter and Lewis) as well as five contiguous counties (Bath, Estill, Mason, Menifee, and Owsley). The pronunciation [mɪnɪz] or sometimes [mɪnɪz] turned out to be widespread in Wisconsin, appearing not only in the southwest, but all over the state, in 15 different counties (Bayfield, Brown, Columbia, Crawford, Door, Eau Claire, Fond du Lac, Juneau, Marathon, Outagamie, Portage, Prairie du Chien, Racine, St. Croix, and Trempealeau). It is only cited in Owen County in the Kentucky LANCS records.

Similarly, we initially thought that [ɔfn] and [ɔfm] were distinctive Kentuck pronunciations for *off of* (LANCS 28, item 1), which is usually [ɔfə] in Wisconsin, but the LANCS records again showed that [ɔfn] and [ɔfm] were at one time widespread in Wisconsin, appearing in ten counties (four in the southwest): Ashland, Brown, Dane, Douglas, Grant, Green, Juneau, Marathon, Pepin, Outagamie, Racine, and Trempealeau. These forms appear in only two of the eastern Kentucky counties (Bath and Estill); [ɔfə] appears everywhere else, including all of the counties which have been so frequently mentioned above (Breathitt, Carter, Estill, Lewis, Mason, Menifee, and Owsley). Thus, these putative Kentuck features turned out only to be archaic, not distinctive to the Kentucks or reflecting their settlement history.

"Kentuck" Grammatical Features

As has been seen, there are several phonological features which, when checked against the LANCS worksheets in Wisconsin and Kentucky, directly manifest the settlement history of the Kentucks in the cutover region and their origins in eastern Kentucky. A more marginal case can be made in terms of grammatical features. Many grammatical features recorded during the interviews were merely nonstandard and did not reflect geographical origins, such as past tense *seed, knowed,* and *throwed,* but a few appeared that did. One such feature is the use of *done* in perfective constructions with an unmarked infinitive or a past participle, as in

> They done give him more time
> They done sold off that land to the Kentucks
> She done taken sick last winter

LANCS map no. 45.4, which is part of the LANCS materials now held at the University of Georgia, shows that this construction is widespread in eastern Kentucky; indeed, it's all over the region, and appears frequently in Indiana as well as in West Virginia, Virginia, North Carolina, and Maryland (as shown in records of the Linguistic Atlas of the Middle and South Atlantic States). However, it is not attested in the Wisconsin LANCS records.

Another grammatical feature (although its grammaticality is in some dispute—cf. Wolfram 1979) is the *a-* prefix, as in *a-goin', a-comin', come a-runnin', a-learnin' and a-teachin',* etc. This form appears several times in our interviews, albeit inconsistently (usually in longer narrative segments), but is not cited elsewhere in the Wisconsin LANCS records. Whatever its meaning, however, it is characteristic of the Appalachian region and would therefore be properly included in this discussion.

Plural deletion also appears sporadically in our interviews, especially in quantitative expressions like the following:

> two or three year__ ago
> sixty-seventy mile__ away
> it [a still] used eight solid cord__ of four-foot wood a day

Such forms also have wide distribution in Kentucky, as well as appearing frequently in records from the Linguistic Atlas of the Middle and South Atlantic States.

"Kentuck" Lexical Features

The LANCS records have also been helpful to some extent in identifying in the speech of residents of the cutover region lexical items that come from eastern Kentucky, but since most of our material was collected through conversation and was not guided by a formal questionnaire, we have had to trust to luck to find citations in LANCS. Accordingly, we also examined Wentworth's *American Dialect Dictionary* (1944). Another useful source was the McDavids' article, "Folk Vocabulary of Eastern Kentucky" (1973), which includes citations from one of the counties of origin (Carter) and three of the contiguous counties (Menifee, Estill, and Owsley). Using all of these sources, we were able to trace some Kentuck lexical items back to eastern Kentucky. The following items were all cited in Wentworth (*bottoms* is also cited in LANCS 24, item 1, as well as McDavid and McDavid 1973; *branch, right,* and *poke* are also cited in McDavid and McDavid):

> *bottoms* or *bottom land* 'low land by a stream'
> *branch* 'creek' (they's a walk-log over the branch)
> *like to* 'about to' (like to split off, like to got shot)
> *meet up with* 'encounter' (we met up later with them fellers)
> *poke* 'bag' (called "old-fashioned," may be a put-on; also a nickname)
> *proud to know you* 'glad to meet you'
> *right* 'pretty, quite' (right smart gait, he's right friendly [dog])
> *soppy* 'pan drippings and biscuits'
> *trafficker* 'sheenie, sharp dealer in guns and valuables'
> *turned and laid off* 'plowed and rows marked for planting'

Conclusion

It seems clear that the continuation of Kentuck English in the cutover region is another example of a classic pattern in secondary (or better, tertiary) migration, when the speakers of a dialect move in substantial numbers and for similar reasons to a new location, and when their subsequent social and economic activities are such as to limit their interaction with the residents of surrounding communities. It doesn't mean, as popular wisdom might suggest, a pure, "frozen," and archaic dialect spoken only in Dogpatch and isolated from modern civilization; most of the speakers have become quite familiar with the conventions of the dominant dialect of their new home while retaining a significant number of forms which reflect their historical origins and maintain their family and community identity when they speak together. Perhaps this study of Kentuck speech also demonstrates the great value of the Linguistic Atlas fieldwork and at least a partial fulfillment of its original purpose—to provide the historical backdrop against which subsequent changes in the dialects of the United States might be better understood; indeed, it is hard to imagine how the speech of the residents of Wisconsin's cutover region could be adequately interpreted without the patient and thorough scholarship of the Atlas fieldworkers.

15

Elements of Midwestern Speech in Oklahoma

BRUCE SOUTHARD

FOR SOME CULTURAL geographers, Oklahoma is an enigma. In *This Remarkable Continent,* a map showing "General Cultural and Popular Regions" identifies Oklahoma as one of the "Regions of Uncertain Status or Affiliation" (Zelinsky 1982: 8–9). Surrounded by "The West" to the west, "The Middle West" to the north, and "The South" to the east and south, Zelinsky's Oklahoma occupies a niche reminiscent of the "No Man's Land" which formed its Panhandle—a land area unclaimed by any state until arbitrarily assigned to Oklahoma Territory by an act of Congress in 1890.

Those cultural geographers who do assign Oklahoma to a particular region present a conflicting melange of possibilities. Information taken from telephone directories, such as business names incorporating "Midwest" or "Southern," identifies the Panhandle and adjoining counties as the "West," the remaining northern one-third of the state as the "Midwest," the southern two-thirds as the "Southwest," and a small triangular area next to Arkansas as the "South" (Zelinsky 1982: 17). Raymond Gastil, however, identifies the lower two-thirds as a separate "Oklahoma" district within the "Western South," while the Panhandle and upper third of the state are placed in the "Western District" of the "Central Midwest" (1975: 174, 205). Finally, Michael Roark, in a "General Culture Area Map of Oklahoma Territory," depicts a "Possible Oklahoman Culture" in the central portion of the state, surrounded to the east and south by a "Southern" culture and to the north and west by a "Midwestern" culture (1979: 354). Roark points out that his analysis is predicated upon a study of Oklahoma Territory as it existed in 1900, and that not "until a study of later twentieth century cultural phenomena is done can this area be confirmed as a hearth [of a new regional culture]" (359). He does, however, embrace Zelinsky's "Doc-

229

trine of First Effective Settlement," which states that "whenever an empty territory undergoes settlement, or an earlier population is dislodged by invaders, the specific characteristics of the first group able to effect a viable, self-perpetuating society are of crucial significance for the later social and cultural geography of the area, no matter how tiny the initial band of settlers may have been" (Zelinsky 1973: 13).

For some dialectologists, Oklahoma is as puzzling as for cultural geographers. *Dialects, USA* presents Oklahoma as an island labeled "Transition Area" floating in a sea of isoglosses purporting to show dialect distribution in the United States (Malmstrom and Ashley 1963). As with cultural geographers, dialectologists who do attempt to classify dialect distribution within the state present differing pictures. E. Bagby Atwood, for example, contends that "in Oklahoma we seem to see a fading out of the Southern vocabulary as we move northward" (1962: 87). He goes on to suggest a possible "arbitrary" division of Oklahoma into northern and southern halves (88).

Gordon Wood, on the other hand, separates the state into two sections along a line that runs roughly from the northeast corner of the state to its southwest corner. The resultant southeast half of the state is identified as belonging to the "Mid Southern" portion of the larger "Southern" dialect area, while the northwest half constitutes a portion of the "Plains Southern" sub-dialect region (1971: 358).

In the conclusion to his own work, Craig Carver carefully points out that his analysis of data collected for the *Dictionary of American Regional English* results in "a broad sketch whose details will have to be filled in with a finer analysis of the atlas and other data collections" (1987: 249). His summary map of the major dialect regions (248) places much of the southeast quadrant of the state in the "Upper South," with the southeastern tip of that quadrant being in the "Lower South." The Panhandle and most of the upper third of the state are placed in the "Southwest" dialect region, while the remainder of the state, almost one-half of Oklahoma's land mass running diagonally from the northeast corner to the south central and southwest, appears to be in the "West Texas" region.[1]

Interestingly, data taken from the protocols for the Linguistic Atlas of Oklahoma (LAO) could be viewed as supporting each of these three characterizations of dialect regions in Oklahoma. I examined 50 Atlas items identified by both Wood (1971) and Carver (1987) as being characteristic of particular regional dialect areas.[2] Map 15.1, which shows the distribution of *seesaw* and *teeter-totter*, divides the state into northern and southern halves, giving Atwood's depiction of dialect distribution within Oklahoma. According to Carver, *teeter-totter* occurs

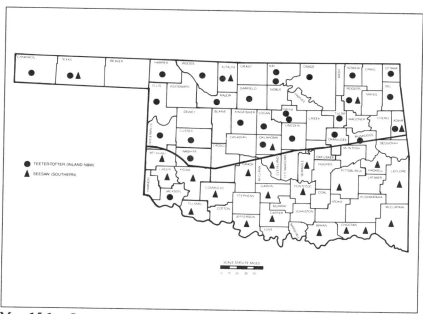

Map 15.1.   ○ teeter-totter (Inland N & W)   △ seesaw

in the Inland North-and-West dialect layer (1987: 274), but he does not characterize *seesaw* as representing a particular area. Kurath, however, points out that *seesaw* is the general term throughout the South, even though it also appears in New England and is gaining currency throughout the United States (1949: 58–59).

Map 15.2 shows the distribution of the Midland-and-West term *mud dauber* and the South II term *dirt dauber.* An isogloss separating the two terms would seem to correspond fairly closely with Wood's diagonal division of the state.

Finally, map 15.3 supports Carver's analysis by isolating both the Lower South term *mosquito hawk* (for *dragon fly*) and the Southern/South Midland term *red worm* (for *earthworm*) (Wood 1971: 30, 36) in the southeast quadrant of the state.

Yet, other terms surveyed present quite different pictures of dialect distribution. Map 15.4, showing the distribution of the South-and-West terms *singletree* and *doubletree,* would seem to indicate that the entire state should be considered part of a South-and-West dialect layer.

Map 15.5, on the other hand, which plots the North-and-West term *jag* (for *part of a load*) and the South II term *piece of a load,* suggests that Oklahoma belongs to a North-and-West dialect layer.

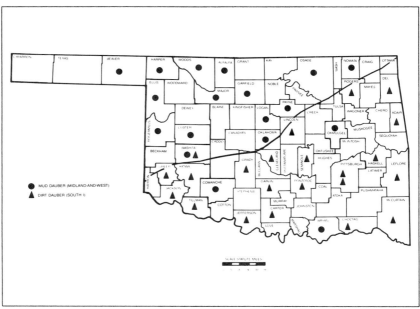

Map 15.2. ○ mud dauber (Midland-and-West)   △ dirt dauber

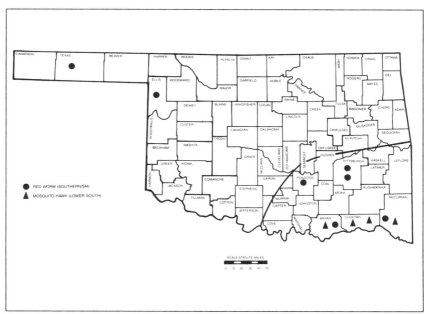

Map 15.3. △ mosquito hawk (Lower South)   ○ red worm (Southern/South Midland)

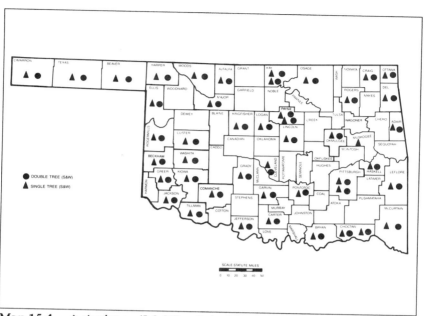

Map 15.4. △ singletree (S & W)   ○ doubletree (S & W)

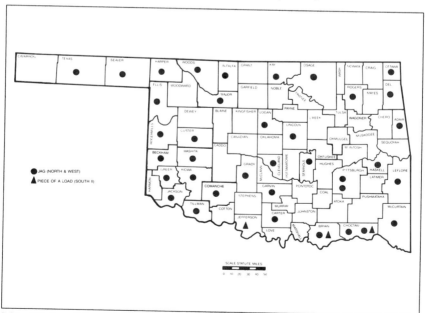

Map 15.5. ○ jag (North & West)   △ piece of a load (South II)

A complete analysis of the LAO data may help resolve these confusing pictures, presenting a clear depiction of dialect distribution which may assist cultural geographers in better defining Oklahoma's place within the regional cultures of the United States. Until that analysis is finished, however, preliminary studies of LAO data suggest an intricate correlation between the settlement history of Oklahoma and its current dialect distribution. The LAO, an autonomous regional project which is part of the larger Linguistic Atlas of the United States and Canada, is particularly significant in identifying dialect distribution within Oklahoma. It represents the most complete and detailed study ever conducted of language within the state. Moreover, it differs in three important ways from other American atlas projects: (1) all data were collected within a four-year span (1960–63) by a single interviewer, W. R. Van Riper, using a consistent interview style; (2) all interviews were recorded on tape and the original tape recordings were placed with the Library of Congress so that other scholars are able to corroborate phonetic transcriptions and calibrate their own transcriptions with those for the LAO; (3) all interviews were transcribed by a single, highly competent phonetician, Raven I. McDavid, Jr., whose interviews and transcriptions constitute a substantial body of the data collected for all the Atlas projects and whose participation ensured a continuity with the other Atlas projects.

Constituting a separate project within the framework of the Linguistic Atlas of the United States and Canada, Oklahoma is particularly important to dialect study, for it may provide a "laboratory case" for the study of language interaction when a sparsely populated area is rapidly settled by a new linguistic stock representing various dialects of one language. With the land runs which began in the late nineteenth century, the western half of Oklahoma ("Oklahoma Territory") was settled literally overnight by English-speaking peoples. The eastern half of the state, which constituted "Indian Territory" at the time of the land runs, soon had an Anglo admixture joining the Indian tribes which had been resettled predominantly from southeastern states. The Anglo settlers in Indian Territory followed more traditional migratory paths and timetables, gradually moving in from Missouri, and Arkansas and Texas in particular.

Map 15.6 depicts the land divisions within Oklahoma immediately prior to statehood in 1907. Indian Territory encompassed land reserved exclusively for Indian nations, particularly the "Five Civilized Tribes" (the Cherokees, the Chickasaws, the Choctaws, the Creeks, and the Seminoles) whose allotments are identified by tribal name on map 15.6.

Earlier, from 1830 to 1855, virtually all of Oklahoma save the

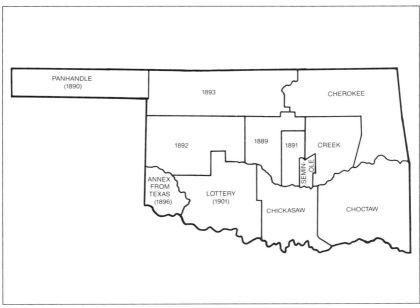

Map 15.6. Oklahoma land divisions prior to 1907.

Panhandle was dedicated by treaty to the Five Civilized Tribes. At the time of the Civil War, however, these tribes signed treaties of alliance with the Confederate States of America and even sent more than 5,000 men to fight on the side of the Confederacy (Gibson 1980: 120). Following the war, the tribes were forced to sign Reconstruction treaties with the United States. These treaties provided for the cession of tribal lands to the federal government; the Seminoles ceded virtually their entire domain (2.17 million acres) to the United States for fifteen cents per acre (Gibson 1980: 128). The other tribes were also forced to cede their westernmost lands, which supposedly were to be used to settle tribes from other parts of the United States.

Ultimately, pressure from Anglos who wanted access to cheap land led to these ceded lands, which constitute most of Oklahoma Territory, being made available via land run for settlement. The dates on map 15.6 identify the areas opened by land run from 1889 to 1893. The Panhandle, as mentioned above, was added to Oklahoma Territory by Congress in 1890 and was open at that time to settlement by homesteaders; it was divided into its present three counties at conferral of statehood in 1907. The area identified on map 15.6 as "Annex" was the former Greer County of Texas. The Supreme Court ruled in 1896 that the Prairie Dog Fork of the Red River, and not its North Fork, constituted the boundary between Texas and Oklahoma Territory and that Greer County be added to Oklahoma Territory; longtime settlers were allowed to file homesteads of 160 acres and to purchase additional land for one dollar per acre (Gibson 1980: 181). Finally, "Lottery" identifies the area of the Kiowa, Comanche, and Apache reservations opened to settlement in 1901 by lottery rather than land run.

Little is known of the type of English spoken or the extent to which it was spoken by the Five Civilized Tribes in Indian Territory prior to statehood. Full bloods apparently tended to remain isolated, speaking their native languages and leading a subsistence type of life, relying on hunting, fishing, and small crops for their livelihood. Their way of life gave rise to the derogatory term *blanket Indian*, which one may still encounter in Oklahoma. The mixed bloods, however, tended to emulate Southern whites, developing large farms and plantations in fertile river valleys and even owning slaves. Because the Indians' original homelands were in what came to be the Confederate States and because the mixed bloods emulated numerous elements of Southern culture, even sending their children to private schools and colleges in the South, one might reasonably expect their language to be generally Southern. The migrants from Texas, Arkansas, and southern Missouri who entered Oklahoma following statehood undoubtedly added to the development of a Southern or South Midland dialect in the former Indian Territory.

In contrast to the fuzzy picture of English in Indian Territory, a great deal is known about the settlers of Oklahoma Territory. Much of this information is summarized in Michael Roark's 1979 dissertation, "Oklahoma Territory: Frontier Development, Migration, and Culture Areas," which contains an extensive study of the origins of migrants to Oklahoma Territory. Although there is some variation from land-run area to land-run area, Roark's analysis of 1900 census data disclosed the following proportions for state of origin of settlers in Oklahoma Territory as a whole: "Lower Midwest 47%, Upper Midwest and Northeast 5%, Upper South 30% and Texas-Lower South 17%. Of the four states with the largest number of migrants three were adjacent to the Territory: Kansas (19%), Missouri (15%), Texas (11%), and Illinois (9%)" (131).

An examination of the land-run area of 1889 discloses particularly pertinent information about this earliest Oklahoma Territory settlement. The 1890 census, taken one year after the 1889 land run, shows a total population in the area of 53,822.[3] Table 15.1 shows the distribution by state of origin for the nine states contributing the greatest

Table 15.1
State of Origin of Settlers of 1889 Land Run

Kansas	10,048	19%
Missouri	7,421	14%
Texas	5,381	10%
Illinois	5,347	10%
Indiana	4,090	8%
Ohio	3,734	7%
Iowa	3,003	6%
Kentucky	2,895	5%
Tennessee	2,507	5%

number of settlers. Population figures are followed by approximate percentage of total population. Roark points out that "grouping the states together shows that 42% of the population of the Territory came from five Midwestern states and that 21% of the population came from three Upper Southern states. This suggests that a Midwestern cultural imprint was significant during the formative period" (1979: 96).[4]

In all of the land-run areas, moreover, the settlers were generally from the Midwest, as table 15.2 discloses, although there was some variation from land run to land run. The 1893 Land Run, for example, was predominantly composed of settlers from the Lower and Upper Midwest. Settlers in the Land Runs of 1889 and 1891 tended to divide into northern and southern halves. Compare Cleveland County, at the southern extreme of the 1889 Land Run area, with the other counties formed from that Land Run, for example. The 1891 Land Run shows a considerable disparity between the northern Lincoln county and the southern Pottawatomie. The 1892 Land Run area tends to divide into eastern and western halves, with such sparsely populated western counties as Roger Mills (6,190) having a considerably greater percentage of Southerners (79.8%) than the more densely populated eastern counties, such as Blain (10,658) with 34.2% from the South. The figures in table 15.2 represent percentages of total population and accordingly do not reflect density of population. Logan County, with a 1900 population of 26,563, for example, had a population more than four times that of Roger Mills County. Accordingly, these data give only approximations as to the influence of different areas of origin.

Land settlement in the Panhandle, Greer County, and the Lottery lands followed a different pattern than did settlement for the areas opened by land run. In both the Panhandle and Greer County, settlers had occupied the lands prior to their addition to Oklahoma Territory, and thus followed more traditional settlement patterns. In the lands

Table 15.2
Origin of Settlers in Oklahoma Territory (Percentages)

Land Run and County	LMW[a]	UMW[b] & NE	Upper South[c]	Texas & Lower South	Other US	Foreign
1889						
Canadian	45.1	13.1	19.9	5.7	1.9	14.8
Cleveland	21.5	3.2	38.0	31.6	0.6	5.6
Kingfisher	43.1	14.0	23.3	8.0	1.0	10.9
Logan	38.6	11.7	27.1	15.5	0.0	7.3
Oklahoma	35.6	9.0	28.8	14.4	1.2	11.5
Payne	52.9	10.1	26.2	6.9	0.5	3.8
1891						
Lincoln	45.1	6.7	30.2	11.4	0.4	6.7
Pottawatomie	23.6	4.3	39.9	26.0	1.2	4.7
1892						
Blaine	32.7	15.5	20.4	13.8	4.9	11.4
Custer	33.2	11.4	29.4	17.3	2.1	6.4
Day	31.7	9.0	22.7	27.2	0.0	9.0
Dewey	40.5	13.2	28.3	14.3	0.0	11.0
Roger Mills	10.4	6.0	36.7	42.6	0.0	4.4
Washita	17.7	3.4	29.4	33.5	2.0	14.4
1893						
Garfield	46.1	16.3	23.8	4.1	0.0	11.0
Grant	58.7	8.1	20.9	1.5	1.0	9.1
Kay	49.7	13.4	24.1	3.6	0.0	8.8
Noble	53.9	10.2	17.0	7.7	0.6	10.6
Woods	56.0	10.1	21.2	1.4	0.0	9.8
Woodward	42.1	17.4	20.5	9.7	3.3	7.7
Panhandle	44.4	14.0	11.1	8.4	5.6	16.7
Greer County	6.2	1.2	34.3	57.3	0.0	1.2
Lottery	not yet open for settlement by Anglos					

Source: Adapted from Roark (1979: 134); classifications from Roark (1979: 6–52).

[a] LMW = Lower Midwest = Central and Southern Ohio, Indiana, and Illinois, Kansas, Iowa, Nebraska, and Northern Missouri
[b] UMW = Upper Midwest = Northern Ohio, Indiana, and Illinois, Michigan, Wisconsin, and Minnesota
[c] Upper South = Kentucky, Tennessee, Southern Missouri, Arkansas, Western Virginia, and North Carolina

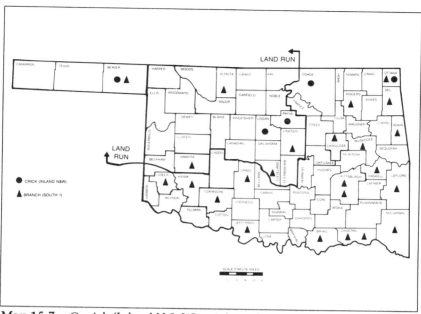

Map 15.7.   ○ crick (Inland N & W)   △ branch (South I)

assigned by lottery, the greatest number of registrants were from Texas and other Southern states.

Despite the complexity of the settlement of Oklahoma, there appear to be two distinct cultural areas within the state: (1) a Southern area composed of Indian Territory, the land annexed from Texas, and the land alloted by lottery; and, (2) a "Midwest" area composed from the land runs of 1889, 1891, 1892, and 1893. The Panhandle may also be added to this area, although its status is less certain because of population shifts prior to 1900 and subsequent migration from the area (its 1960 population being less than that of 1900).

Map 15.7 provides support for this analysis, showing the occurrence of the South I term *branch* 'running stream' and the Inland North-and-West term *crick*. An isogloss separating *branch* from the area where only *creek* or *crick* appear would correspond closely to the line in map 15.7 which separates the land-run area from the remainder of the state.

Map 15.8 shows the distribution of two South I terms, *Christmas gift* 'Christmas morning greeting' and *snap beans* 'string beans', as well as two terms identified with the Lower South, the Inland South *dog irons* and the Atlantic South *fire dogs* 'andirons'. Once again, these Southern terms cluster outside the land-run area.

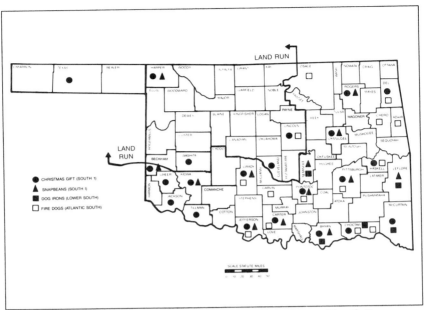

Map 15.8.   ○ Christmas Gift (South I)   △ snap beans (South I)
            □ dog irons (Lower South)   ■ fire dogs (Atlantic South)

Table 15.3 summarizes the number and frequency of possible occurrence of seventeen South I lexical items, five South II items, and eight North-and-West items. The table is separated into the land areas formed by the Indian Territory of 1900, Oklahoma Territory of 1900 (excluding the Panhandle and land annexed from Texas), the land settled by lottery in 1903, the land annexed from Texas, and the Panhandle.

The percentage of occurrence of these terms supports the thesis that the land-run area (Oklahoma Territory) differs in language use from the rest of Oklahoma. The percentage of possible occurrence of total South I and South II terms ranges from a high of 59% in land awarded by lottery to a low of 23% in the Panhandle. Indian Territory shows a frequency of occurrence of 49%, while Oklahoma Territory has a frequency of occurrence of only 28%; land annexed from Texas shows a frequency of 48%.

Other terms not included in table 15.3 show a clear difference of distribution between Oklahoma Territory (OT) and Indian Territory (IT). The Inland North-and-West term *teeter-totter* occurs with 100% frequency in OT, but only 45% in IT. The Inland Upper North-and-West lexical item *cherry pit* occurs with a frequency of 65% in OT, but only

Table 15.3
Lexical Items and Frequency of Possible Occurence
in the Linguistic Atlas of Oklahoma

	Indian Territory (N = 22)	Oklahoma Territory (N = 17)	Lottery Lands (N = 5)	Annexed from Texas (N = 3)	Panhandle (N = 3)
South I Terms					
pully bone	18 (82%)	11 (65%)	2 (40%)	2 (67%)	1 (33%)
comfort	14 (64%)	10 (59%)	5 (100%)	1 (33%)	3 (100%)
light bread	14 (64%)	10 (59%)	3 (60%)	3 (100%)	1 (33%)
branch	14 (64%)	3 (18%)	4 (80%)	1 (33%)	1 (33%)
quarter 'til	13 (59%)	14 (82%)	5 (100%)	2 (67%)	1 (33%)
whetrock	13 (59%)	7 (41%)	3 (60%)	1 (33%)	1 (33%)
seesaw[a]	13 (59%)	3 (18%)	5 (100%)	2 (67%)	1 (33%)
toad frog	13 (59%)	3 (18%)	1 (20%)	2 (67%)	0
snake doctor	13 (59%)	3 (18%)	1 (20%)	2 (67%)	0
cherry seed	12 (55%)	6 (35%)	2 (40%)	0	1 (33%)
tushes	11 (50%)	8 (47%)	4 (80%)	1 (33%)	0
weather board	11 (50%)	7 (41%)	4 (80%)	1 (33%)	3 (100%)
Christmas gift	10 (45%)	3 (18%)	4 (80%)	3 (100%)	1 (33%)
paling fence	9 (41%)	3 (18%)	3 (60%)	3 (100%)	1 (33%)
snap beans	8 (36%)	1 (6%)	3 (60%)	1 (33%)	0
souse	6 (27%)	4 (24%)	4 (80%)	1 (33%)	0
male cow	2 (9%)	2 (12%)	0	0	0
Total	194 (52%)	98 (33%)	53 (62%)	26 (51%)	15 (29%)
South II Terms					
dirt dauber	14 (64%)	3 (18%)	3 (60%)	2 (67%)	0
tow sack	13 (59%)	5 (29%)	4 (80%)	2 (67%)	0
middlins	11 (50%)	1 (6%)	2 (40%)	1 (33%)	0
clabber cheese	4 (18%)	0	2 (40%)	1 (33%)	0
piece of a load	2 (9%)	0	1 (20%)	0	0
Total	44 (40%)	9 (11%)	12 (48%)	6 (40%)	0
South I & II	238 (49%)	107 (29%)	65 (59%)	32 (48%)	15 (23%)
North-and-West Terms					
jag	16 (73%)	11 (65%)	4 (80%)	3 (100%)	2 (67%)
sweet corn	12 (55%)	9 (53%)	2 (40%)	0	2 (67%)
head cheese	11 (50%)	11 (65%)	1 (20%)	2 (67%)	2 (67%)
toad	8 (36%)	11 (65%)	2 (40%)	1 (33%)	2 (67%)
comforter	5 (23%)	5 (29%)	0	2 (67%)	0
hay mow	4 (18%)	7 (41%)	0	0	1 (33%)
baker's bread	2 (9%)	6 (35%)	0	0	0
white bread	0	3 (18%)	0	0	0
Total	58 (33%)	63 (46%)	9 (23%)	8 (33%)	9 (38%)

[a] Based on Wood's classification.

27% in IT. In contrast, the Upper South *surly* (for *bull*) occurs with a frequency of occurrence of 32% in IT, but only 6% in OT. Lower South *mosquito hawk* and *red bug* occur with 14% and 27% frequency in IT, but do not occur in OT. The Inland South *dog irons* occurs with a frequency of 50% in IT, but only 6% in OT, while the comparable Atlantic South *fire dogs* occurs with a 23% frequency in IT, but does not occur in OT.

The frequencies of occurrence for South I, South II, and North-and-West lexical items were subjected to two statistical tests to determine whether the differing percentages were statistically significant. A one-way analysis of variance and a paired *t*-test were conducted for the five land areas of Indian Territory, Oklahoma Territory, lottery land, land annexed from Texas, and the Panhandle. Both statistical procedures test the hypothesis that the means of two groups of observations are equal; because the informants do not constitute a random sample of the population and because two or more responses could be given for each lexical definition, these procedures are suggestive rather than definitive.

Nevertheless, the frequencies of occurrence for the South I, South II, and North-and-West lexical items for Oklahoma Territory were found to be different in a statistically significant manner from the corresponding terms for Indian Territory. Moreover, the differences between Oklahoma Territory and the lottery lands were statistically significant. For South I and South II lexical items, the responses for the Panhandle were different in a statistically significant manner from those for Indian Territory and the lottery lands, and for South II terms only, the Panhandle differed from the land annexed from Texas. The small number of informants in the Panhandle, the lottery lands, and the annexed area, however, make these latter comparisons especially tentative.

Regardless, the statistical data for Oklahoma Territory, combined with information shown in maps 15.7 and 15.8, strongly suggest that an area in north-central Oklahoma, and perhaps extending into the Panhandle, constitutes a dialect area distinct from the remainder of the state. Originally settled by immigrants predominantly from the Lower and Upper Midwest, this area differs from the Upper Southern and Lower Southern areas which constitute the remainder of the state.

Should Zelinsky's "Doctrine of First Effective Settlement" apply to dialect distribution, the importance of this dialect area is profound, for the area encompasses Oklahoma's two major public universities, the University of Oklahoma and Oklahoma State University, as well as the state capitol in Oklahoma City. With governmental and higher educational functions focused in the area, then, one might expect this "Midwestern" dialect area to form the focal area for a prestige dialect which will expand its boundaries into the surrounding Southern dialect areas. The Linguistic Atlas of Oklahoma will constitute an important early picture of dialect distribution within the state which will allow later studies to determine whether this change in dialect distribution does indeed take place.

16

Regional Variation in Missouri

RACHEL B. FARIES and DONALD M. LANCE

THOUGH MISSOURI AND Kansas were not included in any of the regional atlases, these states have been surveyed for regional vocabulary use, and various limited studies have been conducted on both pronunciation and vocabulary. In the 1950s George Pace directed 5 master's theses on 38 counties in the central and northeastern parts of Missouri (Shull 1953; Raithel 1954; Faries 1954; Hoskins 1954; Sanders 1957). These were followed in 1967 by a doctoral dissertation by Rachel B. Faries that covered the entire state and included the data from the master's theses. Gerald Udell surveyed all of Missouri with both DARE and Atlas questionnaires in the late 1960s but has not published results as yet. In the late 1960s professors at Kansas and Kansas State Universities directed their students in systematically collecting vocabulary data in all but four counties, but to date only preliminary studies of the data have been done. Two master's theses (Wasson 1947; Johnson 1976) and a doctoral dissertation (Lusk 1976) have been conducted on the speech in individual cities, Columbia, St. Louis, and Kansas City; only the one in Columbia used the Short Worksheets developed for the Midwest. In 1974 we collected some data from the DARE files on the distribution of dialect forms in Missouri and surrounding states and have published only two short articles on procedures of analysis (Lance and Slemons 1976; Lance 1977). From the time of Vance Randolph onward,[1] articles and short studies have appeared on diverse topics (Wood 1963; Mock 1992; Murray 1987b; Lance 1985; Lance 1986), and recently Thomas Murray (1986a) published a book on St. Louis speech. However, none of the publications to date has included analyses or maps that attempt to show precise locations of dialect divisions within the states of Missouri and Kansas.

The first part of this chapter is based primarily on data from Rachel Faries's doctoral dissertation, which employed the 124 lexical items analyzed in Kurath's *Word Geography of the Eastern United States* (1949). As Atlas studies have been conducted west of the Appalachians, interpretation of the data has been somewhat difficult, particularly in areas that were not settled until the latter part of the nineteenth century. Robert Dakin reported that analysis of the data for the Ohio Valley is difficult because of the admixture of items from a number of areas from which the Midwesterners and Kentuckians had emigrated. The Ohio Valley, he says, is not "simply a transmontane extension of the seaboard Midland—nor even of the western Pennsylvania West Midland" (1971: 31).

While the Ohio Valley may be characterized as a secondary settlement area, states such as Missouri and Kansas are tertiary areas. As each area of the old Northwest and the Louisiana Territory was settled, the immigrants were Americans moving in from primary and secondary settlement areas in New York, Pennsylvania, Kentucky, Virginia, and the Carolinas, and new Americans coming directly from Europe. It is not surprising, then, that dialectologists such as Marckwardt (1957), Allen (1958, 1964, 1973–76), and Dakin (1971) had difficulty drawing dialect boundaries and that Shuy (1962), Frazer (1978a, 1979), and Lance (this volume) have found dialect islands in western Illinois and in Missouri. In the West, Reed (1954) and Metcalf (1972) found that by the time Americans had settled California, the diffusion of dialect items had made it virtually impossible to make clear dialectal divisions on the basis of the words analyzed in Kurath's *Word Geography* or from pronunciations in Kurath and McDavid's *Pronunciation of English in the Atlantic States*—except for drawing a few individual isoglosses for terms such as *bag* and *sack*, with the Midland and Southern word *sack* being more common in Southern than in Northern California, but with the Northern word *bag* in majority usage throughout the state.

In analyzing his data, Allen was able to draw clear isoglosses for many of the items in his survey of the Upper Midwest, but for many others he could not, though there were regionally distributed gradations that correlated with the isoglosses of the other terms; for these terms he displayed the data as percentages of use in each of the five states (Allen 1964: 238–41). In Faries's study of Missouri, only 62 of the 502 regional terms were distributed in such a manner that isoglosses could be drawn; the remainder were scattered throughout the entire state. The only area where there was fairly clear, though loose, bundling of isoglosses was the Ozark Highland; however, individual isoglosses extended from Southern Missouri into Central and Northeastern areas.

The "bundles" were not convincing enough for her to divide the state into distinct dialect regions, as Allen was able to do for the Upper Midwest.

The 502 regional terms surveyed in Missouri represent all of the dialect divisions established by Kurath and others in earlier Atlas studies.[2] See the figures in table 16.1; the index values to the right will be explained below.[3] As one can see from the table, the regional terms that occurred in the greatest frequency were those that Kurath and others had found to originate in the combined Southern and Midland areas, that is, the Coastal South and Pennsylvania and areas settled from Pennsylvania outmigration or transmigration. Other Kurathian areas that were well represented were North plus North Midland, South plus South Midland, and Midland. Thus, as a whole, Missouri must be seen as primarily a Midland state, with particular strength from the North Midland portion of the Midland area.

Table 16.1
Missouri Summary of the Number and Frequency of Expressions Used
in the Major Speech Areas of the Eastern United States

		Number of Expressions		Number of Occurrences
North		103		3,833
North and North Midland		58		7,731
North and Midland		12		3,389
North and South Midland		1		662
North and South		30		1,467
Midland		99		11,308
Entire Midland	37		7,018	
North Midland	50		3,451	
South Midland	12		839	
South		71		1,472
South and Midland		61		12,898
South and South Midland		55		7,800
South and North Midland		6		75
Total		496		50,635

Source: Rachel B. Faries, "A Word Geography of Missouri," PhD diss., University of Missouri, Columbia, 1967.

Note: Northern Index: 9,893; North Midland Index: 11,993; South Midland Index: 10,499; and Southern Index: 9,710.

The earliest American settlers west of the Appalachians migrated via western Virginia and western North Carolina, through the Cumberland gap into Kentucky, later into southern Ohio, Indiana, and Illinois, and in the 1780s and 90s into the Mississippi and Missouri River valleys of Illinois and Missouri.[4] These were the Southerners and South Midlanders, in the terms used in dialect studies. The Southerners were descendants of slave-holding old stock Virginians and Carolinians. The South Midlanders, many of them Ulster Scots, were descendants of Virginians and Carolinians who had originally settled in the western portions of these states. The Southerners were among the first to migrate to new territories, beginning at the turn of the century; they searched for large tracts of land suitable for growing cotton, tobacco, and hemp. The South Midlanders, most of them from Tennessee and western North Carolina, moved in family groups and settled in smaller self-sufficient communities. Map 12.2 (see Lance, this volume) shows the areas that had been settled by 1830.

In the 1830s, settlers from Tennessee, Kentucky, and Virginia continued to move into the land along the Missouri River as far as St. Joseph and into the Springfield Plain in Southwest Missouri. Kentuckians and Virginians from Southern regions that supported slavery settled along the larger tributaries on both sides of the Missouri River. The Mississippi delta area known as the Bootheel was settled largely by "plantation" Tennesseeans from the western part of the state. Emigrants from the Appalachian part of Tennessee settled in the Ozark Highlands away from the large rivers. The Appalachian Tennesseeans were not slave owners, in part because of their limited wealth.

By the time of widespread settlement of the northern and western plains in 1850 to 1860, immigration from Southern states had begun to decline, so these areas were settled primarily by Midwesterners. By 1861 all areas of the state had sufficient population to organize county governments (see map 16.1). Kansas was not settled until after the 1850s; map 16.2 shows the counties that were organized between 1855 and 1862 (Cook, in preparation).

When the Louisiana Purchase (that is, Missouri) was opened for settlement in 1803, there could not have been any immigrants from Ohio, Indiana, and Illinois, because those states were not yet settled themselves. The first permanent settlement in Ohio—Marietta—was founded in 1788, a mere decade before Daniel Boone established his settlement in St. Charles County (Missouri), Moses Austin was granted land in the lead mining region of Washington County, and North Carolina German-Swiss settled in Southeast Missouri. By 1830, a generation after American settlements had been established throughout

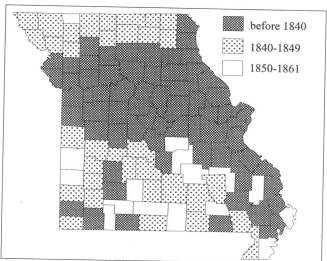

Map 16.1. Missouri counties organized in 1840–1861.

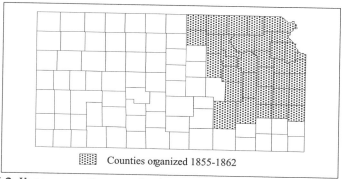

Map 16.2. Kansas counties organized in 1855–1862.

Ohio, Indiana, and Illinois, westward migration into Missouri included people born in these states as well as emigrants from the Pennsylvania and New York.

By the time many of the counties away from the Missouri River were being developed and Kansas was opened for settlement, more immigrants had started coming in from Northern states. After 1865, new immigrants had to sign an oath saying that they had not supported the Confederacy; thus further immigration from the South was effectively halted. The shift to immigration from Northern states, however, had already begun in the decade before the Civil War. Thus, when the northern and western counties and the St. Louis area experienced their greatest growth after the Civil War, new population was distinctly Northern. By 1870 well over half of the Missouri's 1.7 million residents were native-born, most of them of Southern or South Midland heritage. Twenty years later the population was almost doubled, to 3.1 million, many of whom were of Midwest or Northern origin.

The average age of the informants in Faries's study was 75 (they ranged in age from 61 to 105). Thus, most of the informants in this study were born between 1860 and 1900, during the time when Northerners and Midwesterners were immigrating into the northern and western plains of the state. By 1870, during that same period, about 290,000 Missourians had been born in Northern states and about 240,000 in Southern states. By 1890 Northern-born Missourians out-numbered the Southern-born two to one (Meyer 1973).

From the foregoing discussion, one would expect to find Southern and South Midland influence to be strong in the early settlement areas: up the Mississippi River to Hannibal, out the Missouri to the west, and in the Southeast and the Bootheel, with Northern and North Midland terms predominating in the northern and western counties and South Midland in the Ozark Highlands. The bundling of isoglosses mentioned earlier corresponds to this description fairly well, and other analyses discussed below reflect these facts even more graphically.

One of the problems that plague dialect geographers is that scholars collect data from a limited area and then attempt to establish regional boundaries on the basis of their own data alone. Map 16.3 is a composite of maps that have been drawn in six different studies. If the dialectologist does not know what lies across the state line, s/he may draw lines that do not match those drawn by a colleague in the neighboring state. A good example is Wood's (1971) Area G, in two parts; because he did not have access to data from the areas north of the Ohio River, he was unable to see that the northern boundary of the South Midland dialect should be in southern Indiana and Illinois; consequently, his and Dakin's lines (B, C, D) do not match very well. Map 12.3, from Lance's German essay in this volume, would represent an attempt to reach a compromise in "making dialectologists' lines match."

The settlement history of Missouri should lead any researcher to expect exactly the problem that Faries faced in trying to find clear bundles of isoglosses in Missouri. By 1850, when Northerners began immigrating in large numbers, most of the present-day counties had been organized, with Missouri Southerners having settled in every region. The opening of Kansas encouraged further immigration from

Key:
Kurath (1949): The North: 1 Northeastern
New England, 2 Southeastern New England,
3 Southwestern New England, 4 Upstate New York and
Western Vermont, 5 The Hudson Valley, 6 Metropolitan New York
City. The Midland: 7 The Delaware Valley, 9 The Susquehanna Valley,
9 The Upper Potomac and Shenandoah Valleys, 10 The Upper Ohio Valley,
11 Northern West Virginia, 12 Southern West Virginia, 13 Western North
and South Carolina. The South: 14 Delmarvia (Eastern Shore of Maryland and Virginia and Southern Delaware), 15 The Virginia Piedmont,
16 Northern North Carolina, 17 The Cape Fear and the Peedee Valleys, 18 South Carolina.
Marckwardt (1957), Allen (1964): A Inland North, B Midland.
Dakin (1971): B North Midland, C Mixture of North and South Midland, D South Midland.
Wood (1971): E Coastal South, F Gulf South, G Mid South, H Plains South.
Lance (1977): I North Midland, J Mixture of North and South Midland, K South Midland, L Southern.

Map 16.3. Composite map of six Atlas studies.

the corn-belt plains. With the Northern origin of most immigrants after the Civil War, by the end of the century, the North and North Midland dialects should have become predominant in the northern and western counties and in the industrial city of St. Louis, and Northern dialects should have diluted the speech of Southern populations in other areas.

Because the regional terms used in this study are spread over all areas of the state, not much meaning can be attached to the total number of terms of a given Kurathian classification within a particular county. To counterbalance the fact that each and every county contains some terms from all the regional classifications, we devised a formula. When one considers land mass, population, and immigration trends, one may hypothesize that the influence of Northern, North Midland, South Midland, and Southern terms (and combined classifications) may be determined by assigning numerical weights to the words from each regional classification in order to derive "indexes" for the contributions that each dialect has made in a particular county in Missouri, as well as in the state as a whole. For instance, to derive the index of Northernness, one adds together all of the Northern items (4,165 in table 16.1), one-half of the 8,058 North + North Midland items, one-third of the 4,647 North + Midland items, etc.; that is, Midland is half North Midland and half South Midland. Similar formulas were applied to derive "indexes" of North Midlandness, South Midlandness, and Southernness. It is also possible to combine totals to get an index of the influence of, for example, Southern and South Midland together, for generalized Southernness. Indexes for the major classifications are given at the right in table 16.1. The index for North Midland is the largest, 12% higher than for South Midland. The Northern and South-

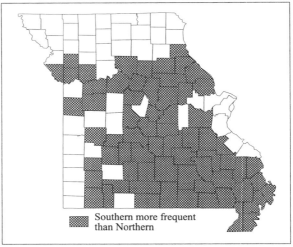

Map 16.4. Southern more frequent than Northern.

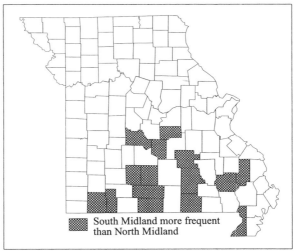

Map 16.5. South Midland more frequent than North Midland.

ern indexes are just about equal and are two-thirds as large as the two Midland indexes.

Maps 16.4 and 16.5 show the regional locations of the strengths of these indexes. On map 16.5 the shading indicates the counties in which the Southernness index is higher than the Northernness index—and the unshaded area is the opposite. A comparison of map 16.5 with the data in map 16.1 shows that the Southern base has remained stronger than the later Northern dialect forms in the counties organized before 1840, in most of the Ozarks, and in the Southeast. The northern three tiers of counties and the Osage Indian area of western Missouri were not heavily settled until after immigration from the North had begun; consequently, their population has a stronger Northern base. The unshaded counties along the Mississippi and Missouri Rivers in eastern Missouri and in portions of western Missouri are a special case: they have substantial German populations, whose speech is strongly North Midland.[5]

Map 16.6 shows areas of South Midland strength, and by extension North Midland. In only 15 counties—all of them in the Ozarks and the Southeast—is the South Midland index stronger than the North Midland. The more mountainous parts of the state were not inviting for North Midland farmers but apparently were attractive to Appalachian South Midlanders. The frequency of North Midland terms throughout the state may depend to a considerable extent on the presence of

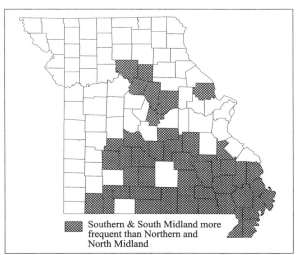

Map 16.6. Southern and South Midland more frequent than Northern and North Midland.

German immigrants, as evidenced in such borrowings and loan translations as *smear case* and *sheep buck*.

Map 16.6 displays the index of Southern and South Midland
combined to show where generalized Southern influence could be
found at the time Faries's informants were developing their language
preferences. The shaded areas are the counties where the combination
of Southern and South Midland dialect items still predominated in the
speech of Missourians born before the turn of the century. (Compare
map 1.3, based on DARE data, in this volume.) Albert B. Cook has
applied the formula to data collected in Kansas and found overwhelm-
ing dominance of North Midland influence, as one might expect from
settlement patterns (personal communication). Though it might be
difficult to validate our formula on some "pure" objective basis, map
16.6 matches both settlement pattern and popular notions about
regional differences extremely well.

Our maps, however, do not represent the last word on Missouri's
dialect geography. It must be kept in mind that when we work with
Atlas and DARE data we are analyzing the speech of many individuals
born in the nineteenth century—2 to 4 generations ago. Change has
occurred since Grandmother's time.

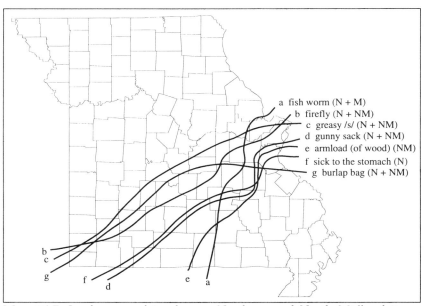

a fish worm (N + M)
b firefly (N + NM)
c greasy /s/ (N + NM)
d gunny sack (N + NM)
e armload (of wood) (NM)
f sick to the stomach (N)
g burlap bag (N + NM)

Map 16.7. Isoglosses and isophones: Northern and North Midland items
(speakers born between 1950 and 1960).

During the current century the North Midland dialect has continued to supplant the original Southern dialects of even rural Missouri. In the late 1970s Lance plotted the distribution of several key North and North Midland terms from questionnaires collected from the students in his classes in American language. The results are shown in map 16.7. North Midland usages now predominate in the Little Dixie area of central Missouri, but Southern usages are still strong in the eastern Ozarks and in the Southeast and the Bootheel. The language of students born after 1960 will no doubt replace many more Southern terms with North-North Midland or general terms.

It is not hard to document change. When Lance first came to Missouri in 1969, many students had answers for well over half of the questions on a questionnaire based on Kurath 1949; now the average undergraduate has never even heard most of the expressions on the questionnaire. In addition there are documentable changes like the ubiquitous "If I would have known you were coming I'd have baked you a cake" and the fact that *anymore* anymore may occur anywhere.

There are also some clear phonological changes. There has been further erosion of phonemic distinctions before /r/. Fifteen years ago, when Lance's colleague Patricia Harris would comment on his accusing her of saying her name wrong—"Herris" rather than "Harris"—about half of her students understood what she was talking about; now they *all* look at her quizzically, with no idea what she has just said. Another change is that, among undergraduates, there is no /ʊ/ before /r/: *poor* and *moor* are "pore" and "more" and *surely* and *Shirley* are homophones, and *Missouri* and *surly* manifest assonance.

In Missouri, we find instability and uncertainty. About twenty years ago, /æ/-raising, /a/-fronting, and /ɪ/- and /ɛ/-lowering were very strong, especially among young people from St. Louis County (West Countians); Harris, after a 13-year hiatus in teaching English language courses, informed Lance that she was surprised that the intensity and frequency of the raising, fronting, and lowering had abated. So this is a potential phonological change that may be erasing itself. Merger of *cot* and *caught* is still alive and well, however. Also noticeable is an increasing monophthongization of the /ai/ and especially /au/ diphthongs, as in *fine* and *house*. The change most noticeable to linguists in the past decade is the centering of all back vowels, with concomitant unrounding, though *put* and *putt* don't merge, perhaps because of a lowering of stressed schwa sound. There is also considerable instability in the loss (or maintenance) of the tense-lax distinction before /l/, as in *fill/feel*, *pull/pool*. These unstable phones make the teaching of phonetic transcription much more difficult.

Even though there have been many changes not only in individual linguistic items but also in the locations of isoglosses and dialect boundaries during the generations of recorded dialect history, it is important for us to continue to analyze existing data from the Atlas studies until we have made an adequate description of the language of the grandparents and great-grandparents of our students, so that future regional studies can be put into appropriate historical and linguistic contexts. We should also cooperate in devising new questionnaires and in systematically recording our students from year to year, saving and adequately labeling the tapes so that future studies can be based on more than the impressionistic comments that we have resorted to in the closing section of this chapter.

The Use of *all the* + Comparative Structure

ERIK R. THOMAS

I N SOME MIDWESTERN dialects, the following hypothetical sentences are possible:

1. Our car broke down, and Croton was *all the further* we got.
2. An hour's *all the longer* that show lasts.
3. That's *all the more comfortable* it ever gets in here.
4. I'm going *all the faster* I can go.

The *all the* + comparative construction is one of the more intriguing grammatical constructions in English, for two reasons. First, it is a well-known dialect feature (McDavid 1958). Secondly, its grammatical function is specialized and somewhat opaque.

Historical Implications

Crozier (1984) believes that the *all the* + comparative construction originated with the *all the* + substantive construction found in most forms of standard English, as in *It's all the evidence we need.* In some dialects, the *all the* + substantive construction can also be used, with the meaning 'only', with the pronoun *one,* and with singular forms of count nouns, such as *daughter,* with which it is not used in standard English in the singular:

5. That's all the daughter he's got.

According to Crozier, this extension continues in Ulster English to the *all the* + positive construction, as in his example, *That's all the far he went.* This construction is completely absent in southern England, however.

In the United States, the *all the* + positive construction is relatively uncommon and largely confined to the South. LAMSAS records (map 17.1) show *all the far* to have been fairly common in eastern Virginia and less common in North Carolina.[1] The entry in DARE shows scattered instances of *all the far* throughout the South, with the heaviest concentrations in Tennessee and Alabama.

Far more frequent in the United States is the *all the* + comparative structure, which Crozier feels was an American innovation. LAMSAS records show a heavy concentration of *all the further/farther* in West Virginia, Pennsylvania south of the northern tier of counties, southern New Jersey, northern Delaware and Maryland, and the Blue Ridge region of Virginia, and they also find the feature to be common in the Carolinas and Georgia. LANCS records (map 17.2), however, show only scattered instances of the structure across Ohio, Indiana, Kentucky, and northern Illinois. *All the further/farther* is somewhat common among LAUM informants (map 17.3) in Iowa and southern Minnesota (map 17.3), but is very rare among LAGS records (map 17.4), with only seven instances of it across the entire LAGS territory, as well as among LANE records (map 17.5). Atwood (1962) records it from only 11% of his informants in Texas and adjacent states.

The DARE entry provides a distribution that is similar but different in some important ways. The heaviest concentrations of *all the further/farther* in DARE do not occur in Pennsylvania and West Virginia, as with the linguistic atlas records, but in Indiana, with 21 of 25 (84.0%) of DARE communities giving the form, followed by Colorado (7 of 9, 77.8%), Ohio (36 of 47, 76.6%), Nebraska (6 of 8, 75.0%), and finally Pennsylvania (42 of 67, 62.7%). Only 4 of 13 West Virginia DARE communities (30.8%) had *all the further/farther*. The only Southern states in which a majority of the communities had *all the further/farther* were South Carolina (13 of 22, 59.1%) and Maryland (10 of 18, 55.6%). Since most of the linguistic atlas interviews (except for those in LAGS and a few in the other projects) were completed before the DARE interviews were begun, one can assume that DARE essentially represents younger generations than the linguistic atlases.[2] A comparison indicates that while *all the further/farther* appears to be declining in the South, it seems to be on the increase in the Inland Upper North. The linguistic atlases found very few instances in upstate New York, Michigan, and Wisconsin, but the DARE entry shows many instances in this area; in fact, 17 of 35, or 48.6%, of Michigan DARE communities had *all the further/farther*. Two Wisconsin LANCS informants reported this construction to be a recent phenomenon.

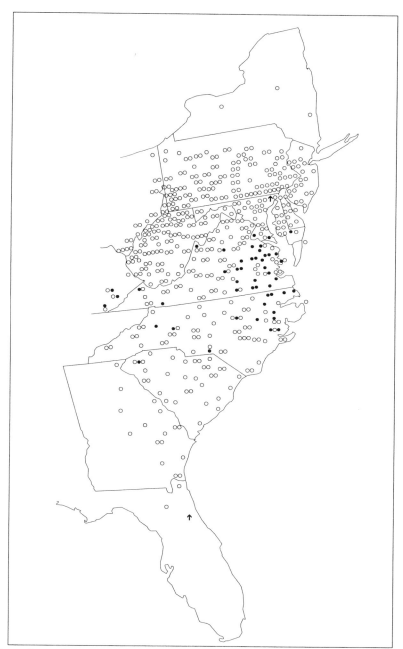

Map 17.1. *All the further* and related constructions in LAMSAS.

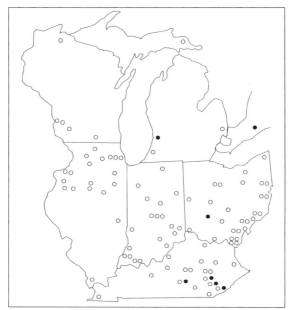

Map 17.2. *All the further* and related constructions in LANCS.

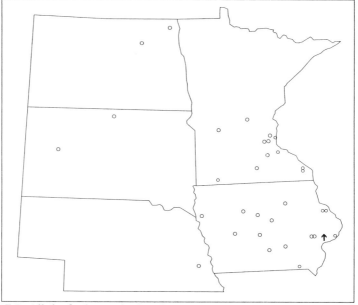

Map 17.3. *All the further* and related constructions in LAUM (vol. 2, p. 275).

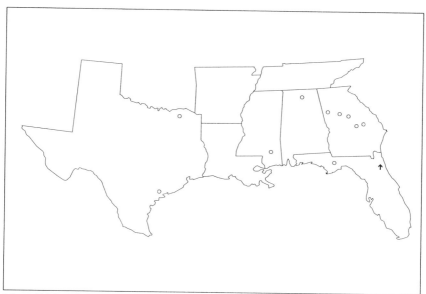

Map 17.4. *All the further* and related constructions in LAGS.

Map 17.5. *All the further* and related constructions in LANE (vol. 1, p. 49).

The linguistic atlases and DARE agree in some important respects as to the distribution of *all the further/farther*. Both show the feature to be practically absent in New England. Both also show a puzzling absence of it in central and southern Illinois. The discrepancy between the high DARE incidence and low LANCS incidence in Ohio and Indiana is problematical, however. It is possible that the LANCS fieldworkers did not probe very deeply for it, especially in light of the fact that its high incidence farther east in the LAMSAS territory ends abruptly where Guy Lowman's fieldwork ends. The DARE question used to elicit the item included the word *all*, which may have cued informants to give the *all the further/farther* construction.

Bryant (1962: 19–20) mentions that better educated informants prefer *as far as* to *all the further/farther*, but I have no other evidence as to the sociolinguistic factors affecting this feature. Linguistic atlas records are unclear in this regard. In short, however, it appears that the *all the* + positive construction was brought to America by Scotch-Irish settlers and became the *all the* + comparative construction. Wentworth (1944) does not list an instance of either one before 1891, but the lack of previous examples only illustrates the lack of dependability of written citations in dating linguistic forms.

While the Midwest seems to have become the stronghold of the *all the* + comparative construction, its continuing currency there is another matter. To test its familiarity there, I devised an experiment in which 98 sixth-graders from a rural junior high school in central Ohio rated three sentences with the construction, which were read to them orally, according to the following scale:

A.   This sounds like something I would say.
B.   This makes sense, but it isn't something I would say.
C.   This makes no sense.

Results for each of the three sentences are shown here:

The road was blocked, and Croton was all the further we could go.

A	23	(23.5%)
B	67	(68.4%)
C	6	(6.1%)
no response	2	(2.0%)

A pound is all the bigger they get.

A	24	(24.5%)
B	39	(39.8%)
C	33	(33.7%)
no response	2	(2.0%)

That's all the more comfortable it gets in here.

A	13	(13.3%)
B	47	(48.0%)
C	36	(36.7%)
no response	2	(2.0%)

The results indicate that only a minority of the sixth graders most likely use *all the* + comparative constructions themselves, but that most of them are at least familiar with the feature. They also indicate that the construction is more commonly used with adjectives forming comparatives with -*er* than with those forming comparatives with *more*. The reliability of the sixth graders in reporting their usages is indicated by the finding that they gave the expected answers to other questions in the experiment; for instance, given the choice between *you guys* and *you all* in a sentence, 80 students (81.6%) chose *you guys* and only 16 (16.3%) chose *you all,* which, as informal questioning of the same students showed, carries a stigma as a Southern feature.

Grammatical Structure

Because texts in which the *all the* + comparative construction appears are rare, my judgments of its grammatical usage must rely on my intuitions. It is usually equated with *as . . . as* or with the superlative, and has approximately the same meaning as those two constructions, but is more limited in its usage than either of those constructions, as the following examples illustrate:

6. He'll talk as long as you listen to him.
7. *He'll talk all the longer you listen to him.
8. That's the furthest distance we can go.
9. *That's the all the further distance we can go.

All the as a modifier is perfectly standard English in certain constructions. The *all the* + substantive form, such as *It's all the evidence we need,* has already been noted. In one particular grammatical structure, *all the* can be used with a comparative adjective in standard English, as in this example:

10. "[My big eyes are] *all the better* to see you with, my dear," said the wolf to Little Red Riding Hood.

Much can function similarly:

11. He feels *much the worse* for his experience.

These uses of *all* and *much* serve to intensify the comparative adjective that they modify. In the *all the* + comparative structure that is the subject of this paper, however, *all* serves to delimit the comparative that it modifies, much as a superlative form would.

An important difference between the superlative and the *all the* + comparative structure is that a superlative can be used to modify a noun, whereas *all the* + comparative normally cannot be. There is one possible exception to this rule, though. In my idiolect, the sentence

12. That's all the better of a shape he's in

can be reduced by the deletion of *of a* to

13. That's all the better shape he's in

where *all the better* becomes reanalyzed as a modifier of *shape.*

Another difference between a superlative and *all the* + comparative is that the comparative cannot take certain simple adverbs as modifiers:

14. That's the very prettiest she can be.
15. *That's all the very prettier she can be.

As with other comparatives, *all the* + comparative can take a *than* clause:

16. That's all the bigger than an apple they get.

Both adjectives and adverbs can take the *all the* + comparative construction, as the following examples demonstrate:

17. An hour's the longest (as long as) that show lasts.
18. An hour's all the longer that show lasts.
19. I'm going as fast as (the fastest) I can go.
20. I'm going all the faster I can go.

As an adjective, the *all the* + comparative construction can be used only as a complement with a form of the verb *be*. As an adverb, conversely, it can be used to modify a variety of verbs:

21. I tried all the harder I could.
22. He's washing dishes all the more quickly that he wants to. (This example is grammatical, but sounds awkward.)

One final constraint on the use of *all the* + comparative is that it cannot be used (in my idiolect, at least) with the adjective *much*:

23. That was the most (as much as) we could do.
24. *That was all the more we could do.

Instead, *all* alone must be used:

25. That was all we could do.

Wentworth, nonetheless, gives one example of usage of *all the more,* indicating that this form is acceptable in some idiolects.

Conclusion

The *all the* + comparative structure exists in American English as a grammatical feature confined to certain dialects, originally those with heavy Scotch-Irish influence in both the Lower North and much of the South but increasingly only those of the Midwest and Pennsylvania, as shown by a comparison of linguistic atlas and DARE records. Although in the past most of the attention given it has been focused on its use with the adjective *far,* it can be used with most adjectives that are inflected in the comparative, as well as with many adverbs. Its semantic content differs little from a superlative or an *as . . . as* construction, but its use is more restricted, except that it can take a *than* clause. Given the lack of research on its constraints, these restrictions are all the better one can define its usage.

Notes

Chapter 1

1. One problem in discussing Midwestern regional speech lies in the regional identity of the area itself, which is perhaps not as strong as that of New England or the South. This becomes apparent when we try to identify the boundaries of the region. Assuming that a region's identity exists largely in the minds of the people who live there, cultural geographer Wilbur Zelinsky (1980) set out to solve this problem by counting regional names in business titles, like "Midwestern Movers" or "Northern Bar and Grill." Examining the telephone directories of 276 major cities nationwide, Zelinsky determined the "conceptual boundaries" of the Midwest by including in the region all those cities where the term "Midwest" made up a plurality of the regional names used by businesses appearing in the yellow pages. This method identified as "Midwestern" the states of Ohio, Indiana, Illinois, Michigan, Wisconsin, Minnesota, South Dakota, Nebraska, Kansas, Missouri, and Oklahoma. But a secondary Midwestern area (where the name "Midwest" was the second most popular) encompasses a larger area including North Dakota and parts of Montana, Wyoming, Colorado, Alberta, Saskatchewan, and slivers of Arkansas, Tennessee, and Kentucky.

Preston's studies in perceptual dialectology also suggest confusion over popular boundaries to the Midwest. New York City respondents included the states of Montana, Wyoming, Colorado, North Dakota, South Dakota, Nebraska, Kansas, Minnesota, Iowa, Missouri, and the western halves of Wisconsin and Illinois. Southern Indiana students, on the other hand, designated only Missouri, Illinois and Indiana as Midwest-speaking (Preston 1989: 114).

2. Linguistic Atlas studies of the Midwest include the Linguistic Atlas of the North Central States, or LANCS (Ohio, Michigan, Indiana, Wisconsin, Illinois, and Kentucky) and the Linguistic Atlas of the Upper Midwest, or LAUM (Iowa, Nebraska, Minnesota, and the Dakotas) (McDavid et al. 1976; Allen 1973, 1975, 1976). The methods of collecting atlas data have been amply discussed elsewhere.

3. Analyzing his own data as well as the LAUM checklists, Houck (1967, 1970) at one point rejected Allen's Northern-Midland boundary in Iowa, arguing that no statistically significant difference existed between respondents on either side of the boundary. After encountering Carver's (1981, 1984) work and continuing further statistical analyses, however, Houck later (1986) suggested that a Northern-Midland dialect boundary does exist in Iowa, but at a lower latitude than Allen had placed it. In fact, his placement of the boundary would continue it in a generally western direction from Illinois, eliminating the northward break at the Mississippi. Houck was not certain enough of those results, however, to publish them in this collection.

4. An important difference between Carver's and my conclusions about the relative influence of Northern/Southern varieties in Illinois may arise from the nature of the DARE grid. As I have noted, it is a wider-meshed grid than that of LANCS, especially in Illinois. Carver's (1986) generalized Northern layer map (map 1.4) overlaps some of my South Midland lines shown here (map 1.3) and elsewhere (Frazer 1987a). But three of the DARE communities in western Illinois are distinctly non-Southern communities. Nauvoo, identified in map 1.4 by isogloss number 8 on the Mississippi just east of the Iowa-Missouri border, was originally a Mormon city which spent several years at virtual war with the rest of Hancock county in the 1840s; after Brigham Young's faction departed for Utah, much of the city was taken over by a French Icarian commune. Quincy, Illinois, which shows up as isogloss 7 in map 1.4, was a Yankee-dominated city from its beginnings. Hardin, in Calhoun County, showing up as 13 just above the St. Louis area, became dominated by Germans. No DARE interviews were conducted in McDonough, Schuyler, Brown, or Pike counties, where Southern settlement was more significant. DARE staff did plan an interview in Pike County, but deadlines expired before that interview was conducted. The Pike County community selected—Pittsfield—was yet another Northern colony, so the addition of that field record would not have solved the problem of Northern bias. Because Western Illinois was short an interview among the DARE data, then, I added the extra reading from "Arthur the Rat" from McDonough County, which in turn strengthens a Southern presence that appears greater on my maps than Carver's.

Chapter 2

1. Of course, this begs the question of whether or not voice characteristics are associated with areal varieties. Since work by Esling and others (e.g., Esling 1981) suggests that vocal quality is connected to regional varieties, the matched guise technique may not be as fail-safe as it was once thought to be. In addition, experiments in which one speaker has been said to accurately represent a large number of varieties (e.g., Giles 1970) are especially suspect; surely such performances capture only the grossest caricatures and are rife with inaccurate representations.

2. Both Indiana and Michigan respondents were subdivided into relatively well-balanced subgroups based on age, status, and gender, but in all the findings reported here, those groups are combined. Data collected from Appalachian immigrants and African Americans in southeastern Michigan were excluded from the findings reported here, and the Indiana respondents were all white.

3. The 7.00–7.99 rating for Washington is a result of many respondents' not distinguishing it from Washington, DC. In this task the states and areas were presented in an alphabetical list, not on a map.

4. Oddly enough, New Hampshire and Delaware belong to this group in the Michigan responses.

5. The confusion of Washington and Washington, DC, shows up even in the factor analysis (group 7).

6. These maps are generalized from the hand-drawn maps of United States dialect areas done by nonlinguist respondents. A microcomputer method of deriving generalized maps from individual ones is discussed in detail in Preston and Howe 1987.

7. Areas drawn by fewer than 15% of the respondents were not represented on the maps.

Chapter 3

1. This discussion is offered as a corollary inquiry and response (with a sociology-of-language emphasis) to many of the issues raised in William R. Van Riper (1973).

2. The approximately retroflex character of the Inland Northern [r] has remained consistent despite the hostility directed toward it by those in a prescriptivist mood since the early decades of this century. George Philip Krapp noted that before consonants and in final position, the preferred [ɹ] sound was being replaced with [r], or the "guttural r, heard in the North Central States and in the Middle West" (1919: 23); he remarked that "Englishmen and Eastern Americans often find this sound offensive" (1919: 23). Prescriptivists writing in later decades have gone so far as to describe the Midwestern [r] as "hot potato speech" (Schaye 1959: 82). Many authors describe Krapp's [ɹ] as conditioned by stress or by neighboring vowels: see Barrows (1922), Gross (1959), McMillan (1963), and Hibbit and Norman (1964). Others writing in a prescriptivist vein reveal, perhaps inadvertently, that Inland Northern [r] and the recommended General American [r] are one and the same: see Barnes (1946), Prator (1957), and Gordon and Wong (1961).

3. Note that the early work of William Labov has a dominant emphasis on no groups higher than those in the upper-middle class. It is interesting to observe that Labov demonstrates that linguistic insecurity is a phenomenon that attaches to the mastery of SWINE, and not to the mastery of the extremely inaccessible upper-class dialects. The sociolinguist Anthony S. Kroch is cur-

rently investigating the character of upper-class Northern dialects; for an orientation to his form of analysis see Kroch (1986).

4. See the remarks by Frazer in this volume (ch. 4, n1, below) concerning Kenyon's peculiar mis-estimate of General American speakers in the Midwest. What could have been his motive in using such figures?

Chapter 4

1. "General American" promoters claimed its distribution to cover the entire North American continent except for the Southeast and the Northeast. By the 1940s, however, linguistic geographers had discovered much diversity in the area supposed to harbor "General American." Alva Leroy Davis's doctoral dissertation (1948) and Hans Kurath's *Word Geography* (1949) showed a major dialect boundary dividing the Midwest. The myth of "General American" was further debunked by Albert Marckwardt (1957), Virginia McDavid (1956), Raven I. and Virginia McDavid (1956, 1960) and Harold Allen (1973–76). Further diversity shown by data from the Dictionary of American Regional English has been demonstrated by James Hartman (1985), Craig Carver (1987), and Frazer (1978).

The most blatant error among "General American" proponents was in Kenyon's 1930 claim of ninety million speakers. According to the 1920 census —the most recent data available in 1930—the population of the entire United States stood at only 105,710,620, leaving fewer than 16 million speakers of other dialects besides "General American." But the population of the South alone makes Kenyon's figure absurd. The population for the South Atlantic region (Delaware, Maryland, D.C., Virginia, the Carolinas, Georgia, and Florida) was given at 13,990,272; the population for the East South Central region (Kentucky, Tennessee, Alabama, Mississippi) was 8,893,302; figures for the West South Central region (Louisiana, Texas, Oklahoma, Arkansas) were 10,242,224). It seems unlikely, in those days of relative regional isolation, that Kenyon could have found enough "General Americans" in the South to round out his figure of 90 million, and his figure seems even more unlikely when we consider the millions of other dialect speakers outside the South—non-rhotic speakers in the Northeast, blacks in the cities, Pennsylvania dialect speakers, Midland speakers in the Midwest, immigrants who did not speak English at all—who did not speak Inland Northern.

2. I am indebted to William Van Riper (1973) for the history of "General American" from 1920 to 1970.

Chapter 5

1. My history of Chicago, necessarily brief and selective, is not flattering. I have lived in the city for forty years. My narrative of earlier days rests largely

on Spear (1967) and on Drake and Cayton (1969), the classic source. Much of the recent history I have seen. Some I lived. My main point: Chicago remains deeply, violently segregated. More of us may work "together," but we still live apart. On an index of residential segregation rising from zero for a perfectly random integration to one hundred for apartheid, Chicago scored 89 in 1960. In 1970, after a decade of national progress in civil rights, the index stood at 93. Change was reluctant to take hold of the city with big shoulders, but by 1980 its segregation rating had dropped—to 92 (see Farley and Allen 1989: 141). Soon scholars and statisticians will analyze the census data for 1990. Decent residents of Chicago hardly need the numbers.

During the last few months in my "integrated" but largely Irish Catholic neighborhood, there has been a resurgence of racist violence in line with trends across the kinder, gentler nation. A black boy across the street from me was knocked silly by three white thugs with a steel pipe that almost put out his eye. Five black teens driving through the community from a nearby movie house had their car stoned by white teenagers three blocks from my house. There was a racially motivated brawl at the public high school precipitated by white students protesting the failure of the local school council to renew a contract for the white principal. The police intervened and took special relish in beating black students. Such incidents are routinely downplayed by the civic-minded in the neighborhood, so I do not know how many I have missed.

Racist street crime by teenagers is a longstanding feature of Chicago's white areas, one of many devices employed to maintain segregation. My community prefers the machinations of its Planning Association, which contrives to steer black families moving into the neighborhood to its modest eastern half. The fancier west remains predominantly white. Nor is the community's enduring racism a mere mask for class hatred: black professionals have trouble being shown the "big houses" in west Beverly.

2. An essay in a collection demonstrating the variety of Midwestern English is not the place to suggest that variation in Chicago can be explained by a simple white/Northern versus black/Southern dichotomy. It cannot. In addition to diversity in the black and white communities, a thorough description of Chicago's Englishes would have to treat the several forms and degrees of "Spanglish" in the city's several Hispanic communities and of "Chinglish" in its Chinatowns, old and new. It could not ignore other modifications of English arising in the new immigrant enclaves of Middle Easterners and Southeast Asians, particularly on the city's North Side. In fact, a good student of language contact could have a field decade in Chicago, for the city is returning, in some measure, to its multi-dialectal and polyglot status of a hundred years ago. New Polish refugees from the repression of Solidarity, Ethiopians fleeing starvation, Haitian boat people and others all add to the uneasily shifting mosaic of language and culture which constitutes Chicago today.

3. In this case, we cannot see very far: there are obvious difficulties in documenting the past of a dialect not often written even in its present form but spoken since long before the advent of audio or video tapes. Written represen-

tations of the dialect by other speakers pose many problems, from the phonetic limitations of ordinary spelling to the technical competence and racial attitudes of the writers. The best records we have, WPA slave narratives, are of variable worth as linguistic data, being devalued, in part, by stereotypes from popular and literary traditions of dialect imitation (Wolfram 1990: 122–26). Although the WPA interviews extend our vision of slave speech perhaps as far back as 1835, that is more than two centuries after the first black slaves were brought to North America and a mere generation before emancipation.

However, lack of strong evidence has not led, in recent years, to a shortage of strong conclusions about the history and structure of black American English. It has become widely accepted opinion—some would say dogma—that "negro dialect differs from other Southern speech because its deep structure is different," having originated "in some proto-creole grammatical structure" (Beryl Bailey 1965: 172); and, more specifically, that "the system of its verbs . . . reveals the greatest difference from white American dialects—as from British dialects—and the closest resemblance to its pidgin and creole ancestors and relatives" (Dillard 1972: 40). The certitude of these and similar pronouncements, which are not seriously challenged often enough, contrasts sharply with the uncertainties of the evidence, which frequently points in rather different directions. To Wolfram, for instance, the slave narratives suggest that "either (1) . . . creolization of VBE . . . was not as extensive as the creole hypothesis maintains, or (2) major . . . decreolization . . . took place . . . earlier than has been thought" (127). Nothing in this paper would contradict his judgment.

4. Obviously, it could still be true that invariant *be* has different sources in BEV and in white folk speech—indeed, in different varieties of each. However, even analysts who suspect that black *be* began, at least in some places, as a relexification of a creole aspect also recognize the likelihood that Scotch-Irish English supplied the *be* for this substitution.

On the basis of evidence taken from WPA interviews with former slaves in Texas and South Carolina, evidence which may be contaminated by linguistic stereotyping (see n3), Brewer argues, for example, that black speakers first used *am* as the relexifier, then replaced it, under the influence of Anglo-Irish, with uninflected *be*. Of course, coastal South Carolina is recognized by all as a creole area, homeland of Gullah. For another attempt to relate the evolution of *be* in the Sea Island creole to that of habitual *be* in BEV, see Rickford (1974). Needless to say, there is no agreement on how typical the developments in Gullah may have been of earlier stages in other varieties of black English. Rickford himself acknowledges the possibility of an Irish impact on the creole.

5. This rule turns out to be semantically satisfying as well as historically grounded. These virtues and its precision and simplicity have not prevented the persistence of a vaguer, problematic account of BEV's perfective *done,* one that originated with William Labov (1972b: 55–57) and that continues to influence his disciples—John Baugh (1983), for example (74–77).

However, in relation to perfective *done,* the "moderate" position that such sociolinguists have attempted to create does not appear to be much more than an artificial, diplomatic compromise between the extremes of creolists and dialect geographers feuding over the history and structure of BEV. The settlement will not withstand examination of the evidence about *(have) done*; it ought to be adjusted, in this case, in the direction of the dialectologists' view that the "peculiarities" of BEV, which are often superficial, are generally derived from Anglo-American dialects, not from an African-American creole.

Baugh (1983), of course, would not agree. Although "it is not altogether clear," according to him, "whether one should look to African-related sources" for ancestors of the perfective *done* found in BEV today or look for them in older English forms, "there are several good reasons," he asserts, "for separating the [contemporary] utterances of black and white speakers" and "for considering a compromise that would account for the distinctions" as having "originally been influenced by African sources" (76). Thus, Baugh is prepared to allow, in the spirit of concession, that black "street speech and white Appalachian communities" do "use *done* in some shared ways" (77). Yet his uncomplicated case for unshared usages fails—and fails in some of the same ways as his mentor's more elaborate one (see Herndobler and Sledd 1976: 187–89 for a critique of Labov's argument). Meanwhile, Baugh's assertion about the partly African history of *done* is bravely advanced without the slightest linguistic evidence or argument to back it up.

Like Labov, Baugh assigns "two main functions" to *done*: shared "perfective functions and an [unshared] intensifier role similar to that of *really*" (77). Of his seven examples of perfective *done* (77–78), Baugh claims "the intensifier function would appear to be best suited to": "So he went to where she was . . . and got the nerve to lie to me . . . talking bout he *done* went to work" (Baugh's ellipses). Skeptics like me, who have heard a fair amount of black speech, from frozen to intimate, and who have never been persuaded of this "intensifier function" for *(have) done,* will immediately suspect that Baugh's instance is a straightforward case of *had done,* with *had* removed according to principles suggested by Labov's own work, principles which allow certain verbals to be deleted in BEV if they can be contracted in Standard English. (Of course, Labov's classic formulation [1972b: 73] was that "the following general principle holds without exception: wherever SE can contract, BEV can delete *is* and *are,* and vice versa; wherever SE cannot contract, BEV cannot delete *is* and *are,* and vice versa." Labov discussed deletion of *have* only peripherally.)

Baugh provides a lengthy anecdote "to place the sentence in its proper context," but the story proves as unconvincing an argument as it is trite in plot and gives no grounds for believing we are dealing with anything here but an ordinary (nonstandard) past perfect. Recall that this sentence is, by his own account, Baugh's best example of the "intensifier role" for perfective *done*.

If *done* has no distinctive intensifier role in BEV, and if it is true elsewhere, as it is in Chicago and seems to be in New York, that *'ve done, 's done,* and *'d done* alternate in BEV with Ø *done* and with *have ('ve), has ('s),* and *had ('d),* then there is no apparent reason to suppose that the underlying rule for perfect aspect in

BEV is any different than it is in some dialects of NSWE: *Perf* → *have* + *en (do* + *en)*. There is good reason, however, to question Baugh's judgment that "It may still be too early to assume [conclude?] that *done* can [now] be analyzed as a general feature of [some] nonstandard American English dialects" (76, bracketed additions mine). And there is one less reason, finally, to see widespread, long-lasting prior creolization in the background of BEV. Indeed, even the brief of moderate proponents of creole influence is weaker, by one point at least.

6. Examples Noseworthy collected in Grand Bank include *I been heard it, I ain't been done it,* and *Have you been eat?* "This puzzling use of the verb 'be'," he says, "suggests that the action took place farther back in the past than any action denoted by . . . 'have' + past participle."

7. These unusual auxiliaries have been described in considerable syntactic detail in Herndobler and Sledd (1976). One purpose of this paper is to present further data in support of the analysis developed in that one (and refuted elsewhere, to my knowledge, by no argument stronger than disregard).

8. Most of the illustrative sentences in this article come from the spontaneous speech or writing of my students at Harold Washington College. None are hypothetical or elicited specimens. They were produced by men and women ranging from their teens to middle age.

9. If perfective *been* does derive from a creole marker of past tense, as often claimed, then a feature of creole deep structure which WPA narratives indicate must have grown quite rare in slave speech by the time of the Civil War has since become a common surface form in contemporary BEV. That is, at the same time that the construction has spread further in black dialects, it has been assimilated closer to the grammar of standard English.

It is interesting to speculate on the sociolinguistic dynamics which may have been at work in the evolution of these usages. Since *been* has also appeared as a past-tense marker in English-based pidgins and creoles of the Pacific (in Hawaii and Australia, for instance), where African influences cannot have been as strong and direct as they were along the routes for Atlantic slave trading, we might consider the possibility that origin of the form in this function owes less to distinctly African substrata than to more general principles that may operate in a variety of sociolinguistic contexts when English dialects' are being pidgin-creolized. How Irish immigrants to Newfoundland evolved perfective *been* (see n6) from the past-tense marker in Cameroon Pidgin or Hawaiian Creole remains somewhat puzzling.

Puzzle or no, perfective *been* seems more thoroughly English than has been admitted, and its putative ancestor, *been* of the past tense, may have been less specifically African than many linguists believe today.

10. Not all mathematical combinations of two modals are permitted. In Chicago's black English, *may, might,* and *must* tend to come first, *can, could, should, will,* and *would* to follow. Double modals in some other American dialects, black and white, seem to obey similar restrictions, apparently the result in Chicago of semantic features distinguishing two groups of the modals and blocking production of many possible pairs.

11. Limitation of forms like *must don't* and *might don't* to black speakers is reported for Jackson, Mississippi by Rebecca Moreton in Labov (1972b: 57); their absence from white speech in Anniston, Alabama is attested in Feagin (1979: 158). Such constructions do not figure in the data from white Texans in Boertien (1986).

12. The intuitions of other linguists about *be + done* have not even been as sharp as Wolfram's. Sometimes lack of data may have dulled their insight. Baugh (1983), for example, admits that *be + done* "appears relatively infrequently in the data [of his interviews]" (78). Examination of my numerous specimens and their systematic links to other auxiliary phrases suggests some corrections to Baugh's scanty and preliminary studies, to his first statement on this matter, for instance, which he repeats three times: "Future Perfective *Be Done*" "occurs with past-tense verbs" (77, 78, 79). Since it is a perfective, *be + done* precedes past participles, not past tenses, both of which are already confused and confusing enough in BEV (and in other dialects as well) without scholars making confusion worse confounded still.

And while we may agree with Baugh that "it is reasonable to assume," on the basis of present understanding, "that this [particular] usage developed among black English speakers" and does not have "any direct association with historical sources beyond the Americas," we might also ask, as a logical consequence, what the evidence is that *be + done* "is perhaps the result" of "relexification for a two-word construction" of "proto-African words" (77–78). If the synchronic data presented in this chapter do suggest historical hypotheses about *be + done,* one could well be that their collocation results from an original combination of English grammatical resources that has occurred in and been confined to the African-American community due to its ongoing segregation from the Anglo-American one, not necessarily because of its distant and limited connection to African linguistic traditions.

In investigations of *be + done,* gaps in their data have thus led sociolinguists to violate one of their cardinal precepts for the study of BEV: the need "to consider the interrelation of [any] feature with other features in the grammar" (Rickford 1986: 40). Baugh (and Rickford) fail to see how closely related *be + done* is to remote *been* and to many other auxiliary constructions exemplified here and systematically explained by subject raising. As a result, they propound an *ad hoc* account of *been* which is reminiscent of one proposed long ago by Loflin (1970), who tried to "account for sentences such as [*The chicken been ate something*] and [*I been washed the dishes*] by postulating a formative *E* of emphatic stress which could be given in the rule rewriting *VP* and which could be converted in a later morphophonemic rule into appropriate realizations. E.g., $E + v + ed \rightarrow been + V + ed$]" (26). Of course, to prove that "the deep structures of [black English] and [standard English] are different," BEV having "no perfective form, *have + En,* comparable to the one posited for" SE (14, 16), Loflin could hardly interpret the *en* in *been* as deriving from *have + en.*

Similarly stressing perfective *been* when it is stressed, and ignoring the rest of BEV's auxiliary system, Baugh argues that "stressed *been* is unique to street speech and Caribbean varieties of creole English" having "unique meanings" because "the stress on *been* is phonemic in black street speech" and "other dialects of English have not employed stress as phonemic (that is, semantic) boundary." It appears to him that "slaves introduced this phonemic stress alternation, since African tone languages exhibit similar . . . modifications of tone [to] constitute different . . . meanings" (80–82).

According to Baugh, an illustration of these unique meanings can be seen in the contrast between *She been married*, referring to "a prior state of affairs," and *She béen married*, indicating "that the marriage is well established and still active" (81). It is apparently no embarrassment to Baugh's theses, which actually derive from Rickford (1975), that precisely the same contrasting senses can be expressed in the English of at least one white Chicagoan by *She's been married* versus *She's béen married*. Unless I'm all wet, the distinctive force of remote perfective *been* is actually imparted by its underlying syntactic structure, which is solidly English, similar to many other constructions in the language, and duplicated, so it would appear, in at least one regional dialect in Newfoundland (see n6, above).

13. Needless to say, important sociolinguistic and political issues from battles in the sixties about forced bidialectalism for black children did carry over into later quarrels about correctness, testing and other matters involved in composition and literacy. (For examples and [jaundiced] commentary see Sledd 1988.)

14. Of course, everything should be done to secure democratic control of television and computer networks so that their own emancipatory potential can be explored and developed. Perhaps requirements of public access to cable TV systems will serve as one popular entrance to these powerful technologies of communication and control.

15. At Harold Washington College, the computerized system of tutorial instruction, PLATO, used to include a number of grammar lessons, one of them aimed explicitly at eradication of invariant *be*. I have not spoken with the philosopher lately to see if he is continuing his campaign, but it has so far not succeeded in eliminating this imperfect form from the language of our student body. Of course, prisoners in the cave are typically slow to learn.

Chapter 6

1. I gratefully acknowledge that this research was supported in part by a faculty development award from the College of Humanities and Fine Arts of the University of Northern Iowa. I would also like to thank Tim Frazer for his helpful comments on an earlier version of this chapter.

2. *Four Recorded Guises*
    1. Network English [*sic*]
        Miss Clark got mad at all of us, so she *made* us sit down and *told* us not to talk.

For an hour all *you could hear was* the clock going tick tock.
She thought I was a rat, and I guess maybe *she was right*.
It got worse in high school.
My best friend *was a girl named Tess . . .*
2. Vernacular Black English
Miss Clark got mad at us, so she *make* us sit down, and *tell* us not to talk.
For hour all *you hear is* the clock going tick tock.
She thought I was a rat and maybe *she right*.
It worse in high school.
My best friend *was Tess who . . .*
3. Network English [*sic*]
Miss Clark got mad at all of us, so she *made* us sit down and *told* us not to talk.
For an hour all *you could hear was* the clock going tick tock.
She thought I was a rat and I guess maybe *she was right*.
It got worse in high school.
My best friend *was a girl named Tess . . .*
4. Black accented English with historical present
Miss Clark got mad at all of us, so she *makes* us sit down, and *tells* us not to talk.
For an hour all *you could hear was* the clock going tick tock.
She thought I was a rat, and I guess maybe *she was right*.
It got worse in high school.
My best friend *was a girl named Tess . . .*

Chapter 7

1. The first permanent white settlers, who arrived in the 1830s, called the area Mount Pleasant. The name was changed to Farmer City in 1868.
2. For example, the urban phenomenon of /æ/-raising, which was observed by Callary (1975) as spreading to downstate Illinois from Chicago, was not observed in Farmer City, even in the most casual speech styles.
3. These include the towns of Mansfield, Le Roy, Dewitt, White Heath, and Mahomet. In general, these minor geographic differences have been ignored, as there was no indication that these students' dialects depended on their town of origin. It is clear that group membership was much more important than these minor political boundaries. Because listing the town of origin would serve to unambiguously identify certain individuals, such information could not be contained in this report. The term Farmer City dialect has been used to refer to all of the idiolects in the Illinois sample, usually without significant loss of accuracy.
4. Somerset (population 10,000) is located about 100 miles south of Lexington, Kentucky. The sample of seven speakers from Somerset is com-

posed of three generations of a large family who live on farms about 10 miles from the city.

5. The inclusion of the six female peer group members would needlessly complicate the figure by adding more cells and connections, without contributing significant information. The girls, however, were important and loyal members of both groups: no girl mentioned a boy of the opposite group as her friend, and vice versa. Readers desiring more specific information concerning the girls' social ties should write to the author.

6. Speaker 17, who insisted that speaker 1 be present at his interview, was unwilling to reveal any of his friendships other than that with speaker 1, even though the latter had not mentioned speaker 17 in his own private interview. Note, however, that speaker 17 was mentioned as a friend by core rednecks 11 and 13. See figure 7.14.

7. As vocal tract measurements were not made for the speakers in this study, the issue is hardly resolved. The ideal study of acoustic variability would combine the careful sociolinguistic methodology of the Farmer City project with reliable vocal tract data for each speaker.

8. It is, of course, an open question whether they exist as phonological rules or as lexically determined realizations.

Chapter 8

1. Portions of this chapter appeared as Murray (1983), Murray (1985), and Murray (1987a: 21–33); a much fuller discussion of the material presented here can be found in Murray (1986a).

2. Flexner (1976: 119), for example, labels the St. Louis-area speakers as using a Southern dialect, while Malmstrom and Ashley (1963: 43) consider the city strictly South Midland; Shuy (1967: 47, map 6) positions it as occurring almost exactly on the boundary separating the North Midlands and South Midlands, though Laird (1970: 156–57) depicts it as a Northern island in the midst of a sea of Highland Southern; and the conclusions of Dakin (1971: 35; cf. also Lance 1974a: 9–10) suggest that the Gateway City exists in a transitional area in which both North Midland and South Midland forms coexist, often in the same speaker.

3. I will not address the ethics and legality of surreptitious recording here; discussions can be found in Murray (1986b) and especially in Larmouth, Murray, and Murray (1992).

4. Strictly speaking, of course, all of St. Louis is something of an ethnic mix, though it still contains areas known to be primarily Italian, German, Irish, and so forth. For fear of skewing my data, these are the areas in which I avoided recording.

5. This does not necessarily mean, of course, that such self-consciousness was entirely absent, nor does it preclude such self-consciousness from interfering with my informants' responses in ways not apparent to me. As an anonymous referee for the University of Alabama Press has pointed out, the data I present for morphology/syntax and lexicon concern *reported* usage, not *actual* or *observed* usage, and should be understood as such.

6. So common is intrusive [r] in the Gateway City that it is not uncommon to see signs in laundromats sporting "warsher broke" or "warsher don't work"—and on one occasion I can recall seeing "warsher don't work" scratched out and replaced with "warsher *doesn't* work" (emphasis in original) by a would-be grammarian who either had a highly-developed linguistic sense of humor or was so used to pronouncing the intrusive [r] that he or she failed to correct it. All of this leads one to muse whether *warsh* will ever become as accepted as *lozenger* (which threatens to replace *lozenge* as the St. Louis standard) or *sherbert* (which is now widely accepted, even by desktop dictionaries, as a variant of *sherbet*).

7. I should perhaps note that all of Faries's informants were classed as "elderly."

8. The "St. Louis only" category is for the Gateway City's pronunciation of *sundae* as [sʌndə] rather than [sʌnde] or [sʌndi]. As far as I have been able to determine, nowhere else in the country is *sundae* pronounced as [sʌndə], and traditional and popular explanations (mostly by non-St. Louisans) for what is usually perceived as an abberant pronunciation have been less than flattering. Quasi-serious attempts to discover the nature of the problem appear at least annually in the feature column of some St. Louis journalist, but none has been convincing. The obvious linguistic explanation, of course, is that *sundae* has fallen prey to the phonological rule reducing unstressed vowels to a centralized vowel. As to why only St. Louisans should apply that rule to *sundae*—if indeed they are the only ones to do so—I have no real explanation. According to Professor Donald Lance of the University of Missouri (personal communications, Nov. 4, 1983, and Feb. 11, 1984), Gateway City folklore dictates that turn-of-the-century soda jerks in a particular South St. Louis drug store invented the pronunciation because they received moral objections to the selling of ice cream sundaes [sʌndez] (which were typically made with Coca-Cola, one of the secret ingredients of which was a derivative of cocaine) on Sundays [sʌndez]. (It was also either illegal or highly objectionable on moral grounds to sell any kind of ice cream—a frivolity—on Sunday.) Apparently the mere thought of creating and vending—on the Christian sabbath—drug-containing concoctions that were homophonous with the holy day of worship was sacrilegious. And rather than cease selling one day a week—which no doubt would have had a profound effect on sales receipts—the merchants of one drug store eased their assailants' objections through the promotion of identically-made but non-homophonous sundaes [sʌndəz].

Chapter 9

1. The social class of each informant was measured individually using the usual rankings—education, employment, income, dwelling, etc.—keeping in mind the many factors in individual life that can subtly affect such a determination. For a full discussion of the problem as it affects the status of women, see Nichols (1983: 64–65).

2. Callary and Labov both believe that complicated vowel shifts occurring across wide areas of phonological space require an acoustic analysis in which the variables are shown on scatter plots, creating a picture of the way the space is used by a particular informant or group. Such an analysis does provide the most accurate picture of sound change but was not possible here. However, for the purposes of the psychosocial correlations made here, an impressionistic analysis reveals the patterns of social and sexual stratification of certain features in the speech of the East Side.

3. I am indebted to James Sledd for the suggestion that raised /æ/ may be regarded as citified by some urban women. He points out that an isogloss might be drawn separating Skokie from its neighbor, Evanston, on the basis of the incidence of raised /æ/ in the speech of the Jewish women in Skokie compared to the absence of this feature in the speech of the female old guard from Evanston. Among Jewish women, raised /æ/ appears to be a prestige feature, whereas among the old guard in Evanston, it is not.

4. In the *Study of the Jewish Population of Chicago* (Chicago Community Inventory: University of Chicago, Philip M. Hauser, Director, 1954), the figure given for the percentage of the population of South Shore which was Jewish is unreliable. The figure is closer to 40%.

Chapter 11

1. All examples given in this chapter were recorded on tape in Columbus, Ohio, and are genuine: none is contrived.

2. Many recently-published dictionaries (*Webster's Ninth New Collegiate,* for example, as well as the second edition of *The American Heritage*) also recognize positive *anymore* in interrogative clauses as "standard English," but my own peculiar experiences with such constructions have led me to wonder whether all Midwestern speakers perceive them as such. I therefore include some instances of interrogative positive *anymore* in the list of sentences that follows.

3. See Malone (1930–31), Maxfield (1931–32), Ferguson (1931–32), Carter (1931–32), Cox (1931–32), Pound (1935), Lyman (1936), Krumpelmann (1939), McCain (1939), Russell (1941), "Editors" (1943), McDavid (1943), Tucker (1944), Gibbons (1944), Wentworth (1944), Dunlap (1945), Moore (1946), Eitner (1949), Klima (1964), Krueger (1965), Davis et al. (1969), Richmond (1972), Labov (1972a, 1972b), Hindle and Sag (1973), Hindle

(1975), Parker (1975), Wolfram and Christian (1976), Crozier (1984), Cassidy et al. (1985), Youmans (1986), Hagerty (1986), and a host of dictionaries and usage handbooks too numerous to mention (though Hagerty 1986, 55–67 provides a concise summary). The earliest of these dates should not be interpreted as a comment on the first appearance of positive *anymore* in the United States, however; indeed, most scholars believe that the usage was brought to America by Scotch-Irish immigrants, who began entering in great numbers through the port of Philadelphia in 1717.

4. I would like to offer my warmest thanks to those many colleagues, students, and informants who gave so selflessly of their time so that this project could be completed. Without all their help, much of my data unquestionably would never have been collected.

5. The research described here was supported in part by grants and sabbaticals provided by the Ohio State University.

6. For the surreptitiously-collected recordings, precise demographic information was available for only 12% of the informants; for all other informants, such information was approximated at the time the data were collected. If such information could not be reasonably approximated, the informant was eliminated from the study.

7. None of the informants from the surreptitiously-collected recordings or the students' folklore projects could participate in these written questionnaires, of course; their various uses of *anymore* were merely tallied in with the totals from the survey respondents.

8. It was hoped that this phrasing would force informants to rely more on their communicative competence and less on their conscious knowledge of right versus wrong, thus eliminating the problem reported above that Hindle and Sag (1973) had with their questionnaire.

9. There was also no variation in my data according to the race of the respondents, but since fewer than 10% of my informants were black, I consider such a fact both insignificant and unreliable.

10. As expounded, for example, by Bailey (1973: 67–86). For those less acquainted with the model, it posits that linguistic change spreads outward from the point of origin in much the same way that shock waves from an earthquake spread outward from the earthquake's focus, or ripples in a pond spread outward from the point at which a rock hits the water. Ideally, the waves in each case are concentric and spread outward at an even speed, but in realistic terms allowances must of course be made for any kind of interference: portions of an earthquake's shock waves may encounter more or less dense substances through which they must pass, which will hinder their outward progression at different rates: portions of the ripples in a pond may come into contact with any number of obstructions, which will slow down or entirely block their progress; and the spread of linguistic change may be hurried along or hindered by such variables as geographic and social barriers, demographic characteristics of potential users, speaker-attitudes, and so on.

11. Implicational scales constitute one method of analyzing linguistic variation (see Bailey 1973). In simplest terms, and for our purposes here, they

can be understood as being based on the notion that since linguistic variables arrive in a given geographic area or social class over a period of time, the appearance of a later-arriving variable in an individual speaker or group of speakers should imply the co-existence of an earlier-arriving variable as well.

12. As a matter of record, it may interest readers that the sentences most often responsible for causing an individual not to fit the implicational pattern in table 11.2 were 15 and 20, which were sometimes ranked higher than ninth and eighth, respectively.

Chapter 12

Portions of the research for this paper were funded by grants from the Chancellor's Year-End Fund in 1980 (Susan Flader, Project Director) and the Weldon Spring Fund of the University of Missouri in 1981 and 1982 (A. E. Schroeder, Project Director).

1. The Missouri Oral History and Folklore Project, begun in 1972, is directed by Adolf E. Schroeder of the University of Missouri–Columbia. The purpose of his study is to gather cultural and folkloric information for Missourians who still maintain Old World traditions; thus the interviews did not specifically elicit dialect information. As part of the project, I also interviewed several individuals in Ste. Genevieve County in 1980 and in Atchison and Nodaway Counties in 1981. For the present study, we copied sample portions of conversations from 33 of these tapes and transcribed them, looking for specific features of South Midland and North Midland pronunciation. Thirteen of the speakers lived within 10 counties with strong German settlement (8 males, 5 females), and 20 lived in counties with proportionately smaller German populations (14 males, 6 females).

2. The 10 counties are Perry, Ste. Genevieve, Jefferson, St. Louis, St. Charles, Franklin, Warren, Gasconade, Osage, Maries, and Cole.

3. The Illinois counties with considerable German populations are Calhoun, Madison, St. Clair, Monroe, Bond, Clinton, and Washington.

4. The five unpublished master's theses were Bettie Bronson Shull, "A Survey of the Vocabulary of Eight Western Missouri Valley Counties" (1953); Erna E. Raithel, "A Survey of the Vocabulary of Eight West Central Missouri Counties" (1954); Rachel B. Faries, "A Survey of the Vocabulary of Seven Eastern Missouri Valley Counties" (1954); Gordon Ray Sanders, "A Vocabulary Survey of Seven Northeast Missouri Counties" (1957). The doctoral dissertation was Rachel B. Faries, "A Word Geography of Missouri" (1967). See Faries and Lance (ch. 16) in this volume.

5. The two main dialect terms for cottage cheese in German are *Schmierkäse* 'spread cheese' and *Quarkkäse* 'curd cheese', the Pennsylvania term coming from the Rhineland dialects. The terms *curds, curd cheese,* besides being possible loan translations, are standard British terms for cottage cheese

that occur in New England and in the Coastal South; there were 11 occurrences in Missouri, only one of which was in the German area.

6. In the analysis of the taped data, I have expanded the "German area" to include the 10 counties mentioned above plus the community in Montgomery County where one informant lives (just across the River from the well-known town Hermann) and the community of Concordia in Lafayette County, because one of the principal features of this particular city is a small Lutheran college; both the college and the city reflect very strong German influence.

Chapter 15

1. Unfortunately, Carver's analysis of Oklahoma may rely entirely on data from the Dictionary of American Regional English, which itself relies much too heavily on informants from the eastern half of the state: of 46 informants from thirteen communities, 32 (70%) are from the former Indian Territory, 4 (9%) from lottery land, 3 (7%) from the Panhandle, and only 7 (15%) from the former Oklahoma Territory.

2. Unless noted otherwise within the text, I will follow Carver's (1987) terminology for dialect areas and will use his terms for identifying individual lexical items as being characteristic of a particular region. Essentially, Carver posits only two dialect regions, the North and the South. These regions, however, are analyzed into numerous layers, whose names I use within this paper without attempting to define them. Those interested in such definitions should consult Carver, especially his concluding chapter (1987, 245–49).

3. Census data are taken from Roark (1979), except for 1900 county totals, which are from the U.S. Census for 1900.

4. Roark's figures actually disclose that the five Midwestern states of Kansas, Illinois, Indiana, Ohio, and Iowa contribute 50% of the population, rather than 42%, and that the three Upper Southern states of Missouri, Kentucky, and Tennessee contribute 24% of the population, rather than 21%. This discrepancy may be accounted for in part by Roark's division of Missouri into Lower Midwest and Upper South portions and by his taking into account the parental home of settlers from Kansas.

Chapter 16

1. For a listing of Vance Randolph's many publications on Ozark language, see Randolph (1987), Randolph and McCann (1987), and Cochran and Luster (1979).

2. The classifications used here are those established in Kurath (1949: 11–49).

3. Faries (1967: 152). For a discussion of her statistics, see 172.

4. Faries (1967: 28). See also Gerlach (1976: 16–18) and Rafferty (1981: 36–37).

5. Lance (1985: 184–85). Timothy Frazer has found that German immigrants in Illinois consciously chose Northern dialects over the local South Midland models and were negatively biased toward both Southern people and Southern accents.

Chapter 17

1. Access to the project files of LAMSAS and LANCS was generously provided by William A. Kretzschmar.

References

Akmajian, A., R. A. Demers, and R. M. Harnisky. 1979. *Linguistics: Introduction to Language and Communication*. Cambridge: MIT P.

Algeo, John. 1985. "The Mirror and the Template: Cloning Public Opinion." Greenbaum 57–64.

Allen, Harold B. 1958. *Minor Dialect Areas of the Upper Midwest*. Publication of the American Dialect Society 30. University: U of Alabama P.

———. 1964. "The Primary Dialect Areas of the Upper Midwest." Marckwardt (1964) 231–41.

———. 1973–76. *The Linguistic Atlas of the Upper Midwest*. 3 vols. Minneapolis: U of Minnesota P.

———. 1985. "Sex-Linked Variation in the Response of Dialect Informants. Part 1: Lexicon." *Journal of English Linguistics* 18: 97–123.

———. 1986a. "Sex-Linked Variation in the Response of Dialect Informants. Part 2: Pronunciation." *Journal of English Linguistics* 19: 4–23.

———. 1986b. "Sex-Linked Variation in the Response of Dialect Informants. Part 3: Grammar." *Journal of English Linguistics* 19: 149–76.

Allen, Harold B., and Michael D. Linn, eds. 1986. *Dialect and Language Variation*. New York: Academic.

Annals of Knox County, Illinois. 1980. Galesburg: Republican Register Reprint.

Atwood, E. Bagby. 1953. *A Survey of Verb Forms in the Eastern United States*. Ann Arbor: U of Michigan P.

———. 1962. *The Regional Vocabulary of Texas*. Austin: U of Texas P.

B. G. Packer Papers, 1920–1930. Department of Agriculture Administration: Immigration Division Records, Archives Division Series 9/1/1– . Madison: State Historical Library of Wisconsin.

Bailey, Beryl L. 1965. "Toward a New Perspective in Negro English Dialectology." *American Speech* 40: 171–77.

———. 1966. *Jamaican Creole Syntax*. Cambridge: Cambridge UP.

Bailey, Charles-James N. 1973. *Variation and Linguistic Theory*. Arlington: Center for Applied Linguistics.

Bailey, Guy, and Marvin Bassett. 1986. "Invariant *Be* in the Lower South." Montgomery and Bailey 158–79.

285

Bailey, Guy, and Natalie Maynor. 1989. "The Divergence Controversy." *American Speech* 64: 12–39.

Barnes, Grace. 1946. *General American Speech Sounds.* Boston: Heath.

Barrows, Sarah T. 1922. *English Pronunciation for Foreigners.* Sacramento: Division of Immigrant Education.

Baugh, Albert C. 1957. *A History of the English Language.* New York: Prentice.

Baugh, John. 1983. *Black Street Speech: Its History, Structure, and Survival.* Austin: U of Texas P.

Bender, James Frederic. 1943. *NBC Handbook of Pronunciation.* New York: Crowell.

Bender, James Frederic, and Thomas Crowell. 1964. *NBC Handbook of Pronunciation.* 3d ed. New York: Crowell.

Blau, Peter M., and Otis Dudley Duncan. 1967. *The American Occupational Structure.* New York: Wiley.

Blunt, Jerry. 1967. *Stage Dialects.* Scranton: Chandler.

———. 1980. *More Stage Dialects.* New York: Harper.

Boertien, Harmon S. 1986. "Constituent Structure of Double Modals." Montgomery and Bailey 294–318.

Boorstin, Daniel. 1973. *The Americans: The Democratic Experience.* New York: Random.

Bracken, James K. 1981. "Sarah Burton Fenn's Diary of a Journey." *Western Illinois Regional Studies* 4: 115–35.

Bradford, William. 1624. "Of Plymouth Plantation." McMichael 33–51.

Brewer, Jeutonne P. 1979. "Nonagreeing *Am* and Invariant *Be* in Early Black English." *SECOL Bulletin* 3: 81–100.

Brink, Wesley R. 1882. *History of Madison County, Illinois.* Edwardsville: Brink.

Bryant, Margaret M., ed. 1962. *Current American Usage.* New York: Funk.

Butters, Ronald. 1989. *The Death of Black English: Divergence and Convergence in Black and White Vernaculars.* Bamberger Beitrage zur Englischen Sprach Wissenschaft. Frankfurt am Main: Lang.

Callary, Robert E. 1975. "Phonological Change and the Development of an Urban Dialect in Illinois." *Language and Society* 4: 155–70.

Carkeet, David. 1979. "The Dialects in *Huckleberry Finn.*" *American Literature* 51: 315–32.

Carmony, Marvin. 1972a. "Aspects of Regional Speech in Indiana." L. Davis 9–24.

———. 1972b. *Indiana Dialects in Their Historical Setting.* Terre Haute: Indiana Council of Teachers of English.

———. 1977. "The Regional Vocabulary of Terre Haute." *Midwestern Journal of Language and Folklore* 3: 3–34.

Carriere, J.-M. 1939. "A Creole Dialect of Missouri." *American Speech* 14: 109–19.

Carter, Charles W., Jr. 1931–32. "*Any more* Again." *American Speech* 7: 235–36.

Carver, Craig. 1981. "The Midland Dialect Nationwide." Paper presented to American Dialect Society, MMLA. Oconomowoc, WI, Nov.

——. 1984. "The Hoosier Apex: A Dialect Contour." Paper presented to American Dialect Society, MMLA. Bloomington, IN, Nov.

——. 1986. "The Influence of the Mississippi River on Northern Dialect Boundaries." *American Speech* 61: 245–61.

——. 1987. *American Regional Dialects: A Word Geography*. Ann Arbor: U of Michigan P.

Cassidy, Frederic G. 1953. *A Method for Collecting Data*. Publication of the American Dialect Society 20. University: U of Alabama P.

Cassidy, Frederic G., et al., eds. 1985– . *Dictionary of American Regional English*. Cambridge: Harvard UP.

Chambers, J. K., and Peter Trudgill. 1980. *Dialectology*. Cambridge: Cambridge UP.

Chapman, Charles C. 1878. *History of Knox County, Illinois*. Chicago: Blakely.

Chicago Commission on Race Relations. 1922. *The Negro in Chicago: A Study of Race Relations and a Race Riot*. Chicago: U of Chicago P.

Churchill, Ward, and Jim Vander Wall. 1988. *Agents of Repression: The FBI's Secret War Against the Black Panther Party and the American Indian Movement*. Boston: South End.

Clark, Thomas. 1972. *Marietta, Ohio: The Continuing Erosion of a Speech Island*. Publication of the American Dialect Society 57. University: U of Alabama P.

Clarke, S. J. 1878. *A History of McDonough County, Illinois*. Springfield: Lust.

Cochran, Robert, and Michael Luster. 1979. *For Love and Money: The Writings of Vance Randolph*. Batesville: Arkansas College Folklore Archives Publications.

Coggeshall, John. 1985. "Goin' to the Dawgs: the Rustification of America." Paper presented to American Folklore Society.

Conniff, Richard. 1988. "In Chattanooga: Anchor Talk." *Time* 7 March: 10–12.

Cook, Albert B., III. 1978. "Perspectives for a Linguistic Atlas of Kansas." *American Speech* 53: 199–209.

——. In preparation. "The Settlement of Kansas." *Word Geography of Kansas*. Ed. Cook.

Countryman, J. 1987. "Why Black English Doesn't Add Up." *New York Times Book Review* 1 Nov: 12–13.

Cox, John Harrington. 1931–32. "*Any more* Again." *American Speech* 7: 236.

Crozier, Alan. 1984. "The Scotch-Irish Influence on American English." *American Speech* 59: 310–31.

Curti, Merle. 1959. *The Making of an American Community*. Stanford: Stanford UP.

Daan, J., and D. P. Blok. 1970. *Von randstattotlandrand*. (Bijdra gen en Mededelingen der Dialecten Commissie Van de Konink liyke Nederlandse Akademie van Wetenschappen te Amsterdam, 37). Amsterdam: N.V. Noord, Hollandsche Uitgevers Maatschappj.

Dakin, Robert F. 1966. "The Dialect Vocabulary of the Ohio River Valley." Diss. U of Michigan.

————. 1971. "South Midland Speech in the Old Northwest." *Journal of English Linguistics* 5: 31–48.

Davis, Alva L. 1948. "A Word Geography of the Great Lakes Region." Diss. U of Michigan.

Davis, Alva L., and Raven I. McDavid, Jr. 1950. "Northwestern Ohio: A Transition Area." *Language* 26: 264–73.

Davis, Alva L., et al. 1969. *A Compilation of the Work Sheets of the Linguistic Atlas of the United States and Canada and Associated Projects.* 2nd ed. Chicago: U of Chicago P.

Davis, Lawrence M., ed. 1972. *Studies in Language and Linguistics in Honor of Raven I. McDavid, Jr.* University: U of Alabama P.

DeCamp, David, and Ian F. Hancock, eds. 1974. *Pidgins and Creoles: Current Trends and Prospects.* Washington: Georgetown UP.

Denning, Gerald. 1988. "Kansas Spanish Fertile in Chicanoisms: A Sociolinguistic Perspective Toward *ojala* + Complementizer Use." Ornstein-Galicia et al. 277–311.

Deutsch, Karl. 1953. *Nationalism and Social Communication.* Cambridge: MIT P.

Dillard, J. L. 1972. *Black English: Its History and Usage in the United States.* New York: Random.

Dingwall, William. 1978. *A Survey of Linguistic Science.* Stamford, CT: Greylock.

DiPaolo, Marianne. 1989. "Double Modals as Single Lexical Items." *American Speech* 64: 195–224.

Donahue, Thomas S. 1985. "'U.S. English': Its Life and Works." *International Journal of the Sociology of Language* 56: 99–112.

Drake, Glendon Frank. 1977. *The Role of Prescriptivism in American Linguistics, 1820–1970.* Amsterdam: Benjamins.

Drake, St. Clair, and Horace R. Cayton. 1969. *Black Metropolis.* Rev. and enl. ed. 2 vols. New York: Harcourt.

Dunbar, Leslie W., ed. 1984. *Minority Report: What Has Happened to Blacks, Hispanics, American Indians, and Other Minorities in the Eighties.* New York: Pantheon.

Dunlap, A. R. 1945. "Observations on American Colloquial Idiom." *American Speech* 20: 12–21.

Eckert, P. 1989. *Jocks and Burnouts: Social Identity in the High School.* New York: Teachers College.

Eckert, P., and W. Labov, eds. 1992. *New Ways of Analyzing Sound Change.* New York: Academic.

Editors. 1943. "Words, words, words." *American Speech* 18: 141.

Eichoff, Jurgen. 1971. "German in Wisconsin." *The German Language in America.* Ed. Glenn G. Gilbert. Austin: U of Texas P, 43–47.

Eisonson, John. 1958. *The Improvement of Voice and Diction.* New York: MacMillan.

Eitner, Walter H. 1949. "Affirmative 'Anymore' in Present-Day American English." *Papers of the Michigan Academy of Science, Arts, and Letters* 35: 311–16.

Elliott, Kennell M. 1978. *History of the Nicolet National Forest Service.* U.S. Forest Service, U.S. Department of Agriculture, and the Forest History Association of Wisconsin.

Emerson, O. F. 1891. *The Ithaca Dialect: A Study of Present English. Dialect Notes* 1.3.

Esling, J. H. 1981. "Methods in Voice Quality Research in Dialect Surveys." Warkentyne 126–38.

Falk, J. 1978. *Linguistics and Language: A Survey of Basic Concepts and Implications.* 2nd ed. New York: Wiley.

Faries, Rachel Bernice. 1954. "A Survey of the Vocabulary of Seven Northeast Central Missouri Counties." Master's thesis. U of Missouri.

———. 1967. "A Word Geography of Missouri." Diss. U of Missouri.

Farley, Reynolds, and Walter R. Allen. 1989. *The Color Line and the Quality of Life in America.* New York: Oxford UP.

Fasold, Ralph, and Roger W. Shuy. 1973. *Analyzing Variation in Language: Papers from the Second Colloquium on Ways of Analyzing Variation.* Washington: Georgetown UP.

Feagin, Crawford. 1979. *Variation and Change in Alabama English: A Sociolinguistic Study of the White Community.* Washington: Georgetown UP.

Ferguson, Charles A., and John J. Gumperz. 1960. "Linguistic Diversity in South Asia." *International Journal of American Linguistics* 26: 3, Part 3.

Ferguson, D. W. 1931–32. "*Any More.*" *American Speech* 7: 233–34.

Finley, Robert W. 1976. *Geography of Wisconsin: A Content Outline.* Madison: U of Wisconsin. Typescript.

Finnie, W. Bruce. 1972. *The Stages of English.* New York: Houghton.

Fischer, John. 1964. "Social Influences on the Choice of a Linguistic Variant." Hymes 483–88.

Fishman, Pamela. 1983. "Interaction: The Work Women Do." Thorne, Kramarae, and Henley 89–101.

Flexner, Stuart Berg. 1976. *I Hear America Talking.* New York: Simon.

Flom, George T. 1925. "English Loan-words in American Norwegian, as Spoken in the Koshkongong Settlement, Wisconsin." *American Speech* 1: 541–48.

Fodor, Jerry, and Jerrold Katz. 1964. *The Structure of Language.* Englewood Cliffs, NJ: Prentice.

Francis, W. Nelson. 1958. *The Structure of American English.* New York: Ronald.

Frazer, Timothy C. 1973. "The Dialect Subareas of the Illinois Midland." Diss. U of Chicago.

———. 1978a. "South Midland Pronunciation in the North Central States." *American Speech* 53: 40–48. Reprinted in Allen and Linn.

———. 1978b. "The Settlement History of the North Central States." Unpublished ms. LANCS.

———. 1978c. "Ohio and the 'North Midland' Dialect Area." *Midwestern Journal of Language and Folklore* 4: 45–52.

———. 1979. "The Speech Island of the American Bottoms: A Problem in Social History." *American Speech* 54: 185–93.

———. 1982. "Joseph Kirkland's *Zury* as Linguistic Evidence." *American Speech* 57: 190–97.

———. 1983a. "Cultural Assimilation in the Post-Frontier Era." *Midwestern Journal of Language and Folklore* 9: 5–23.

———. 1983b. "Sound Change and Social Structure in a Rural Community." *Language in Society* 12: 313–26.

———. 1986. "Microdialectology: Internal Variation in a LANCS Community." *American Speech* 61: 307–17.

———. 1987a. *Midland Illinois Dialect Patterns*. Publication of the American Dialect Society 73. University: U of Alabama P.

———. 1987b. "Attitudes Toward Regional Pronunciation." *Journal of English Linguistics* 20: 89–100.

———. 1987c. "Breaking New Ground in Dialectology." *American Speech* 62: 154–59.

———. 1990. "More on the Semantics of *A*-Prefixing." *American Speech* 65: 89–93.

Fromkin, Victoria, and R. Rodman. 1983. *An Introduction to Language*. 3rd ed. New York: Holt.

Gastil, Raymond D. 1975. *Cultural Regions of the United States*. Seattle: U of Washington P.

Gauchat, L. 1905. "L'Unité phonetique dans le patois d'une commune." *Aus romanischen Sprachen und Literaturen: Festschrift Heinrich Mort*, 175–232. Halle: Max Niemeyer.

Gerlach, Russel L. 1976. *Immigrants in the Ozarks: A Study in Ethnic Geography*. Columbia: U of Missouri P.

Gibbons, V. E. 1944. "Notes on Indiana Speech." *American Speech* 19: 204–06.

Gibson, Arrell Morgan. 1980. *Oklahoma: A History of Five Counties*. Norman: U of Oklahoma P.

Giles, Howard. 1970. "Evaluative Reactions to Accents." *Educational Review* 22: 211–27.

Gilligan, Carol. 1982. *In a Different Voice: Psychological Theory and Women's Development*. Cambridge: Harvard UP.

Gordon, Morton J. 1974. *Speech Improvement*. Englewood Cliffs: Prentice.

Gordon, Morton J., and Helen Wong. 1961. *A Manual for Speech Improvement*. Englewood Cliffs: Prentice.

Greenbaum, Sidney, ed. 1985. *The English Language Today*. New York: Pergamon.

Grootaers, W. A. 1959. "Origin and Nature of the Subjective Boundaries of Dialects." *Orbis* 8: 355–84.

Gross, Hildred A. 1959. *Speech Correction for Junior High Schools*. Detroit: Board of Education.

Gumperz, John J. 1954. "A Swabian Dialect of Washtenaw County, Michigan." Diss. U of Michigan.

Habick, Timothy. 1980. "Sound Change in Farmer City: A Sociolinguistic Study Based on Acoustic Data." Diss. U of Illinois.

Hagerty, Thomas John. 1986. "Attitudes toward English Usage as Applied to the Evolution of Positive *Anymore*." Master's thesis. Ohio State U.

Harris, Jesse W. 1948. "German Language Influences in St. Clair County, Illinois." *American Speech* 23: 106–110.

Hart-Gonzalez, Lucinda. 1988. "Current Population Survey and Household Spanish Maintenance Among Mexican Americans." Ornstein-Galicia et al. 25–44.

Hartman, James. 1966. "Pressures for Dialect Change in Hocking County, Ohio." Diss. U of Michigan.

———. 1985. "Guide to Pronunciation." Cassidy, p. xli–lxi.

Haugen, Einar. 1953. *The Norwegian Language in America*. 3 vols. Philadelphia: U of Pennsylvania P.

Herman, Lewis. 1967. *American Dialects*. New York: Theatre Arts.

Herman, Lewis, and Marguerite Shalett Herman. 1943. *Foreign Dialects*. New York: Theatre Arts.

Hermann, M. E. 1929. Lautveranderungen in der Individualsprache einter Mundart. *Nachrichten der Gesellschaft der Wissenschaften zu Göttingen, Philosophisch-historische Klasse* 11: 195–214.

Hernandez, Ramon R. 1979. "Forest History Association of America." *Proceedings of the 4th Annual Forest History Association of America*. Ed. Ramon Hernandez. Wausau: Forest History Association of Wisconsin.

Herndobler, Robin, and Andrew Sledd. 1976. "Black English: Notes on the Auxiliary." *American Speech* 51: 185–200.

Heymann, C. David. 1983. *Poor Little Rich Girl*. New York: Random.

Heys, S. 1988. "Black English Hurts Academics." *Des Moines Register*. 4 Sept.: 3C.

Hibbit, George W., and Richard A. Norman. 1964. *Guide to Speech Training*. New York: Ronald.

Hindle, Donald. 1975. *Pennsylvania Working Papers on Linguistic Change and Variation*, Vol. 1, no. 5. *Syntactic Variation in Philadelphia: Positive Anymore*. Philadelphia: U.S. Regional Survey.

Hindle, Donald, and Ivan Sag. 1973. "Some More on *Anymore*." Fasold and Shuy 89–111.

Hirsch, Arnold R. 1983. *Making the Second Ghetto: Race and Housing in Chicago, 1940–1960*. Cambridge: Cambridge UP.

History of McLean County, Illinois. 1879. Chicago: Lebaron.

Holbrook, Stewart H. 1950. *The Yankee Exodus: an Account of Migration from New England*. New York: MacMillan.

Hoskins, Jewell Mae. 1954. "A Survey of the Vocabulary of Seven Eastern Missouri Valley Counties." Master's thesis. U of Missouri.

Houck, Charles L. 1967. "A Computerized Methodology for Linguistic Geography: A Pilot Study." *Folia Linguistica* 1: 80–95.

———. 1970. "A Statistical and Computerized Methodology for Analyzing Dialect Materials." Diss. U of Iowa.

———. 1985. "The Iowa Northern-Midland Boundary Revisited: A Computerized and Statistical Analysis." Paper presented to American Dialect Society, MMLA. St. Louis, MO, Nov.

———. 1986. "Multidimensional Scaling as Statistical Analytic Procedure." Paper presented to American Dialect Society, MMLA. Chicago, Nov.

Howren, Robert Ray. 1958. "The Speech of Louisville, Kentucky." Diss. Indiana U.

———. 1972. "The Speech of Louisville, Kentucky." Abstract of Diss. Williamson 683.

Hunter, Albert. 1974. *Symbolic Communities: The Persistence and Change of Chicago's Local Communities*. Chicago: U of Chicago P.

Hymes, Dell, ed. 1964. *Language and Culture in Society*. New York: Harper.

Inkeles, Alex, and David Smith. 1974. *Becoming Modern*. Cambridge: Harvard UP.

Jensen, Richard. 1968. *The Winning of the Midwest*. Chicago: U of Chicago P.

Johnson, Irving. 1935. "A Study of the Amana (Iowa) Dialect." Diss. U of Iowa.

Johnson, J.A. 1868. Letter in *Home Missionary* 61: 6.

Johnson, Robert L. 1976. "A Brief Study of Dialect in St. Louis." Master's thesis. U of Missouri.

Kane, Lucile. 1954. "Selling Cut-over Lands in Wisconsin." *Business History Review* 28: 236–247.

Kehelenback, Alfred P. 1948. *An Iowa Low German Dialect*. Publication of the American Dialect Society 10. University: U of Alabama P.

Kenyon, John S. 1924. *American Pronunciation*. Ann Arbor: U of Michigan P.

———. 1928. "Usage Department." *American Speech* 4: 153, 324.

———. 1930. *American Pronunciation*. 4th ed. Ann Arbor: U of Michigan P.

———. 1934. "Pronunciation." *Webster's New International Dictionary of the English Language*. 2nd ed. Springfield, MA: Merriam, p. xxii–lxxciii.

Kenyon, John S., and Thomas Knott. 1944. *A Pronouncing Dictionary of American English*. Springfield, MA: Merriam.

Kenzer, Robert C. 1987. *Kinship and Neighborhood in a Southern Community*. Knoxville: U of Tennessee P.

Kirkland, Joseph. 1882. *Zury: the Meanest Man in Spring County*. Boston: Houghton.

Klima, Edward S. 1964. "Negation in English." Fodor and Katz 246–323.

Koepfli, Solomon. 1859. *Die Geschicte der Ansiedlung von Highland (The Story of the Settling of Highland)*. Trans. Jenny Laeser Kaeser. Edwardsville: Southern Illinois UP.

Komarovsky, Mirra. 1962. *Blue-Collar Marriage*. New York: Random.

Kornblum, William. 1974. *Blue-Collar Communities*. Chicago: U of Chicago P.

Krapp, George Phillip. 1919. *The Pronunciation of Standard English in America*. New York: Oxford UP.

———. 1925. *The English Language in America*. 2 vols. New York: Ungar.

Kremer, L. 1984. "Die Niederlandisch-Deutsch Staatzgrenze als Subjective Dialektgrenze." *Grenzen en grenz problemen* (Ein bundel studies nitgegren door het nedersaksich instituut van der R. U. Gronengen ter gelgenheid van zijn 30-jaric bestaan = *Nedersaksiche studies* 7, zugleich: Driemaandelijkse Bladen 36), 76–83.

Kroch, Anthony S. 1986. "Toward a Theory of Social Dialect Variation." Allen and Linn 344–61.

Krueger, Jorn R. 1965. "More on Anymore." *American Speech* 40: 159.

Krumpelman, John R. 1939. "West Virginia Peculiarities." *American Speech* 14: 155–56.

Kruse, V. D. 1972. "The Pronunciation of English in Kentucky, Based on the Records of the Linguistic Atlas of the North-Central States." Diss. Illinois Institute of Technology.

Kurath, Hans. 1928. *American Pronunciation*. New York: Society for Pure English.

———, ed. 1939. *Linguistic Atlas of New England*. Providence: Brown UP.

———. 1949. *A Word Geography of the Eastern United States*. Ann Arbor: U of Michigan P.

Kurath, Hans, and Raven I. McDavid, Jr. 1982. *The Pronunciation of English in the Atlantic States*. Ann Arbor: U of Michigan P, 1961. Rpt. University: U of Alabama P.

Labov, William. 1963. "The Social Motivation for a Sound Change." *Word* 19: 273–309.

———. 1966. *The Social Stratification of English in New York City*. Washington, D.C.: Center for Applied Linguistics.

———. 1970. *The Study of Nonstandard English*. Urbana, IL: NCTE.

———. 1971. "Methodology." *A Survey of Linguistic Science*. College Park: U of Maryland P.

———. 1972a. *Sociolinguistic Patterns*. Philadelphia: U of Pennsylvania P.

———. 1972b. *Language in the Inner City*. Philadelphia: U of Pennsylvania P.

———. 1973a. "The Linguistic Consequences of Being a Lame." *Language in Society* 2: 81–115.

———. 1973b. "Where Do Grammars Stop?" *Report of the Twenty-third Annual Round Table Meeting on Linguistics and Language Studies*. Washington: Georgetown UP.

———. 1982. "Objectivity and Commitment in Linguistic Science: The Case of the Black English Trial in Ann Arbor." *Language in Society* 11: 165–202.

———. 1987. "Are Black and White Vernaculars Diverging? Papers from NWAVE XIV Panel Discussion." *American Speech* 62: 5–12.

———. 1992. "The Three Dialects of English." Eckert and Labov n.p.

Labov, William, M. Yeager, and R. Steiner. 1972. *A Quantitative Survey of Sound Change in Progress*. Philadelphia: U.S. Regional Survey.

Ladefoged, P., and D. Broadbent. 1957. "Information Conveyed by Vowels." *Journal of the Acoustical Society of America* 29: 98–104.

Laird, Charlton. 1970. *Language in America*. Englewood Cliffs, NJ: Prentice.

Lambert, Wallace. 1967. "A Social Psychology of Bilingualism." *Journal of Social Issues* 23: 91–109.

Lambert, Wallace, et al. 1960. "Evaluational Reactions to Spoken Language." *Journal of Abnormal Social Psychology* 60: 44–51.

Lance, Donald M. 1974a. "Dialect Divisions in Missouri." Paper presented to American Dialect Society, MMLA. St. Louis, MO, Nov.

———. 1974b. "Missouri and Surrounding States." Paper presented to the annual meeting of the American Dialect Society. New York, Dec.

———. 1975. "Missouri Dialects Revisited." Paper presented to the Missouri Academy of Sciences.

———. 1977. "Determining Dialect Boundaries in the United States by Means of Automatic Cartography." *Germanistiche Linguistik* 3–4: 289–303.

———. 1985. "Dialect Features in the English of Missouri Germans." In *Memory of Roman Jacobson: Papers from the 1984 Mid-America Linguistics Conference.* Columbia: Linguistics Area Program, U of Missouri, 181–91.

———. 1986. "Settlement Patterns, Missouri Germans, and Local Dialects." *The German-American Experience in Missouri: Essays in Commemoration of the Tricentennial of German Immigration to America.* Ed. Howard W. Marshall and James Goodrich. Columbia: Missouri Cultural Heritage Center, U of Missouri.

Lance, Donald M., and Steven B. Slemons. 1976. "The Use of the Computer in Plotting the Geographical Distribution of Dialect Items." *Computers and the Humanities* 10: 221–29.

Landau, Sidney I. 1984. *Dictionaries: The Art and Craft of Lexicography.* New York: Scribner's.

Langacker, Ronald W. 1973. *Language and Its Structure: Some Fundamental Linguistic Concepts.* 2nd ed. New York: Harcourt.

Larmouth, Donald. 1990. "Belgian English in Wisconsin's Door Peninsula." Murray (1990) 135–43.

Larmouth, Donald W., Thomas E. Murray, and Carmin Ross Murray. 1992. *Legal and Ethical Issues in Surreptitious Recordings.* Publication of the American Dialect Society 76. University: U of Alabama P.

Lass, Roger. 1976. *English Phonology and Phonological Theory.* Cambridge: Cambridge UP.

LeMasters, E. E. 1975. *Blue-Collar Aristocracy.* Madison: U of Wisconsin P.

"Letter to Walter Lyon." n.d. *Executive Records Letter Books (October 24, 1899–March 19, 1900).* State Board of Immigration, Archives Division Series 128 (1/1/14). Madison: State Historical Society of Wisconsin.

"Letters to Henry Casson, Secretary of State." 1897. Executive Department of Immigration, Archives Division Series 126 (1/1/14). Madison: State Historical Society of Wisconsin.

Lewis, Brian. 1973. "Swiss German in Wisconsin: The Impact of English." *American Speech* 48: 211–28.

Linn, Michael D. 1980. "Duluth Area English." Paper presented to the American Dialect Society, MMLA. Minneapolis, MN, Nov.

———. 1984. Review of *The Dialect of the Mesabi Range*, by Gary Underwood. *American Speech* 59: 359–62.

———. 1988. "The Origin and Development of Iron Range Dialect in Northern Minnesota." *Studia Anglica Posnaniensa*, 75–87.

————. 1990. "The Development of Dialect Patterns in the Upper Midwest." Murray (1990) 15–30.

Lipset, Seymour M., and Reinhard Bendix. 1959. *Social Mobility in Industrial Society*. Berkeley: U of California P.

Loflin, Marvin D. 1970. "On the Structure of a Verb in a Dialect of American Negro English." *Linguistics* 59: 14–28.

Lowenthal, Leo. 1957. "Historical Perspectives of Popular Culture." In *Mass Culture*, ed. Bernard Rosenberg and David Manning White. Glencoe, IL: Free, 46–58.

Lusk, Melanie. 1976. "Phonological Variation in Kansas City: A Sociolinguistic Analysis of Three-Generation Families." Diss. U of Kansas.

Lyman, Dean B. 1936. "Idioms in West Virginia." *American Speech* 11: 63.

Macaulay, R. K. S. 1976. Review of *The Social Stratification of English in Norwich*, by Peter Trudgill. *Language* 52: 266–70.

Machlin, Evangeline. 1980. *Speech for the Stage*. New York: Theatre Arts.

Malmstrom, Jean, and Annabel Ashley. 1963. *Dialects—U.S.A*. Champaign, IL: NCTE.

Malone, Kemp. 1930–31. "*Any More* in the Affirmative." *American Speech* 6: 460.

Marckwardt, Albert H. 1957. "Principal and Subsidiary Dialect Areas in the North-Central States." Publication of the American Dialect Society 27: 3–15. University: U of Alabama P.

————, ed. 1964. *Studies in Language and Linguistics in Honor of C.C. Fries*. Ann Arbor: English Language Institute.

Markusen, Ann R. 1989. "City on the Skids." *Chicago Reader* 24 November.

Mathews, Lois K. 1909. *The Expansion of New England*. Boston: Houghton.

Maxfield, E.K. 1931–32. "The Speech of Southwestern Pennsylvania." *American Speech* 7: 18–23.

McCain, John Walker, Jr. 1939. "*Anymore*." *American Speech* 14: 304.

McConnell-Ginet, Sally. 1983. "Intonation in a Man's World." Thorne, Kramarae, and Henley 67–68.

McDavid, Raven I., Jr. 1943. "Miscellaneous Notes on Recent Articles." *American Speech* 18: 152–53.

————. 1958. "The Dialects of American English." Francis 480–543.

McDavid, Raven I., et al. 1976. Linguistic Atlas of the North Central States. Unedited field records. Chicago: Regenstein Library, U of Chicago. Microfilm.

McDavid, Raven I., and Virginia Glenn McDavid. 1956. "Regional Linguistic Atlases in the United States." *Orbis* 5: 349–86.

————. 1960. "Grammatical Differences in the North Central States." *American Speech* 35: 5–19.

————. 1973. "The Folk Vocabulary of Eastern Kentucky." *Zeitschrift fur Dialektologie und Linguistik*, Beihefte, NF 9 *(Lexicography and Dialectology: Festgabe for Hans Kurath)*, ed. by Harald Scholler and John Reidy. Wiesbaden, Germany: Franz Steiner Gerlag GmbH, 147–64.

McDavid, Virginia Glenn. 1956. "Verb Forms of the North Central States and Upper Midwest." Diss. U of Minnesota.

———. 1963. "*To* as a Preposition of Location in Linguistic Atlas Materials." Publication of the American Dialect Society 40: 12–19. University: U of Alabama P.

———. 1987. "Sex-Linked Grammatical Variation in Responses of Informants in LANCS." Paper presented to American Dialect Society, MMLA. Columbus, OH, Nov.

McManis, Carolyn, et al., comp. 1987. *Language Files.* 4th ed. Reynoldsburg, OH: Advocate Publishing Group.

McMichael, George, ed. 1974. *Anthology of American Literature.* Vol. 1. New York: MacMillan.

McMillan, James B. 1963. "Pronunciations." *Funk and Wagnalls Standard College Dictionary.* Ed. Ramona R. Michaelis. New York: Harcourt, p. xxii–xxiii.

Meisner, Martin. 1976. "Women and Inequality: At Home—At Work." *Our Generation* 11: 59–71.

Metcalf, Allan A. 1972. "Directions of Change in Southern California English." *Journal of English Linguistics* 6: 28–34.

Meyer, Duane. 1973. *The Heritage of Missouri: A History.* Rev. ed. St. Louis: State Publishing Co.

Miller, Michael I. 1986. "Discovering Chicago's Dialects: A Field Museum Experiment in Adult Education." *Field Museum Natural History Bulletin* 57: 5–11.

———. 1987. "Exploring Black Speech in Chicago." Meeting of the Dictionary Society of America. St. Joseph's University, Philadelphia.

———. 1989. "More Indexes for Investigating Chicago Black Speech." Paper presented to annual meeting of the American Dialect Society.

Milroy, Leslie. 1987. *Language and Social Networks.* New York: Blackwell.

Milroy, Leslie, and P. McGlenaghan. 1977. "Stereotyped Reactions to Four Educated Accents in Ulster." *Belfast Working Papers in Language and Linguistics* 2: 4.

Mock, Carol C. 1992. "The Impact of the Ozark Drawl: The Variable Shift of the English Diphthong /ey/." Eckert and Labov n.p.

Montgomery, Michael, and Guy Bailey, eds. 1986. *Language Variety in the South: Perspectives in Black and White.* University: U of Alabama P.

"Moonshine Legend Colors Crandon History." 1982. *Green Bay Press Gazette* 10 Oct.

Moore, Arthur K. 1946. "New Light on Affirmative 'Anymore'." *American Speech* 21: 301–02.

Morain, Thomas J. 1988. *Prairie Grass Roots.* Ames: Iowa State UP.

Murray, Thomas E. 1983. "Some Sounds of St. Louis: A Social and Stylistic Appraisal." Paper presented to American Dialect Society, MMLA.

———. 1985. "The Language of St. Louis, Missouri: Variation in the Gateway City." Paper presented to the summer conference on English Linguistics.

———. 1986a. *The Language of St. Louis, Missouri: Variation in the Gateway City.* New York: Lang.

———. 1986b. "On Solving the Dilemma of the Hawthorne Effect." Warkentyne 327–40.

———. 1987a. *Aspects of American English.* Columbus, OH: Advocate.

———. 1987b. "You '$#%?$#% Hoosier: Derogatory Names and *the* Derogatory Name in St. Louis, Missouri." *Names* 35: 1–7.

———, ed. 1990. *The Language and Dialect of the Plains.* Special edition of *Kansas Quarterly.*

Nichols, Patricia C. 1983. "Linguistic Choices and Options for Black Women in the Rural South." Thorne, Kramarae, and Henley 54–68.

Niedzielski, N., and D. R. Preston. In preparation. *Folk Linguistics.*

Northern Wisconsin: A Guide Book to Aid the Homeseeker. n.d. Wisconsin State Board of Immigration, Archives Division Series 127 (1/1/14-2). Madison: State Historical Society of Wisconsin.

Noseworthy, Ronald G. 1972. "Verb Usage in Grand Banks." *RLS: Regional Language Studies* 4: 19–24.

Ornstein-Galicia, Jacob L., George K. Greer, and Dennis J. Bixler-Marquez, eds. 1988. *Research Issues and Problems in U.S. Spanish.* Brownsville, TX: Pan American U.

Orr, Elinor. 1987. *Twice as Less: Black English and the Performance of Black Students in Mathematics and Science.* New York: Norton.

Pace, George B. 1965. "On the Eastern Affiliations of Missouri Speech." *American Speech* 40: 47–52.

Pantzer, Kathy Tierney. 1974. "The Kentucks of Fencetown: Outmigration as a Facilitator of Family Structural Change." University of Wisconsin-Green Bay. Typescript.

Parker, Frank. 1975. "A Comment on *Anymore.*" *American Speech* 50: 303–10.

Pederson, Lee. 1964. "Some Structural Differences in the Speech of Chicago Negroes." *Social Dialects and Language Learning.* Ed. Roger W. Shuy. Champaign: NCTE, 28–51.

———. 1965. *The Pronunciation of English in Metropolitan Chicago.* Publication of the American Dialect Society 44. University: U of Alabama P.

———. 1967. "Mark Twain's Missouri Dialects: Marion County Phonemics." *American Speech* 42: 261–78.

———. 1971. "Chicago Words: The Regional Vocabulary." *American Speech* 46: 163–92.

Potter, Edward Earle. 1955. "The Dialect of Northwestern Ohio: A Study of a Transition Area." Diss. U of Michigan.

Pound, Louise. 1935. "Notes and Comments." *American Speech* 10: 159–60.

Power, Richard Lyle. 1953. *Planting Cornbelt Culture.* Indianapolis: Indiana State Historical Society.

Prator, Clifford H. 1957. *Manual of American Pronunciation.* New York: Rinehart.

Preston, D. R. 1982. "Perceptual Dialectology: Mental Maps of United States Dialects from a Hawaiian Perspective." *Working Papers in Linguistics* (U of Hawaii) 14: 5–49.

———. 1985a. "Mental Maps of Language Distribution in Rio Grande do Sul (Brazil)." *The Geographical Bulletin* 27: 46–64.

———. 1985b. "Southern Indiana Perceptions of 'Correct' and 'Pleasant' Speech." Warkentyne 387–411.

———. 1986. "Five Visions of America." *Language in Society* 15: 221–40.

———. 1988. "The Nicest English is in Indiana." *Studia Grammatica Posnaniensia* 14: 169–93.

———. 1989. *Perceptual Dialectology*. Dordrecht: Foris.

———. Forthcoming. "Folk Dialectology." *American Dialect Research*. Ed. D. R. Preston. Philadelphia: Benjamins.

———. In progress. *Folk Views of Language Variety in the United States*.

Preston, D. R., and G. M. Howe. 1987. "Computerized Generalizations of Mental Dialect Maps." *Variation in Language: NWAVE-XV at Stanford*. Ed. Keith Denning, et al. Stanford: Department of Linguistics, Stanford U, 361–67.

Rafferty, Milton D. 1981. *Historical Atlas of Missouri*. Norman: U of Oklahoma P.

Raithel, Erna E. 1954. "A Survey of the Vocabulary of Eight West Central Missouri Counties." Master's thesis. U of Missouri.

Randolph, Vance. 1987. *Ozark Folklore: A Bibliography*. Bloomington: Indiana U Folklore Institute Monograph Series, 1972. Rpt. U of Missouri P.

Randolph, Vance, and George P. Wilson. 1953. *Down in the Holler: A Gallery of Ozark Folk Speech*. Norman: U of Oklahoma P.

Randolph, Vance, and Gordon McCann. 1987. *Ozark Folklore: A Bibliography*. Vol. 2. Columbia: U of Missouri P.

Reed, David W. 1954. *Eastern Dialect Words in California*. Publication of the American Dialect Society 21: 3–15. University: U of Alabama P.

Rennick, Robert. 1984. *Kentucky Place Names*. Lexington: UP of Kentucky.

Rensink, W. G. 1955. "Dialektindeling naar opgaven van medewerkers." *Mededelingen der centrale commissie voor onderzoek van het nederlandse volkseigen* 7: 20–23.

Richmond, W. Edson. 1972. "Folk Speech." *Folklore and Folklife: An Introduction*. Ed. Richard W. Dorson. Chicago: U of Chicago P, 1435–57.

Rickford, John R. 1974. "The Insights of the Mesolect." DeCamp and Hancock 92–117.

———. 1975. "Carrying the New Wave into Syntax: the Case of Black English *Been*." *Analyzing Variation in Language*. Ed. Ralph W. Fasold and Roger W. Shuy. Washington: Georgetown UP, 162–83.

———. 1986. "Some Principles for the Study of Black and White Speech in the South." Montgomery and Bailey 38–62.

Riney, Timothy. 1989. "Black English Vernacular: Policy, Practice and Change." *Proceedings of the 1989 Mid-America Linguistics Conference*. Ed. C. Roberts, T. Riney, and S. Gaies. Cedar Falls: U of Northern Iowa.

Roark, Michael Owen. 1979. "Oklahoma Territory: Frontier Development, Migration, and Culture Areas." Diss. Syracuse U.

Rosenberg, Bernard. 1971. *Mass Culture Revisited*. New York: Van Nostrand.

Rosenberg, Bernard, and David Manning White, eds. 1957. *Mass Culture*. Glencoe, IL: Free.

Russell, I. Willis. 1941. "Notes on American Usage." *American Speech* 16: 17–20.

Ryan, Ellen Bouchard, and Howard Giles. 1982. *Attitudes Towards Language Variation*. London: Arnold.

Sanders, Gordon Ray. 1957. "A Vocabulary Survey of Seven Northeast Missouri Counties." Master's thesis. U of Missouri.

Schaye, Gilbert A. 1959. *Speaking American English*. New York: New York UP.

Scholl, M. L. 1977. "A Social History and Demographic Investigation of the City of Waterloo, IA." Ed.D. thesis. Drake U.

Schroeder, Adolf E. 1976. "The Persistence of Ethnic Identity in Missouri German Communities." *Germanica Americana: Symposium on German-American Literature and Culture*. Ed. Erich Albrecht and J. Anthony Burzle. Lawrence: Max Kade Document and Research Center, U of Kansas.

———. 1979. "Deutsche Sprache in Missouri" (The German Language in Missouri). *Deutsche als Muttersprache in den Vereinigten Staaten* (German as Mother Tongue in the United States). Ed. Leopold Auburger, Heinz Kloss, Heinz Rupp. Vol. 4, Part I. Wiesbaden: Franz Steiner Verlag, 125–59.

Scott, Jerrie, and Geneva Smitherman. 1985. "Language Attitudes and Self-Fulfilling Prophecies in the Elementary School." Greenbaum 302–14.

Shull, Bettie Bronson. 1953. "A Survey of the Vocabulary of Eight Western Missouri Counties." Master's thesis. U of Missouri.

Shuy, Roger W. 1962. *The Northern-Midland Dialect Boundary in Illinois*. Publication of the American Dialect Society 38. University: U of Alabama P.

Shuy, Roger W., Walt Wolfram, and W. K. Riley. 1967. *A Study of Social Dialects in Detroit*. Final Report, Project 6-1347. Washington, DC: Office of Education.

Sledd, Andrew. 1988. "Readin' not Riotin': The Politics of Literacy." *College English* 50: 495–508.

Sledd, James Hinton. 1966. "Breaking, Umlaut, and the Southern Drawl." *Language* 42: 18–41.

———. 1973. "A Note on Buckra Philology." *American Speech* 48: 144–46.

———. 1976. Untitled speech. University of Chicago.

Smith, Harold-Guy. 1929. *Transactions of the Wisconsin Academy of Sciences, Arts, and Letters*, 14. Madison: Wisconsin Academy of Sciences, Arts, and Letters.

Smitherman-Donaldson, Geneva. 1988. "Discriminatory Discourse on Afro-American Speech." Smitherman-Donaldson and Van Dijk 144–175.

Smitherman-Donaldson, Geneva, and Teun Van Dijk, eds. 1988. *Discourse and Discrimination*. Detroit: Wayne State UP.

Spear, Allan H. 1967. *Black Chicago: The Making of a Negro Ghetto, 1890–1920*. Chicago: U of Chicago P.

Stein, Jess, editor-in-chief. 1982. *The Random House College Dictionary*. Rev. ed. New York: Random.

Terrell, Tracy D. 1976. "Some Theoretical Considerations of the Merger of the Low Vowel Phonemes in American English." *Proceedings of the Second Annual Meeting of the Berkeley Linguistics Society*. Ed. Henry Thompson, et al. Berkeley, CA: Institute for Human Learning, 350–59.

"Their Old Kentucky Home is Here." 1978. *Milwaukee Journal* May, Sunday Accent Section.

Thomas, Erik R. 1989. "The Implications of /o/-fronting in Wilmington, North Carolina." *American Speech* 64: 323–33.

Thorne, Barrie, Cheris Kramarae, and Nancy Henley, eds. 1983. *Language, Gender, and Society*. Cambridge, MA: Newbury.

Traugott, Elizabeth Closs. 1972. *A History of English Syntax: A Transformational Approach to the History of English Surface Structure*. New York: Holt.

Trudgill, Peter. 1974. *The Social Differentiation of English in Norwich*. Cambridge: Cambridge UP.

———. 1983. *On Dialect*. New York: New York UP.

Trudgill, Peter, and Jean Hannah. 1982. *International English*. London: Arnold.

Tucker, G. R., and W. E. Lambert. 1969. "White and Negro Listeners' Reactions to Various American Dialects." *Social Forces* 47: 463–68.

Tucker, R. Whitney. 1944. "Notes on the Philadelphia Dialect." *American Speech* 19: 37–42.

Underwood, Gary N. 1981. *The Dialect of the Mesabi Range*. Publication of the American Dialect Society 67. University: U of Alabama P.

U.S. Department of the Census. 1923. *Fourteenth Census of the United States*. Vol. 10. Washington: U.S. Government Printing Office.

Van Goethem, L. D. n.d. *Not Long Ago*. Antigo, WI: Langlade County Historical Society.

Van Riper, William R. 1973. "General American." Reprinted in Allen and Linn, 1986, 123–35.

Vaughn-Cooke, Fay. 1987. "Are Black and White Vernaculars Diverging?" *American Speech* 62: 12–32.

Veltman, Calvin. 1983. *Language Shift in the United States*. Berlin: Mouton.

Visser, F. Th. 1963–73. *An Historical Syntax of the English Language*. 4 vols. Leiden: E. J. Brill.

Warkentyne, W. J., ed. 1986. *Methods V: Papers from the Fifth International Conference on Methods in Dialectology*. Victoria: U of Victoria P.

Warner, W. Lloyd, and James C. Abegglen. 1955. *Big Business Leaders in America*. New York: Harper.

Waskow, Arthur I. 1965. *From Race to Riot to Sit-In*. New York: Doubleday.

Wasson, H. Waldo. 1947. "The Speech of Columbia, Missouri, at Three Age Levels." Master's thesis. U of Missouri.

Weijnen, A. 1968. "Zum Wert Subjektiver Dialektgrenzen." *Lingua* 21: 594–96.

Weinstein, Bryan. *The Civic Tongue*. New York: Longman.

Welligan, J. 1927. "The Life of a Lumberman." *Wisconsin Magazine of History* 13: 263–64.

Wentworth, Harold. 1944. *American Dialect Dictionary*. New York: Crowell.

West, Candace, and Don H. Zimmerman. 1983. "Small Insults: A Study of Interruptions in Cross-Sex Conversations between Unacquainted Persons." Thorne, Kramarae, and Henley 103–18.

Williams, Frederick. 1976. *Explorations of the Linguistic Attitudes of Teachers.* Rowley, MA: Newbury.

Williams, Joseph M. 1975. *Origins of the English Language: A Social and Linguistic History.* New York: Free.

Williamson, Juanita, ed. 1972. *A Various Language.* New York: Holt.

Willibrand, W.A. 1957. "English Loanwords in the Low German Dialect of Westphalia, Missouri." Publication of the American Dialect Society 27: 16–21.

Wilson, Sir James. 1926. *The Dialects of Central Scotland.* London: Oxford UP.

Wilson, William Julius. 1987. *The Truly Disadvantaged.* Chicago: U of Chicago P.

———. 1984. "The Urban Underclass." Dunbar 75–117.

Wise, Claude Merton. 1957. *Applied Phonetics.* Englewood Cliffs, NJ: Prentice.

Wolfram, Walt. 1979. "Toward a Description of A-Prefixing in Appalachian English." *American Speech* 54: 45–56.

———. 1987. "Are Black and White Dialects Diverging?" *American Speech* 62: 40–47.

———. 1990. "Re-Examining Vernacular Black English." *Language* 66: 121–33.

Wolfram, Walt, and Donna Christian. 1976. *Appalachian Speech.* Arlington: Center for Applied Linguistics.

———. 1989. *Dialects and Education: Issues and Answers.* Englewood Cliffs: Prentice.

Wolfram, Walt, and Ralph W. Fasold. 1974. *The Study of Social Dialects in American English.* Englewood Cliffs, NJ: Prentice.

Wolfram, Walt, and Roger W. Shuy. 1974. *The Study of Social Dialects in American English.* Englewood Cliffs, NJ: Prentice.

Wolfram, Walt, et al. 1969. *A Sociolinguistic Description of Detroit Negro Speech.* Washington: Center for Applied Linguistics.

Wood, Gordon R. 1963. "Dialect Contours in the Southern States." *American Speech* 38: 243–56.

———. 1971. *Vocabulary Change.* Carbondale and Edwardsville: Southern Illinois UP.

Youmans, Gilbert. 1986. "Any More on *Anymore*? Evidence from a Missouri Dialect Survey." *American Speech* 61: 61–75.

Zelinsky, Wilbur. 1973. *The Cultural Geography of the United States.* Englewood Cliffs, NJ: Prentice.

———. 1980. "North America's Vernacular Regions." *Annals of the Association of American Geographers* 70: 14–16.

———. 1982. "General Cultural and Popular Regions." *This Remarkable Continent.* Ed. John T. Rooney et al. College Station: Texas A&M P.

Zgusta, Ladislav. 1971. *Manual of Lexicography.* Prague: Academia.

About the Contributors

CRAIG M. CARVER is managing editor of the Dictionary of American Regional English and the author of numerous papers, articles, and books on regional dialects (notably *American Regional Dialects*). He has contributed a piece, "Dialects," to the *Random House Dictionary* and writes a column for the *Atlantic*.

THOMAS S. DONAHUE is professor of linguistics at San Diego State University. He has written a variety of articles on Black English Vernacular, bilingual education, American language policy, American slang, and sociology-of-language issues. He counts among his recent successes an escape from five years of university administrative work.

RACHEL B. FARIES, whose 1967 doctoral dissertation has become an important work in the study of Missouri's linguistic geography, teaches high school English in Illinois and has recently been active as an officer of the Illinois Association of Teachers on English.

TIMOTHY C. FRAZER abandoned Renaissance literature during the turmoil of the 1960s and began the study of dialectology with Raven McDavid. After serving as a DARE fieldworker, Frazer prepared a monograph on settlement history for the Linguistic Atlas of the North Central States. He is the author of *Midland Illinois Dialect Patterns* and articles on dialectology, literature, and onomastics. He and his wife June, both professors of English at Western Illinois University, have co-authored studies on place names and on gendered discourse in television.

TIMOTHY HABICK is an examiner in the reasoning and measurement group at Educational Testing Service, where he works on the reasoning sections of the GRE, the LSAT, and the GMAT. He earned a BA degree (maxima cum laude) in French from La Salle University in 1971 and a PhD degree in linguistics from the University of Illinois, Urbana, in 1980. He travels frequently to China and the Orient.

ROBIN HERNDOBLER is professor of English at Harold Washington College, where she specializes in women's studies and directs the Women's Studies Program. She has published articles on women's issues in a variety of publications including *The Chicago Tribune* and *The Women's Review of Books* and is co-editor of an anthology on women's writing, *Weird Women/Word Women,* a product of the successful writing workshop for women only at Harold Washington College. She is currently at work on a novel about a female wizard, and is preparing a report on the work of a seminar she has directed for teachers at City College on mainstreaming women's studies.

DONALD M. LANCE is professor of English at the University of Missouri-Columbia. He is the author of many papers and articles on language, dialectology, and onomastics. He is co-editor of *Teaching Language Variation,* published by MLA.

DONALD LARMOUTH is professor of linguistics and dean of Arts, Sciences, and Graduate Programs at the University of Wisconsin-Green Bay. He has authored and co-authored articles on statistical methods in dialectology, language policy, applied linguistics, and teaching about language variation. He served as Midwest regional secretary of the American Dialect Society from 1980 to 1990.

MICHAEL I. MILLER is associate professor and former chair of the Department of English and Speech at Chicago State University. He is associate editor of the *Journal of English Linguistics* and the author of several articles on Chicago speech and on Black speech, including a phonological analysis of an apparent Virginia creole from the middle of the nineteenth century. He has temporarily suspended real work in order to serve in the administration at his institution, the only publicly supported black four-year university in Illinois.

THOMAS E. MURRAY has taught linguistics at Kansas State University and at Ohio State University. He is author of *The Language of St. Louis* and many articles and papers on dialectology and onomastics. He recently edited *The Language and Dialects of the Plains,* a special edition of the *Kansas Quarterly.* Murray and his wife, Carmin Ross Murray, are coauthors with Donald Larmouth of a recent PADS volume on the legality and ethics of surreptitious recording.

DENNIS R. PRESTON pioneered the concept of "perceptual dialectology" in the United States. His published work includes his recent monograph *Perceptual Dialectology* and many articles and papers. Preston's forthcoming volume on folk dialectology is supported by the National Science Foundation; he is also editing a volume in the American Dialect Society's centennial collection. Professor Preston teaches at Michigan State University.

MARJORIE REMSING teaches high school English and composition in the Manitowoc school district in Wisconsin and is a graduate of the University of Wisconsin-Green Bay. Her work on "Kentuck" English was part of a senior honors project at the university.

TIMOTHY J. RINEY completed his PhD at Georgetown University in 1988 and from 1988 to 1990 taught linguistics and sociolinguistics at the University of Northern Iowa. Riney co-hosted the 1989 Mid-America Linguistics Conference on Language Planning and has presented papers on topics in sociolinguistics and language acquisition at NWAVE/ADS, AICP&LL, and TESOL. Since 1990, he has been an assistant professor of language at International Christian University in Tokyo.

ANDREW SLEDD teaches at Harold Washington College. His writings have appeared in *American Speech, College English,* and other journals, and have treated both Black English and the morality and political consciousness of the teaching profession.

BRUCE SOUTHARD is associate professor of English at East Carolina University. He has published articles on various aspects of American English and is now completing editorial work on The Linguistic Atlas of Oklahoma, a project begun by William R. van Riper and continued by Raven I. McDavid, Jr. and Southard.

ERIK R. THOMAS is pursuing a doctoral degree in linguistics at the University of Texas at Austin. A native Ohioan, he has written articles on dialectal phonetic variation.

Index